by Doug Lowe

JavaFX® For Dummies®

Published by: **John Wiley & Sons, Inc.,** 111 River Street, Hoboken, NJ 07030-5774, www.wiley.com

Copyright © 2015 by John Wiley & Sons, Inc., Hoboken, New Jersey

Media and software compilation copyright © 2015 by John Wiley & Sons, Inc. All rights reserved.

Published simultaneously in Canada

No part of this publication may be reproduced, stored in a retrieval system or transmitted in any form or by any means, electronic, mechanical, photocopying, recording, scanning or otherwise, except as permitted under Sections 107 or 108 of the 1976 United States Copyright Act, without the prior written permission of the Publisher. Requests to the Publisher for permission should be addressed to the Permissions Department, John Wiley & Sons, Inc., 111 River Street, Hoboken, NJ 07030, (201) 748-6011, fax (201) 748-6008, or online at http://www.wiley.com/go/permissions.

Trademarks: Wiley, For Dummies, the Dummies Man logo, Dummies.com, Making Everything Easier, and related trade dress are trademarks or registered trademarks of John Wiley & Sons, Inc. and may not be used without written permission. All other trademarks are the property of their respective owners. John Wiley & Sons, Inc. is not associated with any product or vendor mentioned in this book.

For general information on our other products and services, please contact our Customer Care Department within the U.S. at 877-762-2974, outside the U.S. at 317-572-3993, or fax 317-572-4002. For technical support, please visit www.wiley.com/techsupport.

Wiley publishes in a variety of print and electronic formats and by print-on-demand. Some material included with standard print versions of this book may not be included in e-books or in print-on-demand. If this book refers to media such as a CD or DVD that is not included in the version you purchased, you may download this material at http://booksupport.wiley.com. For more information about Wiley products, visit www.wiley.com.

Library of Congress Control Number: 2014941051

ISBN 978-1-118-38534-0 (pbk); ISBN 978-1-118-41743-0 (ebk); ISBN 978-1-118-42166-6

Manufactured in the United States of America

10 9 8 7 6 5 4 3 2 1

Table of Contents

Introduction

●·●

*I*n the beginning there was *AWT,* the *Abstract Window Toolkit.* AWT was
Java's first system for displaying window-based user interfaces in Java.
AWT begat *Swing,* which soon became the preferred way to create user-
friendly applications in Java.

But then there was *JavaFX,* the worthy successor to the GUI throne. JavaFX
is designed to create stunning user interfaces that can run on a wide variety
of devices, including traditional desktop and portable computers, tablets,
smartphones, TV set-top boxes, game consoles, and many other types of
devices.

Until recently, JavaFX was the red-headed stepchild of the Java world. It co-
existed with Java, but wasn't an official part of Java. But beginning with Java
version 8, JavaFX is now fully integrated into Java. And while JavaFX and
Swing coexist today, Oracle has made it clear that Swing is in its twilight and
JavaFX represents the future of user-interface programming.

So you're holding the right book in your hands. JavaFX is an essential skill for
every Java programmer to have at his or her disposal, and this book will help
you master that skill.

About This Book

This isn't the kind of book you pick up and read from start to finish, as if it
was a cheap novel. If I ever see you reading it at the beach, I'll kick sand in
your face. Beaches are for reading romance novels or murder mysteries, not
programming books.

Assuming, then, that you have found a more suitable location to read this
book, you can, if you want, read it straight through starting with Chapter 1
and finishing with Chapter 20. However, this sequence isn't necessary. If you
are brand new to JavaFX programming, I suggest you read at least Part I in
sequence so that you'll gain a basic understanding of how JavaFX works.
But after you have the basics down, you can read the chapters in whatever
sequence makes sense for you. If you need to know about adding effects to
a shape, skip straight to Chapter 14. For information about about animation,
skip ahead to Chapter 17.

You don't have to memorize anything in this book. It's a need-to-know book: You pick it up when you need to know something. Need a reminder on how to rotate a shape? Pick up the book. Can't remember the details of the `TilePane` class? Pick up the book. After you find what you need, put down the book and get on with your life.

This book works like a reference. Start with the topic you want to find out about. Look for it in the Table of Contents or in the index. The Table of Contents is detailed enough that you can find most of the topics you're looking for. If not, turn to the index, where you can find even more detail.

Of course, the book is loaded with information — so if you want to take a brief excursion into your topic, you're more than welcome. If you want to know the big picture on the scene graph, read Chapter 7. But if you just want a reminder on how to set the maximum scene size, read just the section on the `Scene` class.

Whenever I describe sample Java code, I present it as follows:

```
@override public void start(Stage primaryStage)
```

And Java class names, keywords, or other language elements are always shown in `monospace type`.

Foolish Assumptions

In this book, I make very few assumptions about what you already may or may not know about JavaFX. But I do have to make two basic assumptions:

✔ You own or have access to a computer on which Java JDK 8 has been installed or on which you have permission to install.

  JavaFX 8 is an integral part of JDK 8, so JDK 8 is a requirement for figuring out JavaFX. If you have not yet installed it, you'll find instructions on how to do so in Chapter 1.

✔ You know the basics of Java programming.

  If you're new to Java, may I suggest one of two books: my own *Java All-In-One For Dummies,* 4th Edition, or Barry Burd's *Java For Dummies*, 6th Edition. Both are published by Wiley.

There are no other prerequisites to this book.

How This Book Is Organized

This book is organized into five parts. Here's a brief description of what you find in each part.

Part I: Getting Started with JavaFX

This part contains the information you need to get started with JavaFX programming. After a brief introduction to what JavaFX is and why it's so popular, you discover the basics of creating simple JavaFX programs. You figure out how to create simple JavaFX scenes populated with common controls such as labels, text field, and buttons. Then, you find out how to write programs that respond to user input, such as when the user clicks a button or enters text into a text field. And finally, you read how to use basic layout managers to control the arrangement of controls in your JavaFX scene.

Part II: JavaFX Controls

The chapters in this part focus on the various types of controls you can use in a JavaFX application. Chapter 7 starts by explaining the details of how the JavaFX scene graph works and presents the details of the class hierarchy used by the various controls. Then, the remaining chapters in this part present information about specific types of controls, ranging from check boxes and radio buttons to tables and menus.

Part III: Enhancing Your Scenic Design

The chapters in this part help you improve the appearance of your applications. First, you read about additional types of layout managers that give you more precise control over the way your user interface is arranged. Then, you discover how to use CSS styles to apply formatting details. Next, you figure out how to incorporate simple shapes into your scenes. And finally, you can read about JavaFX's special effects, which let you embellish your display with shadows, motion blurs, and so on.

Part IV: Making Your Programs Come Alive

The chapters in this part focus on various ways to make your programs more responsive and engaging. You discover how to work with *properties,* which you can use to make one part of your user interface respond to changes in another part of your user interface. Then, you discover how to incorporate media including sound and video. Next, you figure out how to create sophisticated animations that make the objects on the screen dance about. And finally, you read how to create programs that respond to multi-finger gestures on touch-enabled devices.

Part V: The Part of Tens

This wouldn't be a *For Dummies* book without a Part of Tens. Each of the chapters here presents ten items of special interest. Chapter 19 presents ten additional JavaFX controls that didn't fit in Part II. And Chapter 20 presents ten steps to creating a JavaFX application that displays a three-dimensional scene.

Icons Used in This Book

Like any *For Dummies* book, this book is chock-full of helpful icons that draw your attention to items of particular importance. You find the following icons throughout this book:

Danger, Will Robinson! This icon highlights information that may help you avert disaster.

Did I tell you about the memory course I took?

Pay special attention to this icon; it lets you know that some particularly useful tidbit is at hand.

Hold it — overly technical stuff is just around the corner. Obviously, because this is a programming book, almost every paragraph of the next 400 or so pages could get this icon. So I reserve it for those paragraphs that go into greater depth, down into explaining how something works under the covers — probably deeper than you really need to know to use a feature, but often enlightening. You also sometimes find this icon when I want to illustrate a point with an example that uses some Java feature that hasn't been covered so far in the book, but that is covered later. In those cases, the icon is just a reminder that you shouldn't get bogged down in the details of the illustration, and instead focus on the larger point.

Beyond the Book

A lot of extra content that you won't find in this book is available at www. dummies.com. Go online to find the following:

✔ **Online articles covering additional topics at**

    www.dummies.com/extras/javafx

Here you find articles covering additional features of JavaFX that didn't quite fit in the book.

✔ **The Cheat Sheet for this book is at**

    www.dummies.com/cheatsheet/javafx

Here you'll find a convenient summary of some of the most important JavaFX classes.

✔ **Code listings for this book at**

    www.dummies.com/extras/javafx

All the code listings used in this book are available for download.

✔ **Updates to this book, if I have any, are also available at**

    www.dummies.com/extras/javafx

Where to Go from Here

Yes, you *can* get there from here. With this book in hand, you're ready to dive right into to the cool and refreshing water of the JavaFX pool. Browse through the Table of Contents and decide where you want to start. Be bold! Be courageous! Be adventurous! And above all, have fun!

Part I
Getting Started with JavaFX

In this part . . .

- ✔ Figuring out a basic program
- ✔ Handling events
- ✔ Displaying simple scenes
- ✔ Arranging nodes
- ✔ Responding to input controls
- ✔ Visit www.dummies.com for great Dummies content online.

Chapter 1

Hello, JavaFX!

● ●

In This Chapter

▶ Getting a quick overview of what JavaFX is and what you can do with it

▶ Looking at a basic JavaFX program

▶ Downloading, installing, and configuring Java 8 so you can build your own JavaFX programs

▶ Building a JavaFX program the hard way, using nothing but Notepad and a command prompt

▶ Using TextPad to simplify JavaFX programming

▶ Using an IDE, such as Eclipse or NetBeans, for JavaFX programming

● ●

*W*elcome to the wonderful world of JavaFX programming!

This chapter offers a gentle introduction to JavaFX programming. In the next few pages, you find out what JavaFX is, where it came from, and where it's going. You see an example of the classic Hello, World! program implemented in JavaFX. And you discover how to set up your computer to develop your own JavaFX programs using several popular development tools for JavaFX.

Incidentally, I assume that you're already somewhat familiar with Java programming. You don't need to be a master programmer by any means, but you should have a solid understanding of the basics, such as creating programs that work with variables and statements (such as `if` and `for`) as well as creating your own classes and using the various classes that are part of the Java API (Application Programming Interface). I don't take the time to explain such basics in this book, so if you need an introduction to Java before you dive into the details of JavaFX, I suggest you get a copy of my masterpiece, *Java All-in-One For Dummies* (Wiley Publishing, Inc.).

The intent of this chapter is to get you ready to start learning how to write JavaFX programs. As such, you see a brief example of a simple JavaFX program in this chapter, which might not make complete sense at this early stage of your JavaFX journey. Please don't become discouraged. In Chapter 2, I dissect that simple JavaFX program line-by-line so you can see what makes it tick. For this chapter, I focus on the high-level details of what JavaFX is, what you can do with it, and how to get your computer set up for JavaFX programming.

All the code listings used in this book are available for download at www.dummies.com/extras/javafx.

What Is JavaFX?

Simply put, JavaFX is a collection of Java packages that lets you add fancy graphical user interfaces to your Java applications. With JavaFX, you can create traditional windows-style user interfaces that include familiar controls such as labels, buttons, text boxes, check boxes, drop-down lists, and so on. But you can also adorn these user interfaces with fancy effects such as light sources, perspective, and animation. Hence the *FX* in *JavaFX*.

Prior to JavaFX, the main way to create graphical user interfaces in Java was through the Swing API. JavaFX is similar to Swing in many ways, so if you've ever used Swing to create a user interface for a Java program, you have a good head start at learning JavaFX.

JavaFX has been around as an add-on package for a while, but beginning with Java version 8, JavaFX is now an official standard part of the Java platform. Thus, after you install the Java 8 Development Kit (*JDK 8*), you can begin developing your own JavaFX applications with your favorite development tools. Later in this chapter, you discover how to download and install JDK 8, and you figure out how to create a simple JavaFX program using three popular Java development tools: TextPad, Eclipse, and NetBeans.

Because JavaFX is now a standard part of Java, you can run your JavaFX programs on any device that includes version 8 of the Java Runtime Environment (JRE). That includes computers, tablet devices, smartphones, and any other device that can support JDK8.

Oracle has announced that JavaFX will eventually replace Swing. Although Swing is still supported in Java 8 and will be supported for the foreseeable future, Oracle is concentrating new features on JavaFX. Eventually, Swing will become obsolete.

Perusing the Possibilities of JavaFX

One of the basic strengths of JavaFX is its ability to let you easily create complicated graphical user interfaces with all the classic user interface gizmos everyone knows and loves. Thus, JavaFX provides a full range of controls — dozens of them in fact, including the classics such as buttons, labels, text boxes, check boxes, drop-down lists, and menus, as well as more exotic controls such as tabbed panes and accordion panes. Figure 1-1 shows a typical JavaFX user interface that uses several of these control types to create a form for data entry.

Figure 1-1:
A typical
JavaFX
program.

Truthfully, the data-entry form shown in Figure 1-1 isn't very remarkable. In fact, you can easily create data-entry forms like this using Swing with about the same amount of effort. The real advantages of using JavaFX over Swing don't become apparent until you start using some of the more advanced JavaFX features.

For starters, consider the general appearance of the data-entry form shown in Figure 1-1. The appearance of the buttons, labels, text fields, radio buttons, and check boxes are a bit dated. The visual differences between the dialog box shown in Figure 1-1 and one you could've created in Visual Basic on a Windows 95 computer 20 years ago are minor.

Where JavaFX begins to shine is in its ability to easily allow you to improve the appearance of your user interface by using *Cascading Style Sheets (CSS)*. CSS makes it easy to customize many aspects of the appearance of your user interface controls by placing all the formatting information in a separate file dubbed a style sheet. A *style sheet* is a simple text file that provides a set of rules for formatting the various elements of the user interface. You can use CSS to control literally hundreds of formatting properties. For example, you can easily change the text properties such as font, size, color, and weight, and you can add a background image, gradient fills, borders, and special effects such as shadows, blurs, and light sources.

Figure 1-2 shows a variation of the form that was shown in Figure 1-1, this time formatted with CSS. The simple CSS file for this form adds a background image, enhances the text formatting, and modifies the appearance of the buttons.

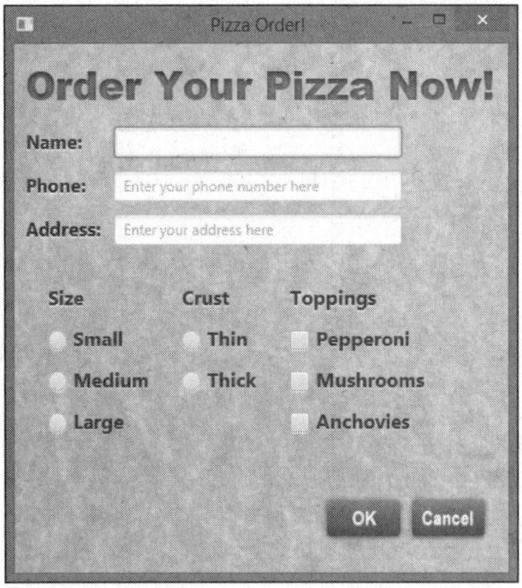

Figure 1-2: JavaFX lets you use CSS to specify formatting for user interface elements.

Besides CSS, JavaFX offers many other capabilities. These are the most important:

- ✔ **Visual effects:** You can add a wide variety of visual effects to your user interface elements, including shadows, reflections, blurs, lighting, and perspective effects.

- ✔ **Animation:** You can specify animation effects that apply transitions gradually over time.

- ✔ **Charts:** You can create bar charts, pie charts, and many other chart types using the many classes of the `javafx.scene.chart` package.

- ✔ **3-D objects:** You can draw three-dimensional objects such as cubes, cylinders, spheres, and more complex shapes.

✔ **Touch interface:** JavaFX can handle touchscreen devices, such as smart-phones and tablet computers with ease.

✔ **Property bindings:** JavaFX lets you create *properties,* which are special data types that can be bound to user interface controls. For example, you can create a property that represents the price of an item being pur-chased and then bind a label to it. Then, whenever the value of the price changes, the value displayed by the label is updated automatically.

You discover all these features and more in later chapters of this book. But for now, it's time to have a look at a simple JavaFX program so you can get a feel for what JavaFX programs look like.

Looking at a Simple JavaFX Program

Figure 1-3 shows the user interface for a very simple JavaFX program that includes just a single button. Initially, the text of this button says `Click me please!` When clicked, the text of the button changes to `You clicked me!` If you click the button again, the text changes back to `Click me please!` Thereafter, each time you click the button, the text cycles between `Click me please!` and `You clicked me!`

Figure 1-3:
The
Click Me
program.

To give you an idea of what JavaFX programming looks like, Listing 1-1 shows the complete listing for this program. I won't explain the details of how this program works — I examine this program in painstaking detail in Chapter 2. For now, I just want you to get the big picture to give you a feel for what JavaFX programming looks like.

Listing 1-1: The Click Me Program

```java
import javafx.application.*;
import javafx.stage.*;
import javafx.scene.*;
import javafx.scene.layout.*;
import javafx.scene.control.*;

public class ClickMe extends Application
{
    public static void main(String[] args)
    {
        launch(args);
    }

    Button btn;

    @Override public void start(Stage primaryStage)
    {
        // Create the button
        btn = new Button();
        btn.setText("Click me please!");
        btn.setOnAction(e -> buttonClick());

        // Add the button to a layout pane
        BorderPane pane = new BorderPane();
        pane.setCenter(btn);
        // Add the layout pane to a scene
        Scene scene = new Scene(pane, 300, 250);

        // Finalize and show the stage
        primaryStage.setScene(scene);
        primaryStage.setTitle("The Click Me App");
        primaryStage.show();
    }

    public void buttonClick()
    {
        if (btn.getText() == "Click me please!")
        {
            btn.setText("You clicked me!");
        }
        else
        {
            btn.setText("Click me please!");
        }
    }
}
```

The following paragraphs give a brief explanation of the key elements of the Click Me program:

✔ As with any other Java program, JavaFX programs begin with a slew of `import` statements that reference the various packages that will be used by the program.

   For this example, five packages are imported. Most JavaFX programs will require these five packages as well as additional packages that provide more advanced features.

✔ All JavaFX programs extend a core class named `Application`, which provides the basic functionality of the program. When you extend the `Application` class, you must override a `start` method; JavaFX calls this method when the application starts.

✔ Like any Java program, a JavaFX program must have a `main` method. In a JavaFX program, the `main` method simply calls the `launch` method of the `Application` class, which in turn launches the application and calls the `start` method.

✔ The user interface elements of a JavaFX program are arranged in a hierarchy of containers. At the highest level is a *stage,* which represents a window. Within the stage is a *scene,* which contains user interface controls. The controls themselves (such as buttons, labels, drop-down lists, and so on) are usually contained in one or more *layout panes* that govern the positional layout of the controls.

   If you study the code in the `start` method, you see that these elements are built from the bottom up:

   • A button is created.

   • The button is added to a layout pane (specifically, a `StackPane`, which is one of several types of layout panes available).

   • The layout pane is added to a scene and then the scene is added to the stage.

   • The stage's `show` method is called to display the application's GUI (Graphical User Interface).

✔ The `buttonClick` method is called whenever the user clicks the button. This method examines the current text displayed by the button and changes the text accordingly. Thus, each time the user clicks the button, the button's text changes from `Click me please!` to `You clicked me!` or vice-versa.

Please don't worry if you find some (or even all) of this program confusing at this point. My intent for this chapter is simply to give you a peek at a simple JavaFX program, but not to overwhelm you with the details of how this program works. As I mention earlier, I will review the details of this program line-by-line in Chapter 2.

In the remaining sections of this chapter, you figure out how to download, install, and configure the Java Development Kit and how to compile and test the Click Me program using popular Java development tools.

Downloading and Installing JavaFX

Actually, the above heading is a bit of a trick. Prior to Java 8, JavaFX was a separate entity from Java. Thus, to use JavaFX, you had to download and install a separate JavaFX package. But beginning with Java 8, JavaFX is now an integral part of Java. So if you've downloaded and installed Java 8, you already have JavaFX.

In the following sections, I discuss how to download, install, and configure the Java 8 Development Kit (JDK 8) so that you can code and test JavaFX programs. If you've already installed JDK 8, you can skip the rest of this section.

Downloading JDK 8

To get to the download page, point your browser to `http://java.oracle.com/technetwork/java` and then follow the appropriate links to download the JDK 8 for your operating system.

When you get to the Java download page, you find links to download the JDK or the JRE. Follow the JDK link; the JRE link gets you only the Java Runtime Environment, not the complete Java Development Kit.

The JDK download comes in two versions:

 ✔ The online version requires an active Internet connection to install the JDK.

   The offline version lets you download the JDK installation file to your computer and install it later.

I recommend that you use the offline version; it installs faster, and you can reinstall the JDK later if you need to without downloading it again.

Installing JDK 8

After you download the JDK file, you can install it by running the executable file you downloaded. The procedure varies slightly depending on your operating system, but basically, you just run the JDK installation program file after you download it, as follows:

- ✔ **On a Windows system,** open the folder in which you saved the installation program and double-click the installation program's icon.

- ✔ **On a Linux or Solaris system,** use console commands to change to the directory to which you downloaded the file and then run the program.

- ✔ **On a Mac,** open the Downloads window and double-click the JDK .dmg file you downloaded. A Finder window appears containing an icon of an open box. Double-click this icon to launch the installer.

After you start the installation program, it prompts you for any information that it needs to install the JDK properly, such as which features you want to install and what folder you want to install the JDK in. You can safely choose the default answer for each option.

Setting the path

After you install the JDK, you need to configure your operating system so that it can find the JDK command-line tools. To do that, you must set the Path environment variable — a list of folders that the operating system uses to locate executable programs. To do this on a Windows system, follow these steps. You must be logged in as an administrator to make the changes described in this procedure.

1. **Open the Control Panel.**

    - *On a Windows 7 or earlier system,* open the Start menu and choose Control Panel.

    - *On a Windows 8 or later system,* click the Start button or press the Windows key, type **Control Panel**, and then press Enter.

2. **Double-click the System icon.**

    The System Properties page appears.

3. **Click the Advanced System Settings link and then click the Environment Variables button.**

    The Environment Variables dialog box appears, as shown in Figure 1-4.

Figure 1-4:
The
Environment
Variables
dialog box.

4. **In the System Variables list, scroll to the `Path` variable, select it, and then click the Edit button.**

A little dialog box pops up to let you edit the value of the `Path` variable.

5. **Add the JDK `bin` folder to the beginning of the `Path` value.**

Use a semicolon to separate the `bin` folder from the rest of the information that may already be in the path.

Note: The name of the `bin` folder may vary on your system, as in this example:

```
c:\Program Files\Java\jdk1.8.0\bin;other directories...
```

6. **Click OK three times to exit.**

The first OK gets you back to the Environment Variables dialog box; the second OK gets you back to the System Properties page; and the third OK closes the System Properties page.

For Linux or Solaris, the procedure depends on which shell you're using. For more information, consult the documentation for the shell you're using. Note that this step is not necessary on Mac systems.

Developing the Click Me Program with Notepad

After you install JDK 8, JavaFX is at your disposal. Strictly speaking, the only other tools besides JDK 8 you need to develop Java programs is a text editor and access to a command prompt. With the text editor, you create the Java source file, saving the file with the extension `.java`. Then, at the command prompt, you use Java's command-line tools to compile and run the program.

Windows comes with the free text-editor Notepad that is adequate enough for creating simple Java source files. *Notepad* is a generic text editor that doesn't know anything about the peculiarities of Java source code. As a result, Notepad doesn't give you any assistance with details such as indenting, matching up left and right braces, or drawing your attention to syntax errors.

Nor will Notepad give you any help with compiling, running, or debugging a Java program. But Notepad does have the advantage of being free and simple to use. And, it's already on your computer, so there's nothing else to install.

Here are the steps for creating the Click Me program using Notepad and Java's command-line tools:

1. **Start Notepad.**

   To do that in Windows 7 or 8:

   a. Click the Start button (or press the Windows key on your keyboard).

   *b. Type **notepad** and then press Enter.*

   Notepad comes to life, presenting you with an empty text editing window.

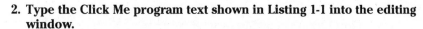

2. **Type the Click Me program text shown in Listing 1-1 into the editing window.**

   Be sure to type the text exactly as it appears in the listing. When you're done, carefully review your work to make sure you typed it correctly.

   Figure 1-5 shows how the Click Me program appears when correctly entered into Notepad. (Note that the Notepad window shown in the figure is not large enough to display the entire source file; you must scroll the window to see the entire file.)

```
                            Untitled - Notepad                    _ □ ×
File  Edit  Format  View  Help
import javafx.application.*;
import javafx.stage.*;
import javafx.scene.*;
import javafx.scene.layout.*;
import javafx.scene.control.*;

public class ClickMe extends Application
{
    public static void main(String[] args)
    {
        launch(args);
    }

    Button btn;

    @Override
    public void start(Stage primaryStage)
    {
        btn = new Button();
        btn.setText("Click me please!");
        btn.setOnAction(e -> buttonClick());

        StackPane pane = new StackPane();
        pane.getChildren().add(btn);
        primaryStage.setTitle("The Click Me App");
        primaryStage.setScene(new Scene(pane, 300, 250));
        primaryStage.show();
    }

    public void buttonClick()
    {
        if (btn.getText() == "Click me please!")
        {
            btn.setText("You clicked me!");
```

Figure 1-5:
The Click
Me program
in Notepad.

3. **Choose File⇨Save to save the file using the name** `ClickMe.java`.

   You can save the file in any folder you wish, but it is very important that
   the name be exactly `ClickMe.java`.

   The name of a Java source file must exactly match the name of the
   class it contains, right down to capitalization. Thus, if you save the file
   as `clickme.java` instead of `ClickMe.java`, the Click Me program
   won't work.

4. **Open a command prompt window.**

   In Windows 7 or 8, to open the window:

   a. *Click the Start button or press the Windows key*

   b. *Type* cmd *and press Enter.*

5. **Use the** `cd` **command to change to the folder in which you saved the
   source file in Step 3.**

   For example, if you saved the file in `C:\Java`, enter the following
   command:

   ```
   cd C:\Java
   ```

6. Use the `javac` command to compile the program.

Enter the following command:

```
javac ClickMe.java
```

Assuming you typed the program exactly right, the `javac` command doesn't display any messages at all. If the program contains any errors, the compiler displays one or more error messages. If that happens, open the source file in Notepad, edit the text to correct the errors, save the file, and then repeat this step until no errors display.

7. Use the `java` command to run the program.

Enter the following command:

```
java ClickMe
```

The window, as shown in Figure 1-6, appears.

Figure 1-6:
The Click Me program in action.

8. Click the `Click Me Please!` button.

When you click the button, the text displayed on the button changes to `You clicked me!`.

9. Close the Click Me program by clicking its Close button.

Congratulations! You've successfully created your first JavaFX program!

Developing the Click Me Program with TextPad

TextPad is an inexpensive ($33) text editor that you can integrate with the Java Development Kit (JDK) to simplify the task of coding, compiling, and running Java programs. It isn't a true integrated development environment (IDE), as it lacks features such as integrated debugging, code generators, and drag-and-drop tools for creating graphical user interfaces.

TextPad is a popular tool for developing Java programs because of its simplicity and speed. It's ideal for learning Java because it's easy to use, so you can concentrate on learning Java rather than on learning how to use a complicated development environment.

You can download a free evaluation version of TextPad from Helios Software Solutions at `www.textpad.com`. You can use the evaluation version free of charge, but if you decide to keep the program, you must pay for it. (Helios accepts credit card payments online.)

If the Java JDK is already installed on your computer, when you install TextPad, TextPad automatically configures itself to compile and run Java programs. If you install the JDK after you install TextPad, you need to configure TextPad for Java by opening the Preferences dialog box (by choosing Configure⟳Preferences), selecting Tools in the tree on the left side of the dialog box, and then choosing Add⟳Java SDK Commands.

After you configure TextPad to compile and run Java programs, you can create the Click Me program by following these steps:

1. **Start TextPad.**

   TextPad automatically opens with an empty source document named Document1.

2. **Choose File⟳Save, type** ClickMe.java, **and then click Save.**

   This saves the file with the name `ClickMe.java`. Saving the file with a name that uses the extension `.java` *before* you enter any text into the file lets TextPad slip into Java editing mode, which makes it easier for you to enter and edit the Java source code for the Click Me program.

3. **Type the text of the Click Me program from Listing 1-1 into the Document1 window.**

The basic text-editing capabilities of TextPad are similar to just about any other text editor you've worked with, so you should have no trouble entering and editing the text of the Click Me program.

As you edit the text, you may notice some of TextPad's useful Java editing features. For example, TextPad automatically indents your code whenever you type an opening bracket, and then reverts to the previous indent when you type a closing bracket. TextPad also uses different colors to indicate keywords, variables, and other Java programming elements.

Figure 1-7 shows how the Click Me program appears in TextPad.

Figure 1-7:
The Click
Me program
in TextPad.

```
1   import javafx.application.*;
2   import javafx.stage.*;
3   import javafx.scene.*;
4   import javafx.scene.layout.*;
5   import javafx.scene.control.*;
6
7   public class HelloFX extends Application
8   {
9       public static void main(String[] args)
10      {
11          launch(args);
12      }
13
14      Button btn;
15
16      @Override
17      public void start(Stage primaryStage)
18      {
19          btn = new Button();
20          btn.setText("Click me please!");
21          btn.setOnAction(e -> buttonClick());
22
23          StackPane pane = new StackPane();
24          pane.getChildren().add(btn);
25          primaryStage.setTitle("The Click Me App");
26          primaryStage.setScene(new Scene(pane, 300, 250));
27          primaryStage.show();
28      }
29
```

4. Choose Tools⇨Compile Java to compile the program.

If you prefer, you can use the keyboard shortcut Ctrl+1. Either way, the changes to your source file are automatically saved and the `javac` command is invoked to compile the program. If the program compiles successfully, the message `Tool completed successfully` appears in the Tool Results pane.

If you made a mistake entering the Click Me program, the compiler generates error messages that display in the Tool Results pane. If you double-click the first line of each error message, TextPad takes you to the spot where the error occurred so you can correct the error.

5. **Choose Tools⇨Run Java Application to run the program.**

   A command prompt window opens and then the Click Me program window opens (refer to Figure 1-6).

6. **Click the `Click Me Please!` button.**

   When you click the button, the text displayed on the button changes to `You clicked me!`.

7. **Close the Click Me program by clicking its Close button.**

   The Click Me program window is closed, but the command prompt window remains visible, displaying the message `Press any key to continue. . .`

8. **Press any key to close the command prompt window.**

   That's all there is to it!

Using an IDE to Create the Click Me Program

An *IDE,* or *integrated development environment,* is a powerful tool that combines sophisticated text-editing features along with the ability to compile, execute, and debug programs in a variety of programming languages. An IDE can keep track of multiple source files that make up a single Java programming project and can even keep track of multiple versions of the source files.

The two most popular IDEs for Java programming are Eclipse and NetBeans. Both are free, and both are comparable in their features. So the choice of which to use is a matter of preference. You can download Eclipse from www.eclipse.org. You can get NetBeans at https://netbeans.org.

In the rest of this chapter, I show you how to create the Click Me program in Eclipse. Although the steps for creating the Click Me program in NetBeans are different, the concepts are the same.

To get started with Eclipse, go to www.eclipse.org, click the Download Eclipse button, and download the current version of Eclipse IDE for Java Developers. Unlike most programs, Eclipse doesn't have a complicated setup program. You just download the Zip file, extract all the files, and then run the Eclipse executable file (eclipse.exe) directly from the folder you extracted it to.

If you're using Windows, you may want to add a desktop shortcut for Eclipse to make it more convenient to start. To do that, open the folder that contains the eclipse.exe file, right-click the file and drag it to the desktop, release the mouse button, and choose Create Shortcut from the menu that appears. Then you can start Eclipse by double-clicking this desktop shortcut.

Here are the steps for creating the Click Me program in Eclipse:

1. **Start Eclipse by running the Eclipse.exe program file or double-clicking its desktop shortcut.**

    Eclipse comes to life, as shown in Figure 1-8.

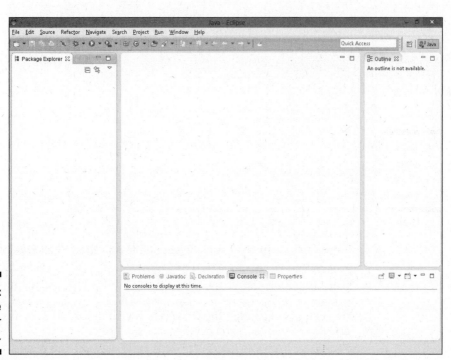

Figure 1-8:
Eclipse awaits your command.

2. **Choose File⇨New⇨Java Project.**

   The New Java Project dialog box appears, as shown in Figure 1-9.

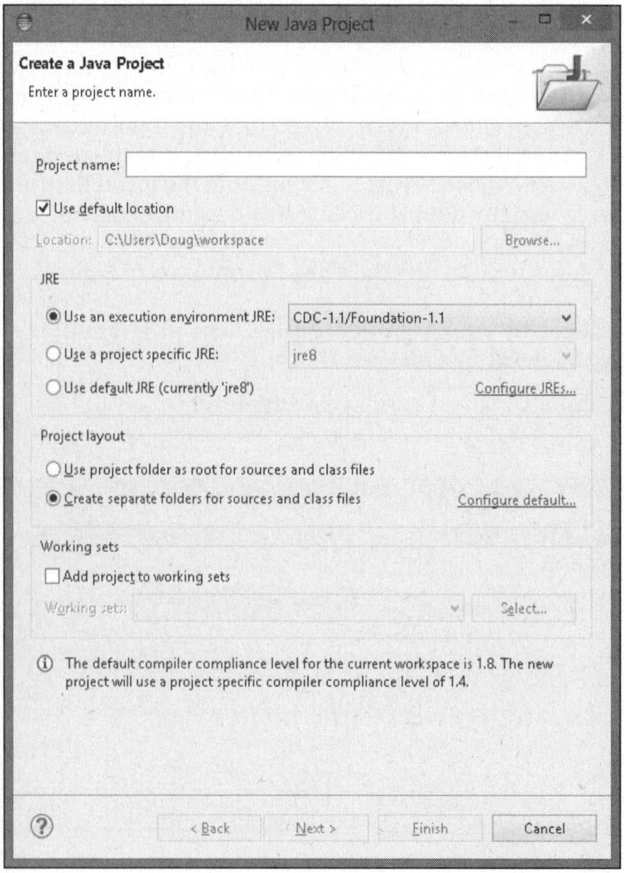

Figure 1-9:
Creating a
new Java
project.

3. **Type** ClickMe **in the Project Name field and then click Finish.**

   Eclipse sets up the project and adds the project to the Package Explorer pane at the left side of the screen, as shown in Figure 1-10. (Initially, the project is collapsed so that just the top line of the project appears. For this figure, I expanded the project to reveal the subfolders named `src` and `JRE System Library`.)

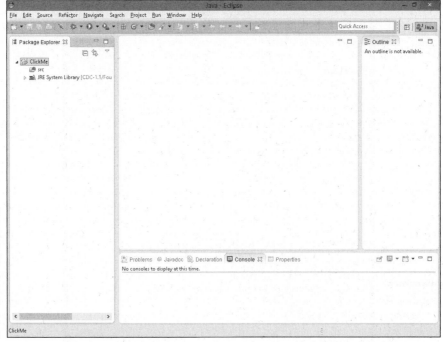

Figure 1-10:
The ClickMe
project
shows up in
the Package
Explorer
pane.

4. **Choose File⇨New⇨Class.**

   The New Java Class dialog box appears, as shown in Figure 1-11.

5. **Type ClickMe in the Name field and then click Finish.**

   Eclipse adds a file named ClickMe.java to the src folder and opens the file in the editing pane, as shown in Figure 1-12. Notice that Eclipse has also added a short stub of code to help you get started with the class.

6. **Delete the code stub in the ClickMe.java file; then type the text from Listing 1-1 into the editing pane.**

   Figure 1-13 shows what the ClickMe.java file looks like when you have correctly entered the program text.

Figure 1-11:
Adding a
class file to
the ClickMe
project.

7. **Choose Run⇨Run to run the program.**

   The Click Me program window opens, as shown earlier in Figure 1-6.

8. **Click the `Click Me Please!` button.**

   When you click the button, the text displayed on the button changes to `You clicked me!`.

9. **Close the Click Me program by clicking its Close button.**

   Congratulations! You have successfully created and run the Click Me program using Eclipse.

Now that you've seen you can develop the simple Click Me program using Notepad and command-line tools, the simple TextPad Java text editor, or a more complicated IDE such as Eclipse, you're ready to start discovering the specifics of how JavaFX programs work. So, in Chapter 2, I detail what every line of this simple program does. Onward and upward!

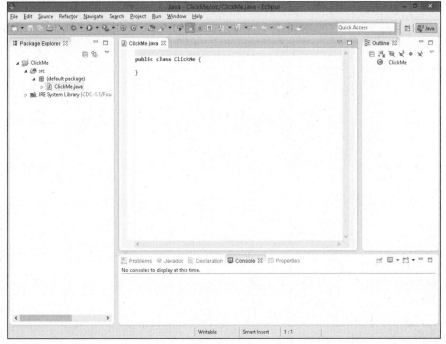

Figure 1-12:
Eclipse
displays
the newly
created
ClickMe.
java file.

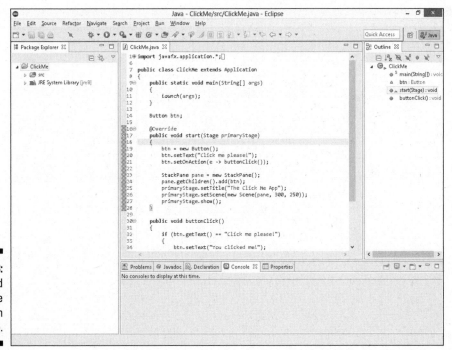

Figure 1-13:
The finished
Click Me
program in
Eclipse.

Chapter 2

Looking Closer at JavaFX Programming

● ●

In This Chapter

▶ Importing the classes you need to create a JavaFX program

▶ Creating a class that extends the JavaFX `Application` class

▶ Using classes such as `Button`, `BorderPane`, and `Scene` to create a user interface

▶ Creating an event handler that will be called when the user clicks a button

▶ Examining an enhanced version of the Click Me program

● ●

*I*n Chapter 1, I introduce you to a simple JavaFX program called the Click Me program and briefly describe how that program works. In this chapter, I put this program under the microscope and examine it in close detail. By the time you finish this chapter, you'll understand how every line of the Click Me program works and why it's required. Then, you'll be ready to start figuring out more nuanced techniques of JavaFX programming.

Looking Again at the Click Me Program

Figure 2-1 shows the Click Me program in action. As you can see, this program displays a simple button that contains the words `Click me please!`. What the figure does not show is that when the user clicks the button, the text on the button becomes `I've Been Clicked!`.

Figure 2-1:
The Click
Me program
in action.

Although this program is simple, it demonstrates most of the essential techniques you need to master to figure out how to write JavaFX programs:

- ✔ It displays a user interface that includes a standard type of user interface control — in this case, a button.
- ✔ It responds to the user's input, generated when the user clicks the button.
- ✔ It updates the display to confirm the user's action.

Many JavaFX programs are variations of this simple theme: Create a user interface, respond to the user's input, and then update the display to reflect the user's input. The user interface displayed by a more realistic JavaFX program will undoubtedly display more than just a single button. The processing performed in response to user input will likely include additional steps, such as looking up information in a database or performing calculations. And the display will undoubtedly be updated in more complicated ways than simply changing the text displayed on a button. But variations on these basic elements are found in most real-world JavaFX programs.

Listing 2-1 shows the actual JavaFX code for the Click Me program. In the remaining sections of this chapter, I explain every line of this program in detail.

Listing 2-1:   The Click Me Program

```java
import javafx.application.*;
import javafx.stage.*;
import javafx.scene.*;
import javafx.scene.layout.*;
import javafx.scene.control.*;

public class ClickMe extends Application
{
    public static void main(String[] args)
    {
        launch(args);
    }

    Button btn;

    @Override public void start(Stage primaryStage)
    {
        // Create the button
        btn = new Button();
        btn.setText("Click me please!");
        btn.setOnAction(e -> buttonClick());

        // Add the button to a layout pane
        BorderPane pane = new BorderPane();
        pane.setCenter(btn);

        // Add the layout pane to a scene
        Scene scene = new Scene(pane, 300, 250);

        // Finalize and show the stage
        primaryStage.setScene(scene);
        primaryStage.setTitle("The Click Me App");
        primaryStage.show();
    }

    public void buttonClick()
    {
        if (btn.getText() == "Click me please!")
        {
            btn.setText("You clicked me!");
        }
        else
        {
            btn.setText("Click me please!");
        }
    }
}
```

Importing JavaFX Packages

Like any Java program, JavaFX programs begin with a series of `import` statements that reference the various JavaFX packages that the program will use. The Click Me program includes the following five `import` statements:

```
import javafx.application.*;
import javafx.stage.*;
import javafx.scene.*;
import javafx.scene.layout.*;
import javafx.scene.control.*;
```

As you can see, all the JavaFX packages begin with `javafx`. The Click Me program uses classes from five distinct JavaFX packages:

- ✔ **`javafx.application`:** This package defines the core class on which all JavaFX applications depend: `Application`. You read more about the `Application` class in the section "Extending the Application Class" later in this chapter.

- ✔ **`javafx.stage`:** The most important class in this package is `Stage` class, which defines the top-level container for all user interface objects. `Stage` is a JavaFX application's highest-level window, within which all the application's user-interface elements are displayed.

- ✔ **`javafx.scene`:** The most important class in this package is the `Scene` class, which is a container that holds all the user interface elements displayed by the program.

- ✔ **`javafx.scene.layout`:** This package defines a special type of user-interface element called a *layout manager*. The job of a layout manager is to determine the position of each control displayed in the user interface.

- ✔ **`javafx.scene.control`:** This package contains the classes that define individual user interface controls such as buttons, text boxes, and labels.

  The Click Me program uses just one class from this package: `Button`, which represents a button that the user can click.

Extending the Application Class

A JavaFX application is a Java class that extends the `javafx.application.Application` class. Thus, the declaration for the Click Me application's main class is this:

```
public class ClickMe extends Application
```

Here, the Click Me application is defined by a class named `ClickMe`, which extends the `Application` class.

Because the entire `javafx.application` package is imported in line 1 of the Click Me program, the `Application` class does not have to be fully qualified. If you omit the `import` statement for the `javafx.application` package, the `ClickMe` class declaration would have to look like this:

```
public class ClickMe
    extends javafx.application.Application
```

The `Application` class is responsible for managing what is called the *lifecycle* of a JavaFX application. The lifecycle consists of the following steps:

1. Create an instance of the `Application` class.

2. Call the `init` method.

   The default implementation of the `init` method does nothing, but you can override the `init` method to provide any processing you want to be performed before the application's user interface displays.

3. Call the `start` method.

   The `start` method is an abstract method, which means that there is no default implementation provided as a part of the `Application` class. Therefore, you must provide your own version of the `start` method. The `start` method is responsible for building and displaying the user interface. (For more information, see the section "Overriding the start Method" later in this chapter.

4. Wait for the application to end, which typically happens when the user signals the end of the program by closing the main application window or choosing the program's exit command.

   During this time, the application isn't really idle. Instead, it's busy performing actions in response to user events, such as clicking a button or choosing an item from a drop-down list.

5. Call the `stop` method.

   Like the `init` method, the default implementation of the `stop` method doesn't do anything, but you can override it to perform any processing necessary as the program terminates, such as closing database resources or saving files.

Launching the Application

As you know, the standard entry-point for Java programs is the `main` method. Here is the `main` method for the Click Me program:

```
public static void main(String[] args)
{
    launch(args);
}
```

As you can see, the `main` method consists of just one statement, a call to the `Application` class' `launch` method.

The `launch` method is what actually starts a JavaFX application. The `launch` method is a `static` method, so it can be called in the static context of the `main` method. It creates an instance of the `Application` class and then starts the JavaFX lifecycle, calling the `init` and `start` methods, waiting for the application to finish, and then calling the `stop` method.

The `launch` method doesn't return until the JavaFX application ends. Suppose you wrote the `main` method for the Click Me program like this:

```
public static void main(String[] args)
{
    System.out.println("Launching JavaFX");
    launch(args);
    System.out.println("Finished");
}
```

Then, you would see `Launching JavaFX` displayed in the console window while the JavaFX application window opens. When you close the JavaFX application window, you would then see `Finished` in the console window.

Overriding the start Method

Every JavaFX application must include a `start` method. You write the code that creates the user interface elements your program's user will interact with in the `start` method. For example, the `start` method in Listing 2-1 contains code that displays a button with the text `Click me please!`

When a JavaFX application is launched, the JavaFX framework calls the `start` method after the `Application` class has been initialized.

The `start` method for the Click Me program looks like this:

```
@Override public void start(Stage primaryStage)
{
    // Create the button
    btn = new Button();
    btn.setText("Click me please!");
    btn.setOnAction(e -> buttonClick());

    // Add the button to a layout pane
    BorderPane pane = new BorderPane();
    pane.setCenter(btn);

    // Add the layout pane to a scene
    Scene scene = new Scene(pane, 300, 250);

    // Finalize and show the stage
    primaryStage.setScene(scene);
    primaryStage.setTitle("The Click Me App");
    primaryStage.show();
}
```

To create the user interface for the Click Me program, the `start` method performs the following four basic steps:

1. Create a button control named `btn`, set its text to `Click me please!`, and specify that a method named `buttonClick` will be called when the user clicks the button.

   For a more detailed explanation of this code, see the sections "Creating a Button" and "Handling an Action Event" later in this chapter.

2. Create a layout pane named `pane` and add the button to it.

   For more details, see the section "Creating a Layout Pane" later in this chapter.

3. Create a scene named `scene` and add the layout pane to it.

   For more details, see the "Making a Scene" section later in this chapter.

4. Finalize the stage by setting the scene, setting the stage title, and showing the stage.

   See the "Setting the Stage" section later in this chapter for more details.

You find pertinent details of each of these blocks of code later in this chapter. But before I proceed, I want to point out a few additional salient details about the start method:

- ✔ The start method is defined as an abstract method in the Application class, so when you include a start method in a JavaFX program, you're actually overriding the abstract start method.

    Although it isn't required, it's always a good idea to include the @override annotation to explicitly state that you're overriding the start method. If you omit this annotation and then make a mistake in spelling the method named (for example, Start instead of start) or if you list the parameters incorrectly, Java thinks you're defining a new method instead of overriding the start method.

- ✔ Unlike the main method, the start method is not a static method. When you call the launch method from the static main method, the launch method creates an instance of your Application class and then calls the start method.

- ✔ The start method accepts one parameter: the Stage object on which the application's user interface will display. When the application calls your start method, the application passes the main stage — known as the *primary stage* — via the primaryStage parameter. Thus, you can use the primaryStage parameter later in the start method to refer to the application's stage.

Creating a Button

The button displayed by the Click Me program is created using a class named Button. This class is one of many classes that you can use to create user interface controls. The Button class and most of the other control classes are found in the package javafx.scene.control.

To create a button, simply define a variable of type Button and then call the Button constructor like this:

```
Button btn;
btn = new Button();
```

In the code in Listing 2-1, the btn variable is declared as a class variable outside of the start method but the Button object is actually created within the start method. Controls are often declared as class variables so that you can access them from any method defined within the class. As you discover in the following section ("Handling an Action Event"), a separate method named buttonClicked is called when the user clicks the button. By defining the btn variable as a class variable, both the start method and the buttonClicked method have access to the button.

To set the text value displayed by the button, call the `setText` method, passing the text to be displayed as a string:

```
btn.setText("Click me please!");
```

Here are a few additional tidbits about buttons:

- ✔ The `Button` constructor allows you to pass the text to be displayed on the button as a parameter, as in this example:

```
Btn = new Button("Click me please!");
```

  If you set the button's text in this way, you don't need to call the `setTitle` method.

- ✔ The `Button` class is one of many classes that are derived from a parent class known as `javafx.scene.control.Control`. Many other classes derive from this class, including `Label`, `TextField`, `ComboBox`, `CheckBox`, and `RadioButton`.

- ✔ The `Control` class is one of several different classes that are derived from higher-level parent class called `javafx.scene.Node`. Node is the base class of all user-interface elements that can be displayed in a scene. A control is a specific type of node, but there are other types of nodes. In other words, all controls are nodes, but not all nodes are controls. You can read more about several other types of nodes later in this book.

Handling an Action Event

When the user clicks a button, an *action event* is triggered. Your program can respond to the event by providing an *event handler,* which is simply a bit of code that will be executed whenever the event occurs. The Click Me program works by setting up an event handler for the button; the code for the event handler changes the text displayed on the button.

As you read in Chapter 3, there are several ways to handle events in JavaFX. For now, I look briefly at one of the simplest methods, which requires simply that you specify that a method be called whenever the event occurs and then provide the code to implement that method.

To specify the method to be called when the user clicks a button, you call the `setOnAction` method of the button class. Here's how it's done in Listing 2-1:

```
btn.setOnAction(e -> buttonClick());
```

If the syntax used here seems a little foreign, that's because it uses a new feature of Java 8 called *Lambda expressions*. As used in this example, there are three elements to this new syntax:

- ✔ The argument e represents an object of type ActionEvent, which the program can use to get detailed information about the event.

  The Click Me program ignores this argument, so you can ignore it too, at least for now.

- ✔ The arrow operator (->) is a new operator introduced in Java 8 for use with Lambda expressions.

- ✔ The method call buttonClick() simply calls the method named buttonClick.

I discuss Lambda expressions in Chapter 3.

After buttonClick has been established as the method to call when the user clicks the button, the next step is to code the buttonClick method. You find it near the bottom of Listing 2-1:

```
public void buttonClick()
{
    if (btn.getText() == "Click me please!")
    {
        btn.setText("You clicked me!");
    }
    else
    {
        btn.setText("Click me please!");
    }
}
```

This method uses an if statement to alternately change the text displayed by the button to either You clicked me! or Click me please!. In other words, if the button's text is Click me please! when the user clicks the button, the buttonClicked method changes the text to You clicked me!. Otherwise, the if statement changes the button's text back to Click me please!.

The buttonClicked method uses two methods of the Button class to perform its work:

- ✔ **getText:** Returns the text displayed by the button as a string
- ✔ **setText:** Sets the text displayed by the button

For more information about handling events, see Chapter 3.

Creating a Layout Pane

By itself, a button is not very useful. You must actually display it on the screen for the user to be able to click it. And any realistic JavaFX program will have more than one control. The moment you add a second control to your user interface, you need a way to specify how the controls are positioned relative to one another. For example, if your application has two buttons, do you want them to be stacked vertically, one above the other, or side by side?

That's where layout panes come in. A *layout pane* is a container class to which you can add one or more user-interface elements. The layout pane then determines exactly how to display those elements relative to each other.

To use a layout pane, you first create an instance of the pane. Then, you add one or more controls to the pane. When you do so, you can specify the details of how the controls will be arranged when the pane is displayed. After you add all the controls to the pane and arrange them just so, you add the pane to the scene.

JavaFX provides a total of eight distinct types of layout panes, all defined by classes in the package `javafx.scene.layout`. The Click Me program uses a type of layout called a *border pane,* which arranges the contents of the pane into five general regions: top, left, right, bottom, and center. The `BorderPane` class is ideal for layouts in which you have elements such as a menu and toolbar at the top, a status bar at the bottom, optional task panes or toolbars on the left or right, and a main working area in the center of the screen.

The lines that create the border pane in the Click Me program are

```
BorderPane pane = new BorderPane();
pane.setCenter(btn);
```

Here, a variable of type `BorderPane` is declared with the name `pane`, and the `BorderPane` constructor is called to create a new `BorderPane` object. Then, the `setCenter` method is used to display the button (`btn`) in the center region of the pane.

Here are a few other interesting details about layout panes:

- ✔ Layout panes automatically adjust the exact position of the elements they contain based on the size of the elements contained in the layout as well as on the size of the space in which the layout pane is displayed.

- ✔ I said earlier that controls are a type of node, and that you would read about other types of nodes later in this book. Well, you just read about one: A layout pane is also a type of node.

✔ Each region of a border pane can contain a node. Because a layout pane itself is a type of node, each region of a border pane can contain another layout pane. For example, suppose you want to display three controls in the center region of a border pane. To do that, you'd create a second layout pane and add the three controls to it. Then, you'd set the second layout pane as the node to be displayed in the center region of the first layout pane.

✔ You read more about the `BorderPane` class and a few other commonly used layout panes in Chapter 5. You also can read about the layout panes that aren't as commonly used in Chapter 13.

Making a Scene

After you create a layout pane that contains the controls you want to display, the next step is to create a scene that will display the layout pane. You can do that in a single line of code that declares a variable of type `Scene` and calls the `Scene` class constructor. Here's how I did it in the Click Me program:

```
Scene scene = new Scene(pane, 300, 250);
```

The `Scene` constructor accepts three arguments:

✔ A node object that represents the *root node* to be displayed by the scene.

A scene can have only one root node, so the root node is usually a layout pane, which in turn contains other controls to be displayed. In the Click Me program, the root note is the border layout pane that contains the button.

✔ The width of the scene in pixels.

✔ The height of the scene in pixels.

Note: If you omit the width and height, the scene will be sized automatically based on the size of the elements contained within the root node.

You can find out about some additional capabilities of the `Scene` class in Chapter 4.

Setting the Stage

If the *scene* represents the nodes (controls and layout panes) that are displayed by the application, the *stage* represents the window in which the scene is displayed. When the JavaFX framework calls your application's `start` method, it passes you an instance of the `Stage` class that represents the application's primary stage — that is, the stage that represents the application's main window. This reference is passed via the `primaryStage` argument.

Having created your scene, you're now ready to finalize the primary stage so that the scene can be displayed. To do that, you must do at least two things:

- ✔ Call the `setScene` method of the primary stage to set the scene to be displayed.
- ✔ Call the `show` method of the primary stage to display the scene.

  After you call the `show` method, your application's window becomes visible to the user and the user can then begin to interact with its controls.

It's also customary to set the title displayed in the application's title bar. You do that by calling the `setTitle` method of the primary stage. The last three lines of the `start` method for the Click Me application perform these functions:

```
primaryStage.setScene(scene);
primaryStage.setTitle("The Click Me App");
primaryStage.show();
```

When the last line calls the `show` method, the `Stage` displays — in other words, the window that was shown in Figure 2-1 displays onscreen.

You can read about additional capabilities of the `Stage` class in Chapter 4.

Examining the Click Counter Program

Now that I've explained the details of every line of the Click Me program, I look at a slightly enhanced version of the Click Me program called the Click Counter program. In the Click Me program that was shown in Listing 1-1 (in Chapter 1), the text displayed on the button changes when the user clicks the button. In the Click Counter program, an additional type of control called a *label* displays the number of times the user has clicked the button.

Figure 2-2 shows the Click Counter program in operation. The window at the top of this figure shows how the Click Counter program appears when you first start it. As you can see, the text label at the top of the window displays the text `You have not clicked the button`. The second window shows what the program looks like after you click the button the first time. Here, the label reads `You have clicked once`. When the button is clicked a second time, the label changes again, as shown in the third window. Here, the label reads `You have clicked 2 times`. After that, the number displayed by the label updates each time you click the button to indicate how many times the button has been clicked.

Figure 2-2:
The Click
Counter
program in
action.

Listing 2-2 shows the source code for the Click Counter program, and the following paragraphs describe the key points of how it works:

Listing 2-2: The Click Counter Program

```
import javafx.application.*;                                    →1
import javafx.stage.*;
import javafx.scene.*;
import javafx.scene.layout.*;
import javafx.scene.control.*;

public class ClickCounter extends Application                   →7
{
    public static void main(String[] args)                      →9
    {
        launch(args);                                           →11
    }
```

```
    Button btn;                                                        →14
    Label lbl;                                                         →15
    int iClickCount = 0;                                               →16

    @Override public void start(Stage primaryStage)                    →18
    {
        // Create the button
        btn = new Button();                                            →21
        btn.setText("Click me please!");                               →22
        btn.setOnAction(e -> buttonClick());                           →23

        // Create the Label
        lbl = new Label();                                             →26
        lbl.setText("You have not clicked the button.");               →27

        // Add the label and the button to a layout pane
        BorderPane pane = new BorderPane();                            →30
        pane.setTop(lbl);                                              →31
        pane.setCenter(btn);                                           →32

        // Add the layout pane to a scene
        Scene scene = new Scene(pane, 250, 150);                       →35

        // Add the scene to the stage, set the title
        // and show the stage
        primaryStage.setScene(scene);                                  →39
        primaryStage.setTitle("Click Counter");                        →40
        primaryStage.show();                                           →41
    }

    public void buttonClick()                                          →44
    {
        iClickCount++;                                                 →46
        if (iClickCount == 1)                                          →47
        {
            lbl.setText("You have clicked once.");                     →49
        }
        else
        {
            lbl.setText("You have clicked "                            →53
                + iClickCount + " times." );
        }
    }

}
```

The following paragraphs explain the key points of the Click Me program:

→ **1:**   The `import` statements reference the `javafx` packages that will be used by the Click Me program.

→ **7:**   The `ClickMe` class extends `javafx.application.Application`, thus specifying that the `ClickMe` class is a JavaFX application.

→ **9:**   As with any Java program, the `main` method is the main entry point for all JavaFX programs.

→ **11:** The `main` method calls the `launch` method, which is defined by the `Application` class. The `launch` method, in turn, creates an instance of the `ClickMe` class and then calls the `start` method.

→ **14:** A variable named `btn` of type `javafx.scene.control.Button` is declared as a class variable. Variables representing JavaFX controls are commonly defined as class variables so that they can be accessed by any method in the class.

→ **15:** A class variable named `lbl` of type `javafx.scene.control.Label` represents the `Label` control so that it can be accessed from any method in the class.

→ **16:** A class variable named `iClickCount` will be used to keep track of the number of times the user clicks the button.

→ **18:** The declaration of the `start` method uses the `@override` annotation, indicating that this method overrides the default `start` method provided by the `Application` class. The `start` method accepts a parameter named `primaryStage`, which represents the window in which the Click Me application will display its user interface.

→ **21:** The `start` method begins by creating a `Button` object and assigning it to a variable named `btn`.

→ **22:** The button's `setText` method is called to set the text displayed by the button to `Click me please!`.

→ **23:** The `setOnAction` is called to create an event handler for the button. Here, a Lambda expression is used to simply call the `buttonClick` method whenever the user clicks the button.

→ **26:** The constructor of the `Label` class is called to create a new label.

→ **27:** The label's `setText` method is called to set the initial text value of the label to `You have not clicked the button`.

→ **30:** A border pane object is created by calling the constructor of the `BorderPane` class, referencing the border pane via a variable named `pane`. The border pane will be used to control the layout of the controls displayed on the screen.

→ **31:** The border pane's `setTop` method is called to add the label to the top region of the border pane.

→ **32:** The border pane's `setCenter` method is called to add the button to the center region of the border pane.

→ **35:** A scene object is created by calling the constructor of the `Scene` class, passing the border pane created in line 30 to the constructor to establish the border pane as the root node of the scene. In addition, the dimensions of the scene are set to 300 pixels in width and 250 pixels in height.

→ **39:** The `setScene` method of the `primaryStage` is used to add the scene to the primary stage.

→ **40:** The `setTitle` method is used to set the text displayed in the primary stage's title bar.

→ **41:** The `show` method is called to display the primary stage. When this line is executed, the window that was shown in Figure 2-1 displays on the screen and the user can begin to interact with the program.

→ **44:** The `buttonClick` method is called whenever the user clicks the button.

→ **46:** The `iClickCount` variable is incremented to indicate that the user has clicked the button.

→ **47:** An `if` statement is used to determine whether the button has been clicked one or more times.

→ **49:** If the button has been clicked once, the label text is set to `You have clicked once`.

→ **53:** Otherwise, the label text is set to a string that indicates how many times the button has been clicked.

That's all there is to it. If you understand the details of how the Click Counter program works, you're ready to move on to Chapter 3. If you're still struggling with a few points, I suggest you spend some time reviewing this chapter and experimenting with the Click Counter program in TextPad, Eclipse, or NetBeans.

The following paragraphs help clarify some of the key sticking points that might be tripping you up about the Click Counter program and JavaFX in general:

- ✔ **When does the program switch from static to non-static?** Like every Java program, the main entry point of a JavaFX program is the static `main` method.

  In most JavaFX programs, the static `main` method does just one thing: It calls the `launch` method to start the JavaFX portion of the program. The `launch` method creates an instance of the `ClickCounter` class and then calls the `start` method. At that point, the program is no longer running in a static context because an instance of the `ClickCounter` class has been created.

- ✔ **Where does the `primaryStage` variable come from?** The `primaryStage` variable is passed to the `start` method when the `launch` method calls the `start` method. Thus, the `start` method receives the `primaryStage` variable as a parameter.

  That's why you won't find a separate variable declaration for the `primaryStage` variable.

- ✔ **How does the `->` operator work?** The `->` operator is used to create what is known as a Lambda expression. *Lambda expressions* are a new feature of Java 8 that are used in situations that would've previously required an anonymous class. Don't worry if you don't understand how the Lambda expression works. I explain them in detail in Chapter 3.

Chapter 3

Handling Events

● ●

In This Chapter

▶ Understanding important event concepts

▶ Working with event-handling classes and interfaces

▶ Extending the `EventHandler` interface

▶ Using inner and anonymous classes for event handling

▶ Using Lambda expressions for event handling

● ●

*I*n Chapter 2, I discuss two programs that display simple scenes that include a button and that respond when the user clicks the button. These programs respond to the event triggered when the user clicks the button by providing an *event handler* that's executed when the event occurs.

In this chapter, you read more details about how event handling works in JavaFX. I discuss how events are generated and how they're dispatched by JavaFX so that your programs can respond to them. You discover the many varieties of events that can be processed by a JavaFX program. And you figure out several programming techniques for handling JavaFX events.

Finally, in this chapter you're introduced to the idea of *property bindings,* which let you write code that responds to changes in the value of certain types of class fields, dubbed *property fields*. In JavaFX, property bindings are sometimes used in situations that would've called for an event handler in `Swing`.

Although event handling is used mostly to respond to button clicks, it can also be used to respond to other types of user interactions. You can use event handling, for example, to write code that's executed when the user makes a selection from a combo box, moves the mouse over a label, or presses a key on the keyboard. The event-handling techniques in this chapter work for those events as well.

Examining Events

An *event* is an object that's generated when the user does something note-worthy with one of your user-interface components. Then this event object is passed to a special method you create, called an event handler. The *event handler* can examine the event object, determine exactly what type of event occurred, and respond accordingly. If the user clicks a button, the event handler might write any data entered by the user via text fields to a file. If the user passes the mouse cursor over a label, the event handler might change the text displayed by the label. And if the user selects an item from a combo box, the event handler might use the value that was selected to look up information in a database. The possibilities are endless!

An event is represented by an instance of the class `javafx.event.Event` or one of its many subclasses. Table 3-1 lists the most commonly used event classes.

Table 3-1	Commonly Used Event Classes	
Event Class	*Package*	*Description*
ActionEvent	javafx.event	Created when the user performs an action with a button or other component. Usually this means that the user clicked the button, but the user can also invoke a button action by tabbing to the button and pressing the Enter key. This is the most commonly used event class, as it represents the most common types of user-interface events.
InputEvent	javafx.scene.input	Created when an event that results from user input, such as a mouse or key click, occurs.
KeyEvent	javafx.scene.input	Created when the user presses a key on the keyboard. This event can be used to watch for specific keystrokes entered by the user. (KeyEvent is a subclass of InputEvent.)

Event Class	Package	Description
MouseEvent	javafx. scene.input	Created when the user does something interesting with the mouse, such as clicking one of the buttons, dragging the mouse, or simply moving the mouse cursor over another object. (MouseEvent is a subclass of InputEvent.)
TouchEvent	javafx. scene.input	Created when a user initiates a touch event on a device that allows touch input.
WindowEvent	javafx.stage	Created when the status of the window (stage) changes.

Here are four important terms you need to know:

✔ **Event:** An object that's created when the user does something noteworthy with a component, such as clicking it.

✔ **Event source:** The object on which the event initially occurred.

✔ **Event target:** The node that the event is directed at.

This is usually the button or other control that the user clicked or otherwise manipulated. (In most cases, the event source and the event target are the same.)

✔ **Event handler:** The object that listens for events and handles them when they occur.

The event-listener object must implement the EventHandler interface, which defines a single method named handle (see Table 3-2). The EventHandler interface is defined in the package javafx.event.

Table 3-2   **The EventHandler Interface**

Method	Description
void handle<T event>	Called when an event occurs

Handling Events

Now that you know the basic classes and interfaces that are used for event handling, you're ready to figure out how to wire them to create a program that responds to events.

In this section, I discuss how to implement the event handler by coding the program's `Application` so that in addition to extending the `Application` class, it also implements the `EventHandler` interface. In subsequent sections of this chapter, I discuss alternative techniques to implement event handlers that are more concise and, in many cases, easier to work with.

Note that the programs that were shown in Chapters 1 and 2 use the concise Lambda expressions technique, and most of the programs featured throughout the rest of this book also use Lambda expressions. But it's important that you know the other techniques so that you have a complete understanding of how event handling actually works.

Here are three steps you must take to handle a JavaFX event:

1. **Create an event source.**

   An *event source* is simply a control, such as a button, that can generate events. Usually, you declare the variable that refers to the event source as a private class field, outside the `start` method or any other class methods:

   ```
   private Button btn;
   ```

   Then, in the `start` method, you can create the button like this:

   ```
   btn = new Button();
   btn.setText("Click me please!");
   ```

2. **Create an event handler.**

   To create an event handler, you must create an object that implements the `EventHandler` interface and provides an implementation of the `handle` method.

   Here are four ways to create an event handler:

   - Add `implements EventHandler` to the program's `Application` class and provide an implementation of the `handle` method.

     You figure out how to use this technique in the section "Implementing the EventHandler Interface."

   - Create an inner class that implements `EventHandler` within the `Application` class.

You figure out how to use this technique in the section "Handling Events with Inner Classes."

- Create an anonymous class that implements `EventHandler`.

  I show you how to use this technique in the section "Handling Events with Anonymous Inner Classes."

- Use a Lambda expression to implement the `handle` method.

  You read about how to use this technique in the section "Using Lambda Expressions to Handle Events."

3. **Register the event handler with the event source.**

   The final step is to register the event handler with the event source so that the `handle` method is called whenever the event occurs.

   Every component that serves as an event source provides a method that lets you register event handlers to listen for the event. For example, a `Button` control provides a `setOnAction` method that lets you register an event handler for the action event. In the `setOnAction` method, you specify the event handler object as a parameter. The exact way you do that depends on which of the various techniques you used to create the event handler.

Implementing the EventHandler Interface

To see how all these elements work together in a complete program, Figure 3-1 shows the output from a simple program called AddSubtract1. This program displays a label and two buttons, one titled Add and the other titled Subtract. The label initially displays the number 0. Each time the user clicks the Add button, the value displayed by the label is increased by one; each time the user clicks the Subtract button, the value is decreased by one.

Listing 3-1 shows the complete code for this program.

Figure 3-1:
The Add-
Subtract1
program.

Listing 3-1:   The AddSubtract1 Program

```
import javafx.application.*;
import javafx.stage.*;
import javafx.scene.*;
import javafx.scene.layout.*;
import javafx.scene.control.*;
import javafx.event.*;                                              →6

public class AddSubtract extends Application
    implements EventHandler <ActionEvent>                            →9
{
    public static void main(String[] args)                          →11
    {
        launch(args);
    }

    Button btnAdd;                                                   →16
    Button btnSubtract;
    Label lbl;
    int iCounter = 0;                                               →19

    @Override public void start(Stage primaryStage)                 →21
    {
        // Create the Add button
        btnAdd = new Button();                                      →24
        btnAdd.setText("Add");
        btnAdd.setOnAction(this);                                   →26

        // Create the Subtract button
        btnSubtract = new Button();                                 →29
        btnSubtract.setText("Subtract");
        btnSubtract.setOnAction(this);

        // Create the Label                                         →33
        lbl = new Label();
        lbl.setText(Integer.toString(iCounter));

        // Add the buttons and label to an HBox pane
        HBox pane = new HBox(10);                                   →38
        pane.getChildren().addAll(lbl, btnAdd, btnSubtract);        →39

        // Add the layout pane to a scene
        Scene scene = new Scene(pane, 200, 75);                     →42

        // Add the scene to the stage, set the title
        // and show the stage
        primaryStage.setScene(scene);                               →46
        primaryStage.setTitle("Add/Sub");
        primaryStage.show();
    }
```

```
    @Override public void handle(ActionEvent e)              →51
    {
        if (e.getSource()==btnAdd)                           →53
        {
            iCounter++;
        }
        else
        {
            if (e.getSource()==btnSubtract)                  →59
            {
                iCounter--;
            }
        }
        lbl.setText(Integer.toString(iCounter));             →64
    }
}
```

The following paragraphs point out some key lines of the program:

→ **6:** The program must import the `javafx.event` package, which defines the `ActionEvent` class and the `EventHandler` interfaces.

→ **9:** As in any JavaFX program, the `AddSubtract1` class extends the `Application` class. However, the `AddSubtract1` class also implements the `EventHandler` interface so that it can define a `handle` method that will handle `ActionEvent` events that are generated by the buttons.

The `EventHandler` interface is a generic interface, which means that you must specify the specific event type that the interface will implement. In this case, the class will handle `ActionEvent` events.

→ **11:** The `main` method is required as usual. This method simply calls the `launch` method to create an instance of the `AddSubtract` class, which in turn calls the `start` method.

→ **16:** Two buttons (`btnAdd` and `btnSubtract`) and a label (`lbl`) are defined as class fields so that they can be accessed throughout the class.

→ **19:** The `iCounter` variable keeps track of the value displayed by the label. The value will be incremented when the user clicks the `btnAdd` button and decremented when the user clicks the `btnSubtract` button.

→ **21:** The `start` method is called when the application is started.

→ **24:** This line and the next line create the Add button and set its text to display the word *Add*.

→ **26:** This line sets the current object as the event handler for the `btnAdd` button. The `this` keyword is used here because the `AddSubtract` class implements the `EventHandler`. In effect, the `AddSubtract` class itself handles any events that are created by its own controls.

→ **29:** These lines create the Subtract button, set its text to the word *Subtract,* and set the current object (`this`) as the event handler for the button.

→ **33:** These two lines create the label and set its initial text value to a string equivalent of the `iCounter` variable.

→ **38:** For this program, a border pane is not the appropriate type of layout pane. Instead, for this program, use a new type of layout pane called an `HBox`. An `HBox` pane arranges any controls you add to it in a horizontal row. The parameter `10` indicates that the controls should be separated from one another by a space ten pixels wide.

→ **39:** This line adds the label and the two buttons to the horizontal box. The code required to do this is admittedly a bit convoluted. First, you must call the `getChildren` method to get a list of all the child nodes that are in the `HBox`. Then, you call the `addAll` method to add one or more controls. In this case, three controls are added: the label (`lbl`), the Add button (`btnAdd`), and the Subtract button (`btnSubtract`).

→ **42:** This line creates a new scene, using the `HBox` pane as its root node.

→ **46:** This line sets the scene created in line 42 as the primary scene for the stage, sets the stage title, and then shows the stage.

→ **51:** The `handle` method must be coded because the `AddSubtract` class implements the `EventHandler` interface. This method is called by either of the button objects whenever the user clicks one of the buttons. The `ActionEvent` parameter is the event generated by the button click and passed to the `handle` method.

→ **53:** The `getSource` method of the `ActionEvent` parameter is called to determine the event source. If the event source is `btnAdd`, the `iCounter` variable is incremented.

→ **59:** If, on the other hand, the event source is `btnSubtract`, the `iCounter` variable is decremented.

→ **64:** The label's text value is set to the string equivalent of the `iCounter` variable.

Handling Events with Inner Classes

An *inner class* is a class that's nested within another class. Inner classes are commonly used for event handlers. That way, the class that defines the application doesn't also have to implement the event handler. Instead, it includes an inner class that handles the events.

Listing 3-2 shows the AddSubtract2 program, which uses an inner class to handle the action event for the buttons.

Listing 3-2:   The AddSubtract2 Program with an Inner Class

```
import javafx.application.*;
import javafx.stage.*;
import javafx.scene.*;
import javafx.scene.layout.*;
import javafx.scene.control.*;
import javafx.event.*;

public class AddSubtract2 extends Application                          →8
{
    public static void main(String[] args)
    {
        launch(args);
    }

    Button btnAdd;
    Button btnSubtract;
    Label lbl;
    int iCounter = 0;

    @Override public void start(Stage primaryStage)
    {
        // Create a ClickHandler instance
        ClickHandler ch = new ClickHandler();                         →23

        // Create the Add button
        btnAdd = new Button();
        btnAdd.setText("Add");
        btnAdd.setOnAction(ch);                                       →28

        // Create the Subtract button
        btnSubtract = new Button();
        btnSubtract.setText("Subtract");
        btnSubtract.setOnAction(ch);                                  →33
```

(continued)

Listing 3-2 *(continued)*

```
            // Create the Label
            lbl = new Label();
            lbl.setText(Integer.toString(iCounter));

            // Add the buttons and label to an HBox pane
            HBox pane = new HBox(10);
            pane.getChildren().addAll(lbl, btnAdd, btnSubtract);

            // Add the layout pane to a scene
            Scene scene = new Scene(pane, 200, 75);

            // Add the scene to the stage, set the title
            // and show the stage
            primaryStage.setScene(scene);
            primaryStage.setTitle("Add/Sub");
            primaryStage.show();
        }

    private class ClickHandler                                      →53
            implements EventHandler <ActionEvent>
        {
            @Override public void handle(ActionEvent e)             →56
            {
                if (e.getSource()==btnAdd)
                {
                    iCounter++;
                }
                else
                {
                    if (e.getSource()==btnSubtract)
                    {
                        iCounter--;
                    }
                }
                lbl.setText(Integer.toString(iCounter));
            }
        }
    }

}
```

This program works essentially the same way as the program shown
in Listing 3-1, so I don't review every detail. Instead, I just highlight the
differences:

→ **8:** The `AddSubtract2` class still extends `Application` but doesn't
implement `EventHandler`.

→ **23:** This statement creates an instance of the `ClickHandler` class
(the inner class) and assigns it to the variable `ch`.

→ **28:** This statement sets ch as the action listener for the Add button.

→ **33:** This statement sets ch as the action listener for the Subtract button.

→ **53:** The ClickHandler class is declared as an inner class by placing its declaration completely within the AddSubtract2 class. The ClickHandler class implements the EventHandler interface so that it can handle events.

→ **56:** The handle method here is identical to the handle method in the AddSubtract1 program (see Listing 3-1) but resides in the inner ClickHandler class instead of in the outer class.

Handling Events with Anonymous Inner Classes

An *anonymous inner class,* usually just called an *anonymous class,* is a class that's defined on the spot, right at the point where you need it. Because you code the body of the class right where you need it, you don't have to give it a name; that's why it's called an *anonymous* class.

Anonymous classes are often used for event handlers to avoid the need to create a separate class that explicitly implements the EventHandler interface.

One advantage of using anonymous classes for event handlers is that you can easily create a separate event handler for each control that generates events. Then, in the handle method for those event handlers, you can dispense with the if statements that check the event source.

Consider the event handler for the AddSubtract2 program shown earlier in Listing 3-2: It must check the event source to determine whether to increment or decrement the iCounter variable. By using anonymous classes, you can create separate event handlers for the Add and Subtract buttons. The event handler for the Add button increments iCounter, and the event handler for the Subtract button decrements it. Neither event handler needs to check the event source because the event handler's handle method will be called only when an event is raised on the button with which the handler is associated.

Listing 3-3 shows the AddSubtract3 program, which uses anonymous inner classes in this way.

Listing 3-3: The AddSubtract3 Program with Anonymous Inner Classes

```java
import javafx.application.*;
import javafx.stage.*;
import javafx.scene.*;
import javafx.scene.layout.*;
import javafx.scene.control.*;
import javafx.event.*;

public class AddSubtract3 extends Application
{
    public static void main(String[] args)
    {
        launch(args);
    }

    Button btnAdd;
    Button btnSubtract;
    Label lbl;
    int iCounter = 0;

    @Override public void start(Stage primaryStage)
    {
        // Create the Add button
        btnAdd = new Button();
        btnAdd.setText("Add");
        btnAdd.setOnAction(
            new EventHandler<ActionEvent>()                    →26
            {
                public void handle(ActionEvent e)              →28
                {
                    iCounter++;                                →30
                    lbl.setText(Integer.toString(iCounter));
                }
            } );

        // Create the Subtract button
        btnSubtract = new Button();
        btnSubtract.setText("Subtract");
        btnSubtract.setOnAction(
            new EventHandler<ActionEvent>()                    →39
            {
                public void handle(ActionEvent e)              →41
                {
                    iCounter--;
                    lbl.setText(Integer.toString(iCounter));
                }
            } );
```

```
        // Create the Label
        lbl = new Label();
        lbl.setText(Integer.toString(iCounter));

        // Add the buttons and label to an HBox pane
        HBox pane = new HBox(10);
        pane.getChildren().addAll(lbl, btnAdd, btnSubtract);

        // Add the layout pane to a scene
        Scene scene = new Scene(pane, 200, 75);

        // Add the scene to the stage, set the title
        // and show the stage
        primaryStage.setScene(scene);
        primaryStage.setTitle("Add/Sub");
        primaryStage.show();
    }
}
```

The following paragraphs highlight the key points of how this program uses anonymous inner classes to handle the button events:

→ **26:** This line calls the setOnAction method of the Add button and creates an anonymous instance of the EventHandler class, specifying ActionEvent as the type.

→ **28:** The handle method must be defined within the body of the anonymous class.

→ **30:** Because this handle method will be called only when the Add button is clicked (not when the Subtract button is clicked), it does not need to determine the event source. Instead, the method simply increments the counter variable and sets the label text to display the new value of the counter.

→ **39:** This line calls the setOnAction method of the Subtract button and creates another anonymous instance of the EventHandler class.

→ **41:** This time, the handle method decrements the counter variable and updates the label text to display the new counter value.

Using Lambda Expressions to Handle Events

Java 8 introduces a new feature that in some ways is similar to anonymous classes, but with more concise syntax. More specifically, a Lambda expression lets you create an anonymous class that implements a specific type of interface — a *functional interface* — which has one and only one abstract method.

The `EventHandler` interface used to handle JavaFX events meets that definition: It has just one abstract method, `handle`. Thus, `EventHandler` is a functional interface and can be used with Lambda expressions.

A Lambda expression is a concise way to create an anonymous class that implements a functional interface. Instead of providing a formal method declaration that includes the return type, method name, parameter types, and method body, you simply define the parameter types and the method body. The Java compiler infers the rest based on the context in which you use the Lambda expression.

The parameter types are separated from the method body by a new operator — the *arrow operator* — which consists of a hyphen followed by a greater-than symbol. Here's an example of a Lambda expression that implements the `EventHandler` interface:

```
e ->
    {
        iCounter++;
        lbl.setText(Integer.toString(iCounter);
    }
```

In this case the Lambda expression implements a functional interface whose single method accepts a single parameter, identified as e. When the method is called, the `iCounter` variable is incremented and the label text is updated to display the new counter value.

Here's how you'd register this Lambda expression as the event handler for a button:

```
btnAdd.setOnAction( e ->
    {
        iCounter++;
        lbl.setText(Integer.toString(iCounter));
    } );
```

One of the interesting things about Lambda expressions is that you don't need to know the name of the method being called. This is possible because a functional interface used with a Lambda expression can have only one abstract method. In the case of the `EventHandler` interface, the method is named `handle`.

You also do not need to know the name of the interface being implemented. This is possible because the interface is determined by the context. The `setOnAction` method takes a single parameter of type `EventHandler`. Thus, when you use a Lambda expression in a call to `setOnAction`, the Java compiler can deduce that the Lambda expression will implement the `EventHandler` interface. And because the only abstract method of `EventHandler` is the `handle` method, the compiler can deduce that the method body you supply is an implementation of the `handle` method.

In a way, Lambda expressions take the concept of anonymous classes two steps further. When you use an anonymous class to set an event handler, you must know and specify the name of the class (`EventHandler`) and the name of the method to be called (`handle`), so the only sense in which the class is anonymous is that you don't need to provide a name for a variable that will reference the class. But when you use a Lambda expression, you don't have to know or specify the name of the class, the method, or a variable used to reference it. All you have to do, essentially, is provide the body of the `handle` method.

Listing 3-4 shows the AddSubtract4 program, which uses Lambda expressions to handle the button clicks.

Listing 3-4: The AddSubtract4 Program with Lambda Expressions

```
import javafx.application.*;
import javafx.stage.*;
import javafx.scene.*;
import javafx.scene.layout.*;
import javafx.scene.control.*;
import javafx.event.*;

public class AddSubtract4 extends Application
{
    public static void main(String[] args)
    {
        launch(args);
    }

    Button btnAdd;
    Button btnSubtract;
    Label lbl;
    int iCounter = 0;

    @Override public void start(Stage primaryStage)
    {
        // Create the Add button
        btnAdd = new Button();
        btnAdd.setText("Add");
        btnAdd.setOnAction( e ->                              →25
            {
                iCounter++;
                lbl.setText(Integer.toString(iCounter));
            } );

        // Create the Subtract button
        btnSubtract = new Button();
        btnSubtract.setText("Subtract");
        btnSubtract.setOnAction( e ->                         →34
```

(continued)

Listing 3-4 *(continued)*

```
        {
            iCounter--;
            lbl.setText(Integer.toString(iCounter));
        } );

        // Create the Label
        lbl = new Label();
        lbl.setText(Integer.toString(iCounter));

        // Add the buttons and label to an HBox pane
        HBox pane = new HBox(10);
        pane.getChildren().addAll(lbl, btnAdd, btnSubtract);

        // Add the layout pane to a scene
        Scene scene = new Scene(pane, 200, 75);

        // Add the scene to the stage, set the title
        // and show the stage
        primaryStage.setScene(scene);
        primaryStage.setTitle("Add/Sub");
        primaryStage.show();
    }
}
```

This program works essentially the same way as the program shown in Listing 3-3, so I just point out the features directly related to the use of the Lambda expression:

→ **25:** This statement uses a Lambda expression to add an event handler to the Add button. The method body of this Lambda expression increments the counter variable and then sets the label text to reflect the updated value.

→ **34:** This statement uses a similar Lambda expression to create the event handler for the Subtract button. The only difference between this Lambda expression and the one for the Add button is that here the counter variable is decremented instead of incremented.

Note that in this example, the Lambda expressions for the two event handlers are simple because very little processing needs to be done when either of the buttons in this program are clicked. What would the program look like, however, if the processing required for one or more of the button clicks required hundreds of lines of Java code to implement? The Lambda expression would become unwieldy. For this reason, I often prefer to isolate the actual processing to be done by an event handler in a separate method. Then, the Lambda expression itself includes just one line of code that simply calls the method.

Listing 3-5 shows another variation of the AddSubtract5 program implemented using that technique. Note that the technique used in Listing 3-5 is the technique that most of the remaining programs in this book use.

Listing 3-5:   The AddSubtract5 Program with Lambda Expressions

```
import javafx.application.*;
import javafx.stage.*;
import javafx.scene.*;
import javafx.scene.layout.*;
import javafx.scene.control.*;
import javafx.event.*;

public class AddSubtract5 extends Application
{
    public static void main(String[] args)
    {
        launch(args);
    }

    Button btnAdd;
    Button btnSubtract;
    Label lbl;
    int iCounter = 0;

    @Override public void start(Stage primaryStage)
    {
        // Create the Add button
        btnAdd = new Button();
        btnAdd.setText("Add");
        btnAdd.setOnAction( e -> btnAdd_Click() );          →25

        // Create the Subtract button
        btnSubtract = new Button();
        btnSubtract.setText("Subtract");
        btnSubtract.setOnAction( e -> btnSubtract_Click() );  →30

        // Create the Label
        lbl = new Label();
        lbl.setText(Integer.toString(iCounter));

        // Add the buttons and label to an HBox pane
        HBox pane = new HBox(10);
        pane.getChildren().addAll(lbl, btnAdd, btnSubtract);
```

(continued)

Listing 3-5 *(continued)*

```
                // Add the layout pane to a scene
                Scene scene = new Scene(pane, 200, 75);

                // Add the scene to the stage, set the title
                // and show the stage
                primaryStage.setScene(scene);
                primaryStage.setTitle("Add/Sub");
                primaryStage.show();
        }

        private void btnAdd_Click()                                →50
        {
                iCounter++;
                lbl.setText(Integer.toString(iCounter));
        }

        private void btnSubtract_Click()                           →56
        {
                iCounter--;
                lbl.setText(Integer.toString(iCounter));
        }

}
```

The following paragraphs highlight the important points of this version of the program:

→ **25:** The setOnAction method for the Add button uses a Lambda expression to specify that the method named btnAdd_Click should be called when the user clicks the button.

→ **30:** The setOnAction method for the Subtract button uses a Lambda expression to specify that the method named btnSubtract_Click should be called when the user clicks the button.

→ **50:** The btnAdd_Click method increments the counter and updates the label's text to reflect the updated counter value.

→ **56:** Likewise, the btnSubtract_Click method decrements the counter and updates the label's text accordingly.

Chapter 4

Setting the Stage and Scene Layout

In This Chapter

▶ Looking at some useful methods of the Stage and Scene classes

▶ Alternating scenes within a single stage

▶ Displaying additional stages as message and confirmation boxes

▶ Discovering the proper way to exit a JavaFX program

O for a Muse of fire, that would ascend
The brightest heaven of Invention,

A kingdom for a stage, princes to act,
And monarchs to behold the swelling scene!

So begins William Shakespeare's play *Henry V,* and so also begins this chapter, in which I explore the various ways to manipulate the appearance of a JavaFX application by manipulating its stage and its swelling scenes.

Specifically, you read important details about the Stage class and the Scene class so that you can control such things as whether the window is resizable and if so, whether it has a maximum or a minimum size. You also read how to coerce your programs into displaying additional stages beyond the primary stage, such as an alert or confirmation dialog box. And finally, you read the proper way to end a JavaFX program by handling the events generated when the user closes the stage.

Examining the Stage Class

A stage, which is represented by the `Stage` class, is the topmost container in which a JavaFX user interface appears. In Windows, on a Mac, or in Linux, a stage is usually a window. On other types of devices, such as a smartphone or tablet, the stage may be the full screen or a tiled region of the screen.

When a JavaFX application is launched, a stage known as the *primary stage* is automatically created. A reference to this stage is passed to the application's `start` method via the `primaryStage` parameter:

```
@Override public void start(Stage primaryStage)
{
    // primaryStage refers to the
    // application's primary stage.
}
```

You can then use the primary stage to create the application's user interface by adding a scene, which contains one or more controls or other user-interface nodes.

In many cases, you will need to access the primary stage outside of the scope of the `start` method. You can easily make this possible by defining a class field and using it to reference the primary stage. You see an example of how to do that later in this chapter, in the section "Switching Scenes."

The primary stage initially takes on the default characteristics of a normal windowed application, which depends on the operating system within which the program will run. You can, if you choose, change these defaults to suit the needs of your application. At the minimum, you should always set the window title. You may also want to change details, such as whether the stage is resizable and various aspects of the stage's appearance.

The `Stage` class comes equipped with many methods that let you manipulate the appearance and behavior of a stage. Table 4-1 lists the ones you're most likely to use.

Table 4-1 **Commonly Used Methods of the Stage Class**

Method	*Description*
`void close()`	Closes the stage.

`void initModality(Modality modality)`	Sets the modality of the stage. This method must be called before the `show` method is called. The modality can be one of the following:
	
	`Modality.NONE`
	`Modality.APPLICATION_MODAL`
	`Modality.WINDOW_MODAL`

`void initStyle(StageStyle style)`	Sets the style for the stage. This method must be called before the `show` method is called. The style can be one of the following:
	
	`StageStyle.DECORATED`
	`StageStyle.UNDECORATED`
	`StageStyle.TRANSPARENT`
	`StageStyle.UNIFIED`
	`StageStyle.UTILITY`

`void getMaxHeight(double maxheight)`	Gets the maximum height for the stage.
`void getMaxWidth(double maxwidth)`	Gets the maximum width for the stage.
`void getMinHeight(double maxheight)`	Gets the minimum height for the stage.
`void getMinWidth(double maxwidth)`	Gets the minimum width for the stage.
`void setFullScreen(boolean fullscreen)`	Sets the fullscreen status of the stage.
`void setIconified(boolean iconified)`	Sets the iconified status of the stage.
`void setMaximized(boolean maximized)`	Sets the maximized status of the stage.

(continued)

Table 4-1 *(continued)*

Method	Description
void setMaxHeight(double maxheight)	Sets the maximum height for the stage.
void setMaxWidth(double maxwidth)	Sets the maximum width for the stage.
void setMinHeight(double maxheight)	Sets the minimum height for the stage.
void setMinWidth(double maxwidth)	Sets the minimum width for the stage.
void setResizable(boolean resizable)	Sets the fullscreen status of the stage.
void setScene(Scene scene)	Sets the scene to be displayed on the stage.
void setTitle(String title)	Sets the title to be displayed in the stage's title bar, if a title bar is visible.
void show()	Makes the stage visible.
void showAndWait()	Makes the stage visible and then waits until the stage is closed before continuing.
void toFront()	Forces the stage to the foreground.
void toBack()	Forces the stage to the background.

The following paragraphs point out some of the ins and outs of using the Stage class methods listed in Table 4-1:

✔ **For many (if not most) applications, the only three methods from Table 4-1 you need to use are setScene, setTitle, and show.**

- Every stage *must* have a scene.

- Every stage *should* have a title.

- There's not much point in creating a stage if you don't intend on showing it to the user.

The other methods in the table let you change the appearance or behavior of the stage, but the defaults are acceptable in most cases.

✔ **If you want to prevent the user from resizing the stage, use the** `setResizable` **method like this:**

```
primaryStage.setResizable(false);
```

Then, the user can't change the size of the window. (By default, the stage is resizable. Thus, you don't need to call the `setResizable` method unless you want to make the stage non-resizable.)

✔ **If the stage is resizable, you can set the minimum and maximum size for the window.** For example:

```
primaryStage.setResizable(true);
primaryStage.setMinWidth(200);
primaryStage.setMinHeight(200);
primaryStage.setMaxWidth(600);
primaryStage.setMaxHeight(600);
```

In this example, the user can resize the window, but the smallest allowable size is 200-x-200 pixels and the largest allowable size is 600-x-600 pixels.

✔ **If you want to display the stage in a maximized window, call** `setMaximized`:

```
primaryStage.setMaximized(true);
```

A maximized window still has the usual decorations (a title bar, window borders, and Minimize, Restore, and Close buttons). If you want the stage to completely take over the screen with no such decorations, use the `setFullScreen` method instead:

```
primaryStage.setFullScreen(true);
```

When your stage enters fullscreen mode, JavaFX displays a message advising the user on how to exit fullscreen mode.

✔ **If, for some reason, you want to start your program minimized to an icon, use the** `setIconified` **method:**

```
primaryStage.setIconified(true);
```

✔ **For more information about the** `close` **method,** see the section "Exit, Stage Right" later in this chapter.

✔ **The** `initModality` **and** `initStyle` **methods are interesting because they can be called only** *before* **you call the** `show` **method.** The `initModality` method allows you to create a modal dialog box — that is, a window that must be closed before the user can continue using other functions within the program. And the `initStyle` method lets you create windows that do not have the usual decorations such as a title bar or Minimize, Restore, and Close buttons. You typically use these methods when you need to create additional stages for your application beyond the primary stage. You can read more about how that works later in this chapter, in the section "Creating a Dialog Box."

Examining the Scene Class

Like the `Stage` class, the `Scene` class is fundamental to JavaFX programs. In every JavaFX program, you use at least one instance of the `Scene` class to hold the user-interface controls that your users will interact with as they use your program.

Table 4-2 lists the more commonly used constructors and methods of the `Scene` class.

Table 4-2	Commonly Used Constructors and Methods of the Scene class
Constructor	*Description*
`Scene(Parent root)`	Creates a new scene with the specified root node.
`Scene(Parent root, double width, double height)`	Creates a new scene with the specified root node, width, and height.
Method	*Description*
`double getHeight()`	Gets the height of the scene.
`double getWidth()`	Gets the width of the scene.
`double getX()`	Gets the horizontal position of the scene.
`double getY()`	Gets the vertical position of the screen.
`void setRoot(Parent root)`	Sets the root node.

The following paragraphs explain some of the more interesting details of the constructors and methods of the `Scene` class:

- ✔ **All the `Scene` class constructors require that you specify the root node.**

   You can change the root node later by calling the `setRoot` method, but it's not possible to create a scene without a root node.

- ✔ **You might be wondering why the root node is an instance of the `Parent` class rather than an instance of the `Node` class.** The `Parent` class is actually a subclass of the `Node` class, which represents a node that can have child nodes. There are several other subclasses of `Node`, which represent nodes that can't have children; those nodes can't be used as the root node for a scene.

✔ **You can set the scene's initial size when you create it by specifying the** `Width` **and** `Height` **parameters.**

If you don't set the size, the scene will determine its own size based on its content.

✔ **You can retrieve the size of the scene via the** `getHeight` **and** `getWidth` **methods.**

There are no corresponding `set` methods that let you set the height or width.

✔ **In general, the size of the scene determines the size of the stage,** provided that that scene is not smaller than the minimum size specified for the stage or larger than the maximum size.

✔ **If the user resizes the stage, the size of the scene is resized accordingly.**

Switching Scenes

The primary stage of a JavaFX program (or any other stage, for that matter) can have only one scene displayed within it at any given time. However, that doesn't mean that your program can't create several scenes and then swap them as needed. For example, suppose you're developing a word-processing program and you want to let the user switch between an editing view and a page preview view. You could do that by creating two distinct scenes, one for each view. Then, to switch the user between views, you simply call the stage's `setScene` method to switch the scene.

In Chapter 2, you read about a ClickCounter program whose scene displays a label and a button and then updates the label to indicate how many times the user has clicked the button. Then, in Chapter 3, you saw several variations of an AddSubtract program whose scene displayed a label and two buttons: One button added one to a counter when clicked, the other subtracted one from the counter.

Listing 4-1 shows a program named SceneSwitcher that combines the scenes from the ClickCounter and AddSubtract programs into a single program. Figure 4-1 shows this program in action:

✔ **When the SceneSwitcher program is first run,** it displays the ClickCounter scene as shown on the left side of the figure.

✔ **When the user clicks the Switch Scene button,** the scene switches to the AddSubtract scene, as shown in the right side of the figure.

Figure 4-1:
The Scene-
Switcher
program.

Listing 4-1:   The SceneSwitcher Program

```
import javafx.application.*;
import javafx.stage.*;
import javafx.scene.*;
import javafx.scene.layout.*;
import javafx.scene.control.*;
import javafx.event.*;

public class SceneSwitcher extends Application
{
    public static void main(String[] args)
    {
        launch(args);
    }

    // class fields for Click-Counter scene              →15
    int iClickCount = 0;
    Label lblClicks;
    Button btnClickMe;
    Button btnSwitchToScene2;
    Scene scene1;

    // class fields for Add-Subtract scene               →22
    int iCounter = 0;
    Label lblCounter;
    Button btnAdd;
    Button btnSubtract;
    Button btnSwitchToScene1;
    Scene scene2;

    // class field for stage
    Stage stage;                                         →31

    @Override public void start(Stage primaryStage)
    {
        stage = primaryStage;                            →35

        // Build the Click-Counter scene                 →37

        lblClicks = new Label();
        lblClicks.setText("You have not clicked the button.");
```

```
    btnClickMe = new Button();
    btnClickMe.setText("Click me please!");
    btnClickMe.setOnAction(
        e -> btnClickMe_Click() );

    btnSwitchToScene2 = new Button();
    btnSwitchToScene2.setText("Switch!");
    btnSwitchToScene2.setOnAction(
        e -> btnSwitchToScene2_Click() );

    VBox pane1 = new VBox(10);
    pane1.getChildren().addAll(lblClicks, btnClickMe,
        btnSwitchToScene2);

    scene1 = new Scene(pane1, 250, 150);


    // Build the Add-Subtract scene                              →59

    lblCounter = new Label();
    lblCounter.setText(Integer.toString(iCounter));

    btnAdd = new Button();
    btnAdd.setText("Add");
    btnAdd.setOnAction(
        e -> btnAdd_Click() );

    btnSubtract = new Button();
    btnSubtract.setText("Subtract");
    btnSubtract.setOnAction(
        e -> btnSubtract_Click() );

    btnSwitchToScene2 = new Button();
    btnSwitchToScene2.setText("Switch!");
    btnSwitchToScene2.setOnAction(
        e -> btnSwitchToScene1_Click() );

    HBox pane2 = new HBox(10);
    pane2.getChildren().addAll(lblCounter, btnAdd,
        btnSubtract, btnSwitchToScene2);

    scene2 = new Scene(pane2, 300, 75);

    // Set the stage with scene 1 and show the stage              →84
    primaryStage.setScene(scene1);
    primaryStage.setTitle("Scene Switcher");
    primaryStage.show();
}


// Event handlers for scene 1                                     →91
```

(continued)

Listing 4-1 *(continued)*

```
public void btnClickMe_Click()
{
    iClickCount++;
    if (iClickCount == 1)
    {
        lblClicks.setText("You have clicked once.");
    }
    else
    {
        lblClicks.setText("You have clicked "
            + iClickCount + " times." );
    }
}


private void btnSwitchToScene2_Click()
{
    stage.setScene(scene2);
}



// Event handlers for scene 2                              →112

private void btnAdd_Click()
{
    iCounter++;
    lblCounter.setText(Integer.toString(iCounter));
}

private void btnSubtract_Click()
{
    iCounter--;
    lblCounter.setText(Integer.toString(iCounter));
}

private void btnSwitchToScene1_Click()
{
    stage.setScene(scene1);
}

}
```

The following paragraphs point out some key sections of the program:

→ 15: This section of the program defines class fields that will be used by the scene for the Click-Counter portion of the program. These fields include `iClickCount`, used to count the number of times the user has clicked the Click Me! Button; the label used to display the count of how many times the Click Me! button has been clicked; the Click Me! button itself; and the button used to switch to the Add-Subtract scene. Also included is a `Scene` field named `scene1` that will be used to reference the Click Counter scene.

→ **22:** These lines define class variables used by the Add-Subtract portion of the program, including the counter (iCounter), the label used to display the counter, the two buttons used to increment and decrement the counter, the button used to switch back to the Click-Counter scene, and a Scene field named scene2 that will be used to reference the Add-Subtract scene.

→ **31:** A class field named stage is used to hold a reference to the primary stage so that it can be accessed throughout the program.

→ **35:** This line sets stage class field to reference the primary stage.

→ **37:** This section of the program builds the Click-Counter scene. First, it creates the label and buttons displayed by the scene. Then it creates a VBox layout pane (which lays out its controls in a vertical stack) and adds the label and buttons to the pane. Finally, it creates the scene using the VBox pane as its root.

→ **59:** This section of the program builds the Add-Subtract scene by creating the label and the buttons displayed by the scene, arranging them in an HBox layout pane, and creating the scene using the HBox pane as its root.

→ **84:** These lines set the Click-Counter scene as the root scene for the primary stage, sets the stage title, and then shows the stage.

→ **91:** This section of the program provides the event handlers for the buttons in the Click-Counter scene. The event handler for the Click Me! button increments the click counter, then sets the label to display an appropriate message. The handler for btnSwitchToScene2 simply switches the scene of the primary stage to scene2, which instantly switches the display to the Add-Subtract scene as shown in the right side of Figure 4-1.

→ **112:** This section of the program provides the event handlers for the buttons in the Add-Subtract scene. The event handler for the Add and Subtract buttons increment or decrement the counter and update the text displayed by the label. The handler for btnSwitchToScene1 switches the scene back to scene1, which switches the display back to the Click-Counter scene shown in the left right side of Figure 4-1.

Creating a Dialog Box

Every JavaFX program has at least one stage — the primary stage. In addition to the primary stage, most JavaFX programs at some point find the need to create additional stages to

✔ **Display informational or warning messages** (commonly called *alert boxes* or a *message boxes*)

✔ **Ask for confirmation from the user before performing a task**

✔ **Show complex dialog boxes that ask the user to enter data or select options**

Many GUI programming packages or languages contain provisions for creating such dialog boxes. For example, Swing includes a built-in class called JOptionPane that makes it easy to create a simple alert box. With the JOptionPane class, you can create a simple alert box, such as the one shown in Figure 4-2, with a single call to the static showMessageDialog method, like this:

```
JOptionPane.showMessageDialog(null,
    "Thanks for stopping by", "Say Thanks",
    JOptionPane.INFORMATION_MESSAGE);
```

Figure 4-2:
The Click-
Counter
program in
action.

Unfortunately (and a little inexplicably), JavaFX provides no such facility. To display a similar message box in JavaFX, you must write code to create a new stage, create a new scene, create a label or other type of text control to display the message, create an OK button, create a layout pane, add the controls to the layout pane, add the pane to the scene, add the scene to the stage, set the stage's modality to WINDOW_MODAL, and then display the stage. You end up needing well over a dozen lines of code to do this.

That's a lot of work to display a simple message box. Fortunately, it doesn't take a lot of effort to create a simple class that you can use to display common message, alert, or confirmation boxes. You can use the class throughout your project, or you can place the class in a package so you can import it into any JavaFX project.

Listing 4-2 shows a simple class named MessageBox that has one method, show, which you can call to display a dialog box that displays a message. To display a message box, simply call the show method, like this:

```
MessageBox.show("Hello!", "Greetings!");
```

The show method accepts two parameters — the message to be displayed and the title displayed in the dialog box.

Listing 4-2: The MessageBox Class

```
import javafx.application.*;
import javafx.stage.*;
import javafx.scene.*;
import javafx.scene.layout.*;
import javafx.scene.control.*;
import javafx.geometry.*;

public class MessageBox                                           →8
{
    public static void show(String message, String title)        →10
    {
        Stage stage = new Stage();                               →12
        stage.initModality(Modality.APPLICATION_MODAL);          →13
        stage.setTitle(title);                                   →14
        stage.setMinWidth(250);                                  →15

        Label lbl = new Label();                                 →17
        lbl.setText(message);

        Button btnOK = new Button();                             →20
        btnOK.setText("OK");
        btnOK.setOnAction(e -> stage.close());                   →22

        VBox pane = new VBox(20);                                →24
        pane.getChildren().addAll(lbl, btnOK);
        pane.setAlignment(Pos.CENTER);                           →26

        Scene scene = new Scene(pane);                           →28
        stage.setScene(scene);
        stage.showAndWait();                                     →30
    }
}
```

The following paragraphs highlight the key points of this program:

→ **8:**   The `MessageBox` class creates and shows a simple dialog box that displays a message.

→ **10:**   The `show` method accepts two parameters — the message to be displayed and the title for the dialog box.

→ **12:**   The `show` method creates a new stage by calling the `Stage` class constructor.

→ **13:**   The `initModality` method is called to specify that the stage will be displayed in application modal mode, which means that when displayed, the stage will block all events from reaching any other stages in the application. Thus, the user must close the message box before using any part of the rest of the application's user interface.

→ **14:**   The message box title is set to the `title` parameter passed to the `show` method.

→ **15:** The message box's minimum width is set to 250 pixels. The actual width of the message box will be increased automatically if necessary based on the length of the message to be displayed.

→ **17:** A label control is created and its text set to the value of the `message` parameter.

→ **20:** A button is created; its text is set to the string `OK`.

→ **22:** An event handler is created by using a Lambda expression to call the `close` method of the `stage` object. Thus, when the user clicks OK, the stage is closed. This, in turn, causes the message box to disappear.

→ **24:** A `VBox` layout pane is created, and the label and button are added to it.

→ **26:** The `setAlignment` method of the `VBox` class is called to specify that the label and button should be centered within the `VBox` layout pane. (You can read more about this method and other methods of the `VBox` class in Chapter 5.)

→ **28:** A `scene` object is created using the layout pane as its root node. Then, in the next line, the `setScene` method of the primary stage is called to establish the scene to be displayed on the stage.

→ **30:** The `showAndWait` method is called to display the message box. This method doesn't return until the stage has been closed, which ensures that the message box is modal — no other part of the program will receive events until the user has closed the message box.

To demonstrate how you might use the `MessageBox` class, the program shown in Listing 4-3 is a variation of the ClickCounter program that was originally discussed in Chapter 2. The original version of this program displayed a label and a button, using the label to display a count of how many times the user has clicked the button. This version of the program dispenses with the label and instead uses the `MessageBox` class to display a message indicating how many times the user has clicked the button.

Listing 4-3:   The ClickCounter Program

```
import javafx.application.*;
import javafx.stage.*;
import javafx.scene.*;
import javafx.scene.layout.*;
import javafx.scene.control.*;

public class ClickCounter extends Application
{
    public static void main(String[] args)
    {
        launch(args);
    }

    int iClickCount = 0;
```

```
@Override public void start(Stage primaryStage)
{
    // Create the button
    btn = new Button();
    btn.setText("Click me please!");
    btn.setOnAction(e -> buttonClick());

    // Add the button to a layout pane
    BorderPane pane = new BorderPane();
    pane.setCenter(btn);

    // Add the layout pane to a scene
    Scene scene = new Scene(pane, 250, 150);

    // Add the scene to the stage, set the title
    // and show the stage
    primaryStage.setScene(scene);
    primaryStage.setTitle("Click Counter");
    primaryStage.show();
}

public void buttonClick()
{
    iClickCount++;
    if (iClickCount == 1)
    {
        MessageBox.show("You have clicked once.", "Click!");
    }
    else
    {
        MessageBox.show("You have clicked "
            + iClickCount + " times." , "Click!");
    }
}
}
```

This program is nearly identical to the version that was presented in Chapter 2 (in Listing 2-2). In fact, here are the only two differences:

✔ No label is defined in this program because a message box, not a label, is used to display the number of times the button has been clicked.

✔ In the buttonClick method of the Chapter 2 version, the label's setText method was called to display the number of times the button has been clicked. In this version, MessageBox.show is used instead.

Figure 4-2 shows the new version of the ClickCounter program in action. Here, you can see the message box displayed when the user clicks the button the first time. (In this example, I moved the message box to the side a little so that you can see the primary stage beneath it. When you actually run the program, the message box is centered over the primary stage.)

Creating a Confirmation Box

A *confirmation box* is a dialog box that asks the user for confirmation before proceeding with some action. For example, if the user of a word processing program closes the program without first saving changes to the current document, the program typically asks the user whether he really wants to quit without saving changes. A confirmation box displays a text message, which is often as simple as "Are you sure?" along with two buttons, typically labeled Yes and No or OK and Cancel.

Creating a confirmation box is a little more complicated than creating a message box because the confirmation box must let the main program know which button the user clicked. The most common way to do that is to call a method that displays the confirmation box and returns a result value that indicates the user's selection.

In this section, I look at a simple class called ConfirmationBox that has a static method named show. This method displays a message and two buttons and returns a Boolean value true if the user clicks the first button and false if the user clicks the second button.

The show method accepts four parameters:

✔ The message to be displayed

✔ The title for the confirmation box

✔ The text to be displayed on the first button

✔ The text to be displayed on the second button

Here's an example of how you might use this class to display a confirmation box:

```
boolean confirm = ConfirmationBox.show(
    "Are you sure?", "Confirmation",
    "Yes", "No");
```

Figure 4-3 shows the confirmation box displayed by the preceding statement. If the user clicks the Yes button, the show method returns true; otherwise, the show method returns false.

Listing 4-4 shows the source for the ConfirmationBox class.

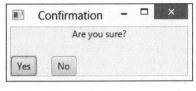

Listing 4-4:   The ConfirmationBox Class

```
import javafx.application.*;
import javafx.stage.*;
import javafx.scene.*;
import javafx.scene.layout.*;
import javafx.scene.control.*;
import javafx.scene.text.*;
import javafx.event.*;
import javafx.geometry.*;

public class ConfirmationBox                                      →10
{

    static Stage stage;                                          →13
    static boolean btnYesClicked;                                →14

    public static boolean show(String message, String title,     →16
        String textYes, String textNo)
    {
        btnYesClicked = false;

        stage = new Stage();                                     →21
        stage.initModality(Modality.APPLICATION_MODAL);
        stage.setTitle(title);
        stage.setMinWidth(250);

        Label lbl = new Label();                                 →26
        lbl.setText(message);

        Button btnYes = new Button();                            →28
        btnYes.setText(textYes);
        btnYes.setOnAction(e -> btnYes_Clicked() );

        Button btnNo = new Button();                             →32
        btnNo.setText(textNo);
        btnNo.setOnAction(e -> btnNo_Clicked() );
```

(continued)

Listing 4-4 *(continued)*

```
        HBox paneBtn = new HBox(20);                              →36
        paneBtn.getChildren().addAll(btnYes, btnNo);

        VBox pane = new VBox(20);                                 →39
        pane.getChildren().addAll(lbl, paneBtn);
        pane.setAlignment(Pos.CENTER);

        Scene scene = new Scene(pane);                            →43
        stage.setScene(scene);
        stage.showAndWait();
        return btnYesClicked;                                     →46
    }

    private static void btnYes_Clicked()                          →49
    {
        stage.close();
        btnYesClicked = true;
    }

    private static void btnNo_Clicked()                           →55
    {
        stage.close();
        btnYesClicked = false;
    }

}
```

The following paragraphs explain some of the key points of this class:

→ **10:** The `ConfirmationBox` class represents a dialog box that asks the user for a Yes/No confirmation.

→ **13:** The stage is defined using a class field so that it will be available to the event handlers for the buttons, which are implemented in separate methods that will be called via Lambda expressions.

→ **14:** A `boolean` class field named `btnYesClicked` indicates whether the user clicks the Yes or No button.

→ **16:** The `show` method returns a `boolean` value and accepts four parameters: the message to display, the dialog box title, the text to display on the first button (the Yes button), and the text to display on the second button (the No button).

→ **21:** The stage is created using APPLICATION_MODAL modality so that no events are processed elsewhere in the program until the user closes the confirmation box. The title is assigned the value passed via the title parameter.

→ **26:** A label is created and assigned the value passed via the message parameter.

→ **28:** The Yes button is created and assigned the text value passed via the textYes property. The setOnAction method uses a Lambda expression to call a method named btnYes_Clicked when the user clicks this button.

→ **32:** The No button is created and assigned the text value passed via the textNo property. The setOnAction method uses a Lambda expression to call a method named btnNo_Clicked when the user clicks this button.

→ **36:** The buttons are added to an HBox layout pane so they will appear side by side in the confirmation box.

→ **39:** The label and the HBox are added to a VBox layout pane so the label will appear centered above the buttons in the confirmation box.

→ **43:** The scene is created using the VBox pane as its root node. Then, the scene is added to the stage and the stage is displayed.

→ **46:** When the user closes the confirmation box, the show method returns the value of btnYesClicked to indicate which button the user clicked.

→ **49:** The btnYes_Clicked method is called if the user clicks the Yes button. In this method, the stage is closed and the btnYesClicked class field is set to true.

→ **55:** The btnNo_Clicked method is called if the user clicks the No button. Here, the stage is closed and the btnYesClicked class field is set to false.

Exit, Stage Right

Because I started this chapter by quoting Shakespeare, I thought it'd be nice to end it by quoting Snagglepuss, the famous pink mountain lion from the old Hanna-Barbera cartoons. He'd often leave the scene by saying, "Exit, stage left" or "Exit, stage right."

Heavens to Mergatroyd!

There's a right way and a wrong way to exit the stage, even. And so far, none of the programs presented in this book have done it the right way. The only mechanism the programs you've seen so far have provided to quit the program is for the user to click the standard window close button, typically represented by an X in the upper-right corner of the window's title bar. That is almost always the wrong way to exit a program.

In most cases, the correct way to exit a program involves the following details:

✔ **Adding a button, menu command, or other way for the user to signal that she wishes to close the program.**

Many programs include a button labeled Exit or Close, and programs that use a menu usually have an Exit command.

✔ **Optionally displaying a confirmation box that verifies whether the user really wants to close the program.** You can do that by using the `ConfirmationBox` class shown in the preceding section or by using a similar class.

Depending on the program, you might want to display this dialog box only if the user has made changes to a document, database, or other file that have not yet been saved.

✔ **If the user really does want to close the program, the program should perform any necessary clean-up work,** such as

• Saving changes to documents, databases, or other files.

• Properly closing databases and other resources.

✔ **After you've done any necessary clean-up work, you can close the application by calling the primary stage's `close` method.**

✔ **The verification and clean-up steps should be taken whether the user attempts to close the program** by using a button or menu command you've provided in your user interface or by clicking the built-in window close button.

In the following sections, you read about how to add a Close button to your application, how to prevent the window close button from unceremoniously terminating your application, and how to put these two elements together in a complete program.

Creating a Close button

To add a button or other user-interface element that allows the user to close the button, all you have to do is provide an action event handler that calls the stage's `close` method.

For example, suppose you create a Close button using the following code:

```
Button btnClose = new Button();
btnClose.setText("Close");
btnClose.setOnAction( e -> primaryStage.close() );
```

In this case, the action event handler simply calls `primaryStage.close()` to close the application.

If you want to do more than simply call the `close` method in the action event handler, you may want to isolate the event handler in a separate method, as in this example:

```
btnClose.setOnAction( e -> btnClose_Clicked());
```

Because the `btnClose_Clicked` method will need to access the primary stage to close it, you need to define a class field of type `Stage` and use it to reference the primary stage. Then, your `btnClose_Clicked` method can easily perform additional tasks. For example:

```
private void btnClose_Click()
{
    boolean reallyQuit = false;
    reallyQuit = ConfirmationBox.show(
        "Are you sure you want to quit?",
        "Confirmation",
        "Yes", "No");
    if (reallyQuit)
    {
        // Perform cleanup tasks here
        // such as saving files or freeing resources
        stage.close();
    }
}
```

In this example, a confirmation box is displayed to make sure the user really wants to exit the program.

Shakespeare's Best Stage Direction

So far in this chapter, I've quoted William Shakespeare once and Snagglepuss once. Both quotes are appropriate for the topic of this chapter: The Shakespeare quotation from *Henry V* refers to stages and scenes, and the Snagglepuss quotation refers to the proper way to exit the stage. Even so, quoting Snagglepuss as often as Shakespeare seems a little out of balance. Thus, I think it's best to throw in another Shakespeare quote to save what little respect I may still have from my college English professors.

Shakespeare's plays are liberally sprinkled with stage directions. Most of them are very brief, such as *Enter Tybalt* or *Exit Romeo* found in *Romeo and Juliet*. A few are a bit more detailed, such as *Enter several of both houses, who join the fray,* also from *Romeo and Juliet.* And

sometimes they're a bit ambiguous, such as *Enter a messenger with two heads and a hand* from *Titus Andronicus.*

But in my opinion, the most interesting of all Shakespeare's stage directions is found in *The Winter's Tale,* when Antigonus is thwarted from rescuing Perdita following a shipwreck: *Exit, pursued by a bear.*

When you exit the stage because you're pursued by a bear, you don't get to collect your things or accomplish any of the other important tasks you had set out to do, such as saving the princess or saving the important changes the user made to a document. Instead, you just turn and run, which is pretty much what happens when the user clicks the window close button unless you properly handle the `CloseRequest` event.

Handling the CloseRequest event

Providing a Close button is an excellent way to allow your users to cleanly exit from your program. However, the user can bypass your exit processing by simply closing the window — that is, by clicking the window close button, usually represented as an X in the upper-right corner of the window border. Unless you provide otherwise, clicking this button unceremoniously terminates the application, bypassing all your nice code that confirms whether the user wants to save his work, closes any open resources, and otherwise provides for a graceful exit.

Fortunately, you can easily avoid such ungraceful exits. Whenever the user attempts to close the window within which a JavaFX stage is displayed, JavaFX generates a `CloseRequest` event, which is sent to the stage. You can provide an event handler for this event by calling the `setOnCloseRequest` method of the `Stage` class. Then, the event handler is called whenever the user tries to close the window.

You might be tempted to create a single method that can serve as the event handler for both the Action event of your Close button and the CloseRequest event, like this:

```
btnClose.setText("Close");
btnClose.setOnAction( e -> btnClose_Click () );
primaryStage.setOnCloseRequest( e -> btnClose_Click () );
```

Here, the intent is to handle the CloseRequest event exactly as if the user had clicked the btnClose button.

That's a good idea, but it doesn't work if the btnClose_Click event displays a confirmation box and closes the stage only if the user confirms that she really wants to quit the program. That's because when the event handler for the CloseRequest event ends, JavaFX automatically closes the stage if the event handler doesn't explicitly close the stage.

To prevent that from happening, you call the consume method of the CloseRequest event object. Consuming the event causes it to be stopped in its tracks within the event handler, thus preventing JavaFX from automatically closing the stage when the event handler ends.

In the Lambda expression passed to the setOnCloseRequest method, the CloseRequest event object is represented by the argument e. Thus, you can consume the CloseRequest event by calling e.consume().

An easy way to provide a method that handles both the Action event for a Close button and the CloseRequest event for a stage is to craft the Lambda expression for the setOnCloseRequest method so that it consumes the event before calling the method that will handle the event:

```
btnClose.setText("Close");
btnClose.setOnAction( e -> btnClose_Click () );
primaryStage.setOnCloseRequest(
    e -> {
            e.consume();
            btnClose_Click ();
        } );
```

Here, the event handler for the CloseRequest event first consumes the event and then calls btnClose_Click. The btnClose_Click method, in turn, displays a confirmation box and closes the stage if the user confirms that this is indeed what he wishes to do.

Putting it all together

Now that you know how to add a Close button to a scene and how to handle the `CloseRequest` event, I look at a program that puts together these two elements to demonstrate the correct way to exit a JavaFX program.

This section presents a variation of the ClickCounter program that includes a Close button in addition to the Click Me! button. When the user clicks the Click Me! button, a message box displays to indicate how many times the button has been clicked. But when the user attempts to exit the program, whether by clicking the Close button or by simply closing the window, the `ConfirmationBox` class that was shown in Listing 4-4 is used to ask the user whether she really wants to exit the program. Then, the stage is closed only if the user clicks the Yes button in the confirmation box.

The source code for this program is shown in Listing 4-5.

Listing 4-5: The ClickCounter Exit program

```
import javafx.application.*;
import javafx.stage.*;
import javafx.scene.*;
import javafx.scene.layout.*;
import javafx.scene.control.*;
import javafx.geometry.*;

public class ClickCounterExit extends Application
{
    public static void main(String[] args)
    {
        launch(args);
    }

    Stage stage;
    int iClickCount = 0;

    @Override public void start(Stage primaryStage)
    {
        stage = primaryStage;

        // Create the Click Me button
        Button btnClickMe = new Button();
        btnClickMe.setText("Click me please!");
        btnClickMe.setOnAction(e -> btnClickMe_Click());

        // Create the Close button
        Button btnClose = new Button();
        btnClose.setText("Close");
        btnClose.setOnAction(e -> btnClose_Click() );
```

→27

```
        // Add the buttons to a layout pane
        VBox pane = new VBox(10);
        pane.getChildren().addAll(btnClickMe, btnClose);
        pane.setAlignment(Pos.CENTER );

        // Add the layout pane to a scene
        Scene scene = new Scene(pane, 250, 150);

        // Finish and show the stage
        primaryStage.setScene(scene);
        primaryStage.setTitle("Click Counter");
        primaryStage.setOnCloseRequest( e ->                        →43
            {
                e.consume();
                btnClose_Click();
            } );
        primaryStage.show();
    }

public void btnClickMe_Click()
    {
        iClickCount++;
        if (iClickCount == 1)
        {
            MessageBox.show("You have clicked once.", "Click!");
        }
        else
        {
            MessageBox.show("You have clicked "
                + iClickCount + " times." , "Click!");
        }
    }

public void btnClose_Click()                                       →65
    {
        boolean confirm = false;
        confirm = ConfirmationBox.show(
            "Are you sure you want to quit?", "Confirmation",
            "Yes", "No");
        if (confirm)
        {
            // Place any code needed to save files or
            // close resources here.

            stage.close();
        }
    }
}
```

The following paragraphs describe the sections of this program that are responsible for making sure the program exits cleanly:

→ **27:** These lines create the Close button. The Lambda expression in the call to setOnAction causes the method named btnClose_ Click to be called if the user clicks the button.

→ **43:** This statement creates an event handler for the CloseRequest event, which is raised if the user attempts to close the window by clicking the window close button. The event handler first consumes the CloseRequest event and then calls the btnClose_ Click method. Thus, from the user's perspective, clicking the window close button is the same as clicking the Close button.

→ **65:** The btnClose_Click method displays a confirmation box to ask the user whether he really wants to quit. If so, the stage is closed. I added comments to show where you'd insert any code needed to save files or do any other cleanup work that might be required in a more realistic program.

Chapter 5

Using Layout Panes to Arrange Your Scenes

. . . .

In This Chapter

▶ Using four popular layout pane classes: HBox, VBox, FlowPane, and BorderPane

▶ Adjusting the size of layout panes and the nodes they contain

▶ Fiddling with various options for spacing out the nodes in a layout pane

. . . .

Controlling the layout of components in a scene is often one of the most difficult aspects of working with JavaFX. In fact, at times it can be downright exasperating. Often the components almost seem to have minds of their own. They get stubborn and refuse to budge. They line up on top of one another when you want them to be side by side. You make a slight change to a label or text field, and the whole scene seems to rearrange itself. At times, you want to put your fist through the monitor.

I recommend against putting your fist through your monitor. You'll make a mess, cut your hand, and have to spend money on a new monitor — and when you get your computer working again, the components *still* won't line up the way you want them to be.

The problem isn't with the components; it's with the *layout panes,* which determine where each component appears in its frame or panel. Layout panes are special classes whose sole purpose in life is to control the arrangement of the nodes that appear in a scene. JavaFX provides several distinct types of layout panes; each type uses a different approach to controlling the arrangement of nodes. The trick to successfully lay out a scene is to use the layout panes in the correct combination to achieve the arrangement you want.

Working with Layout Panes

Understanding layout panes is the key to creating JavaFX frames that are attractive and usable.

Introducing four JavaFX layout panes

JavaFX provides many different layout panes for you to work with. I explain the following four in this chapter:

- ✔ **HBox:** This layout pane arranges nodes horizontally, one next to the other. You use it to create controls arranged neatly in rows.

- ✔ **VBox:** This layout pane arranges nodes vertically, one above the other. You use it to create controls arranged neatly in columns.

- ✔ **FlowPane:** This layout pane arranges nodes next to each other until it runs out of room; then, it wraps to continue layout nodes. You can configure a `FlowPane` to arrange nodes horizontally in rows or vertically in columns.

- ✔ **BorderPane:** This layout pane divides the pane into five regions: Top, Left, Center, Right, and Bottom. When you add a node, you can specify which region you want to place the node in.

To give you a general idea of the results that can be achieved with each of these four layout panes, Figure 5-1 shows four sample windows that each use one of the layout panes.

Chapter 11 discusses additional types of layout panes.

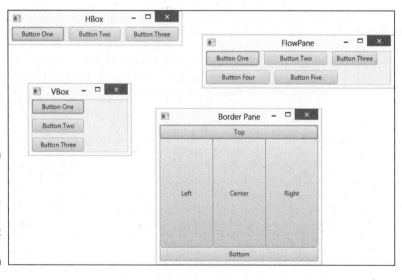

Figure 5-1:
Four commonly used types of layout panes.

Creating layout panes

The basic process of working with layout panes is simple. Here is the general procedure for creating a layout node:

1. Create the controls or other nodes you want to add to the pane.

   For example, if the layout pane will contain two buttons, you should create the two buttons using code similar to this:

   ```
   Button btnOK = new Button();
   btnOK.setText("OK");
   btnOK.setOnAction( e -> btnOK_Click() );
   Button btnCancel = new Button();
   btnCancel.setText("Cancel");
   btnCancel.setOnAction( e -> btnCancel_Click() );
   ```

2. Create a layout pane by calling its constructor.

   For example:

   ```
   HBox pane = new HBox();
   ```

3. Fine-tune any of the settings required by the layout pane.

   Each type of layout pane has a unique assortment of parameters that govern the details of how nodes are laid out within the pane. For example, the HBox pane lets you set the number of pixels that will be used to separate each node in the pane. You can set this value as follows:

   ```
   HBox.setSpacing(10);
   ```

4. Add each of the nodes that will appear in the layout pane.

   Each type of layout pane provides a method for adding nodes to the pane. For the HBox pane, you must first call the getChildren method to get a list of all the nodes that have been added to the pane. Then, you call the addAll method to add one or more nodes to the pane. For example:

   ```
   pane.getChildren().addAll(btnOK, btnCancel);
   ```

5. Create the scene, specifying the layout pane as the scene's root node.

   For example:

   ```
   Scene scene = new Scene(pane, 300, 400);
   ```

   In this example, pane is added as the root node for the scene.

Combining layout panes

You can combine several layout panes to create layouts that are more complicated than a single layout pane can provide. For example, suppose you want to create a layout that has a horizontal row of buttons at the bottom and a vertical column of buttons at the right. To do that, you could create an HBox for the buttons at the bottom and a VBox for the buttons at the right. Then, you could create a BorderPane and add the HBox to the bottom region and the VBox to the right region.

Combinations like this are possible because all the layout panes inherit the base class javafx.scene.layout.Pane, which in turn inherits the class javafx.scene.node. In other words, all panes are also nodes. Each node that you add to a layout pane can be another layout pane. You can nest layout panes within layout panes as deeply as you need to achieve the exact layout you need for your application.

Using the HBox Layout

The HBox class provides one of the simplest of all JavaFX's layout managers: It arranges one or more nodes into a horizontal row. Table 5-1 presents the most commonly used constructors and methods of the HBox class.

Table 5-1	HBox Constructors and Methods
Constructor	**Description**
HBox()	Creates an empty HBox.
HBox(double spacing)	Creates an empty HBox with the specified spacing.
HBox(Node. . . children)	Creates an HBox with the specified child nodes. This constructor lets you create an HBox and add child nodes to it at the same time.
HBox(double spacing, Node. . . children)	Creates an HBox with the specified spacing and child nodes.

Method	*Description*
`ObservableList<Node>` `getChildren()`	Returns the collection of all child nodes that have been added to the `HBox`. The collection is returned as an `ObservableList` type, which includes the method `addAll`, letting you add one or more nodes to the list.
`static void setAlignment(Pos alignment)`	Sets the alignment for child nodes within the `HBox`. See Table 5-5 for an explanation of the `Pos` enumeration. For more information, see the section "Aligning Nodes in a Layout Pane" later in this chapter.
`static void setHgrow(Node child, Priority priority)`	Sets the growth behavior of the given child node. See Table 5-3 for an explanation of the `Priority` enumeration. For more information, see the section "Adding Space by Growing Nodes" later in this chapter.
`static void setMargin(Node child, Insets value)`	Sets the margins for a given child node. See Table 5-2 for the constructors of the `Insets` class. For more information, see the section "Adding Space with Margins" later in this chapter.
`void setPadding(Insets value)`	Sets the padding around the inside edges of the `Hbox`. See Table 5-2 for the constructors of the `Insets` class. For more information, see the section "Spacing Things Out" later in this chapter.
`void setSpacing(double value)`	Sets the spacing between nodes displayed within the `HBox`. For more information, see the section "Spacing Things Out" later in this chapter.

The HBox class is defined in the javafx.scene.layout package, so you should include the following import statement in any program that uses an HBox:

```
import javafx.scene.layout.*;
```

The easiest way to create an HBox is to first create the nodes that you want to place in the HBox and then call the HBox constructor and pass the nodes as arguments. For example:

```
Button btn1 = new Button("Button One");
Button btn2 = new Button("Button Two");
Button btn3 = new Button("Button Three");
HBox hbox = new HBox(btn1, btn2, btn3);
```

If you prefer to create the HBox control in an initially empty state and later add the controls, you can do so like this:

```
HBox hbox = new HBox();
Hbox.getChildren().addAll(btn1, btn2, btn3);
```

Here, the getChildren method is called, which returns a collection of all the children added to the HBox pane. This collection is defined by the class ObservableList, which includes a method named addAll that you can use to add one or more nodes to the list.

Spacing Things Out

By default, child nodes in a layout pane are arranged immediately next to one another, with no empty space in between. If you want to provide space between the nodes in the pane, you can do so in four ways:

- ✔ Adding spacing between elements within the pane
- ✔ Adding padding around the inside edges of the pane
- ✔ Adding margins to the individual nodes in the pane
- ✔ Creating spacer nodes that can grow to fill available space

In this section, I show you how to add spacing and padding to an pane. Then, the next three sections show you how to use the other two techniques.

Note that although I illustrate the techniques in these sections using the HBox layout pane, the techniques apply to other types of panes as well.

To set the spacing for an HBox pane, you can use the spacing parameter on the HBox constructor or by calling the setSpacing method. For example, this statement creates an HBox pane with a default spacing of 10 pixels:

```
HBox hbox = new HBox(10);
```

This example creates an HBox pane with 10-pixel spacing and adds three buttons:

```
HBox hbox = new HBox(10, btn1, btn2, btn3);
```

And this example creates an HBox pane using the default constructor, and then calls the setSpacing method to set the spacing to 10 pixels:

```
HBox hbox = new HBox();
Hbox.setSpacing(10);
```

Although spacing adds space between nodes in an HBox pane, it doesn't provide any space between the nodes and the edges of the pane itself. For example, if you set the spacing to 10 pixels and add three buttons to the pane, the three buttons will be separated from one another by a gap of 10 pixels. However, there won't be any space at all between the left edge of the first button and the left edge of the pane itself. Nor will there be any space between the top of the buttons and the top of the pane. In other words, the three buttons will be crowded tightly into the pane.

To add space around the perimeter of the layout pane, use the setPadding method. This method takes as a parameter an object of type Insets, which represents the size of the padding (in pixels) for the top, right, bottom, and left edge of an object. You can create an Insets object using either of the two constructors listed in Table 5-2. The first provides an even padding for all four edges of an object; the second lets you set a different padding value for each edge.

To set the padding to a uniform 10 pixels, call the setPadding method like this:

```
hbox.setPadding(new Insets(10));
```

To set a different padding value for each edge, call it like this:

```
hbox.setPadding(new Insets(20, 10, 20, 10));
```

In this example, the top and bottom padding is set to 20 and the right and left padding is set to 10.

Table 5-2	Insets Constructors
Constructor	*Description*
`Insets(double value)`	Creates an `Insets` object that uses the same value for the top, right, bottom, and left margins.
`Insets(double top, double right, double bottom, double left)`	Creates an `Insets` object that uses the specified top, right, bottom, and left margins.

The `Insets` enumeration is defined in the `javafx.geometry` package, so you should include the following `import` statement in any program that uses `Insets`:

```
import javafx.geometry.*;
```

Adding Space with Margins

Another way to add space around the nodes in a layout pane is to create margins around the individual nodes. This technique allows you to set a different margin size for each node in the layout pane, giving you complete control over the spacing of each node.

To create a margin, call the `setMargin` method for each node you want to add a margin to. You might think that because each node can have its own margin, the `setMargin` method would belong to the `Node` class. Instead, the `setMargin` method is defined by the `HBox` class. The `setMargin` method accepts two parameters:

- The node you want to add the margin to
- An `Insets` object that defines the margins you want to add

Here's an example that sets a margin of 10 pixels for all sides of a button named `btn1`:

```
HBox hbox = new HBox();
hbox.setMargin(btn1, new Insets(10));
```

The setMargin method is a static method of the HBox class, so when you call it, you can reference the HBox class itself rather than an actual instance of an HBox. Thus, the following code will work equally as well:

```
Hbox.setMargin(btn1, new Insets(10));
```

(Yes it's a subtle difference: In the first example, hbox refers to an instance of the HBox class; in the second example, HBox refers to the class itself.)

Here's an example that sets a different margin for each side of the pane:

```
Hbox.setMargin(btn1, new Insets(10, 15, 20, 10));
```

In this example, the top margin is 10 pixels, the right margin is 15 pixels, the bottom margin is 20 pixels, and the left margin is 10 pixels.

Note that margins, spacing, and padding can work together. Thus, if you create a 5-pixel margin on all sides of two buttons, add those two buttons to a pane whose spacing is set to 10 pixels and whose padding is set to 10 pixels, the buttons will be separated from one another by a space of 20 pixels and from the inside edges of the pane by 15 pixels.

Adding Space by Growing Nodes

A third way to add space between nodes in an HBox is to create a node whose sole purpose is to add space between two HBox nodes. Then, you can configure the spacer node that will automatically grow to fill any extra space within the pane. By configuring only the spacer node and no other nodes in this way, only the spacer node will grow. This has the effect of pushing the nodes on either side of the spacer node apart from one another.

For example, suppose you want to create an HBox layout pane that contains three buttons. Instead of spacing all three buttons evenly within the pane, you want the first two buttons to appear on the left side of the pane and the third button to appear on the right side of the pane. The amount of space between the second and third buttons will depend entirely on the size of the pane. Thus, if the user drags the window to expand the stage, the amount of space between the second and third buttons should increase accordingly.

The easiest way to create a spacer node is by using the Region class. The Region class is the base class for both the Control class, from which controls such as Button and Label derive. It is also the based class for the Pane class, from which all the layout panes described in this chapter and in Chapter 11 derive.

For my purposes here, I just use the simple default constructor of the Region class to create a node that serves as a simple spacer in a layout pane. I don't provide a specific size for the region. Instead, I configure it so that it will grow horizontally to fill any unused space within its container.

To do that, you use the static setHgrow method of the HBox class, specifying one of the three constant values defined by an enumeration named Priority enumeration. Table 5-3 lists these constants and explains what each one does.

Table 5-3	The Priority enumeration
Constant	*Description*
Priority.NEVER	Indicates that the width of the node should never be adjusted to fill the available space in the pane. This is the default setting. Thus, by default, nodes are not resized based on the size of the layout pane that contains them.
Priority.ALWAYS	Indicates that the width of the node should always be adjusted if necessary to fill available space in the pane. If you set two or more nodes to ALWAYS, the adjustment will be split equally among each of the nodes.
Priority. SOMETIMES	Indicates that the node's width may be adjusted if necessary to fill out the pane. However, the adjustment will be made only if there are no other nodes that specify ALWAYS.

The Priority enumeration is defined in the javafx.scene.layout package; the same package that defines the layout managers that require it. So you don't need to include an additional import statement to use the Priority enumeration.

The following example creates three buttons and a spacer, sets the margins for all three buttons to 10 pixels, and then adds the three buttons and the spacer to an HBox such that the first two buttons appear on the left of the HBox and the third button appears on the right:

```
// Create the buttons
Button btn1 = new Button("One");
Button btn2 = new Button("Two");
Button btn3 = new Button("Three");

// Create the spacer
Region spacer = new Region();
```

```
// Set the margins
hBox.setMargin(btn1, new Insets(10));
hBox.setMargin(btn2, new Insets(10));
hBox.setMargin(btn3, new Insets(10));

// Set the Hgrow for the spacer
hBox.setHgrow(spacer, Priority.ALWAYS);

// Create the HBox layout pane
HBox hbox = new HBox(10, btn1, btn2, spacer, btn3);
```

Figure 5-2 shows how this pane appears when added to a stage. So that you can see how the spacer works, the figure shows three incarnations of the pane, each with the window dragged to a different size. Notice how the spacing between the second and third buttons is adjusted automatically so that the first two buttons are on the left side of the pane and the third button is on the right.

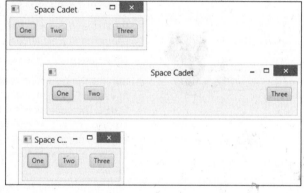

Figure 5-2:
Using a spacer node to space out buttons in an HBox pane.

Like the `setMargin` method, the `setHGrow` method is a static class of the `HBox` class. Thus, you can call it from an instance of the `HBox` class (as in the preceding example), or you can call it from the `HBox` class itself. In other words, the second two lines in the following code segment are redundant:

```
HBox pane = new HBox();
pane.setHGrow(spacer, Priority.ALWAYS);
HBOX.setHGrow(spacer, Priority.ALWAYS);
```

Using the VBox Layout

The VBox class is similar to the HBox class, but instead of arranging nodes horizontally in a row, it arranges them vertically in a column. Table 5-4 shows the most commonly used constructors and methods of the VBox class.

Table 5-4	VBox Constructors and Methods
Constructor	*Description*
VBox()	Creates an empty VBox.
VBox(double spacing)	Creates an empty VBox with the specified spacing.
VBox(Node. . . children)	Creates an VBox with the specified child nodes. This constructor lets you create a VBox and add child nodes to it at the same time.
VBox(double spacing, Node. . . children)	Creates a VBox with the specified spacing and child nodes.
Method	*Description*
ObservableList<Node> getChildren()	Returns the collection of all child nodes that have been added to the VBox. The collection is returned as an ObservableList type, which includes the method addAll, letting you add one or more nodes to the list.
static void setAlignment(Pos alignment)	Sets the alignment for child nodes within the VBox. See Table 5-5 for an explanation of the Pos enumeration. For more information, see the section "Aligning Nodes in a Layout Pane" later in this chapter.
static void setMargin(Node child, Insets value)	Sets the margins for a given child node. See Table 5-2 for the constructors of the Insets class. For more information, see the section "Adding Space with Margins" earlier in this chapter.

Method	Description
`void setPadding(Insets value)`	Sets the padding around the inside edges of the `VBox`. See Table 5-2 for the constructors of the `Insets` class. For more information, see the section "Spacing Things Out" earlier in this chapter.
`static void setVgrow(Node child, Priority priority)`	Sets the growth behavior of the given child node. See Table 5-3 for an explanation of the `Priority` enumeration. For more information, see the section "Adding Space by Growing Nodes" earlier in this chapter.

The `VBox` class is defined in the `javafx.scene.layout` package, so you should include the following `import` statement in any program that uses a `VBox`:

```
import javafx.scene.layout.*;
```

Here's an example that creates three buttons and uses a `VBox` to arrange them into a column:

```
Button btn1 = new Button("Button One");
Button btn2 = new Button("Button Two");
Button btn3 = new Button("Button Three");
VBox vbox = new VBox(btn1, btn2, btn3);
```

You can accomplish the same thing by using the default constructor and calling the `getChildren` method, as in this example:

```
VBox vbox = new VBox();
Vbox.getChildren().addAll(btn1, btn2, btn3);
```

As with the `HBox` class, you can use spacing, padding, margins, and spacer nodes to control the spacing of nodes within a `VBox`. Here's an example that sets 10 pixels of vertical space between nodes and 10 pixels of padding on each edge of the pane:

```
Button btn1 = new Button("One");
Button btn2 = new Button("Two");
Button btn3 = new Button("Three");
VBox vbox = new VBox(10, btn1, btn2, btn3);
vbox.setPadding(new Insets(10));
```

Here's an example that creates a column of three buttons, with one button at the top of the column and two at the bottom, with 10 pixels of spacing and padding:

```
// Create the buttons
Button btn1 = new Button("One");
Button btn2 = new Button("Two");
Button btn3 = new Button("Three");

// Create the spacer
Region spacer = new Region();

// Set the Vgrow for the spacer
VBox.setVgrow(spacer, Priority.ALWAYS);

// Create the VBox layout pane
VBox vbox = new VBox(10, btn1, spacer, btn2, btn3);
vbox.setPadding(new Insets(10));
```

Aligning Nodes in a Layout Pane

Both the HBox and the VBox layout panes have a setAlignment method that lets you control how the nodes that are contained within the pane are aligned with one another. The setAlignment method accepts a single argument, which is one of the constants defined by the Pos enumeration, described in Table 5-5.

Table 5-5	The Pos enumeration	
Constant	*Vertical Alignment*	*Horizontal Alignment*
Pos.TOP_LEFT	Top	Left
Pos.TOP_CENTER	Top	Center
Pos.TOP_RIGHT	Top	Right
Pos.CENTER_LEFT	Center	Left
Pos.CENTER	Center	Center
Pos.CENTER_RIGHT	Center	Right
Pos.BOTTOM_LEFT	Bottom	Left
Pos.BOTTOM_CENTER	Bottom	Center
Pos.BOTTOM_RIGHT	Bottom	Right

Constant	Vertical Alignment	Horizontal Alignment
Pos.BASELINE_LEFT	Baseline	Left
Pos.BASELINE_CENTER	Baseline	Center
Pos.BASELINE_RIGHT	Baseline	Right

The Pos enumeration is defined in the javafx.geometry package, so you should include the following import statement in any program that uses Insets:

```
import javafx.geometry.*;
```

The following example shows how you might create a vertical column of three buttons, centered within the pane:

```
Button btn1 = new Button("Number One");
Button btn2 = new Button("Two");
Button btn3 = new Button("The Third Button");
VBox vbox = new VBox(10, btn1, btn2, btn3);
vbox.setPadding(new Insets(10));
vbox.setAlignment(Pos.CENTERED);
```

When this pane is added to a scene and then shown in a stage, the results resemble the window shown in Figure 5-3.

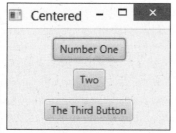

Figure 5-3:
Three buttons centered in a VBox layout pane.

Making Nodes the Same Width

When you place a set of buttons or other controls in a layout pane, you may want the buttons to all have the same width to create a neat, even appearance. This is especially true when you place them in a vertical column in a VBox pane because the vertical column will draw attention to any differences in the widths of the buttons.

You can easily dictate that the buttons all have the same width by setting the maximum width of each of the buttons to `Double.MAX_VALUE`. Here's a revised version of the preceding example in which the three buttons are set to the same width:

```
Button btn1 = new Button("Number One");
Button btn2 = new Button("Two");
Button btn3 = new Button("The Third Button");
btn1.setMaxWidth(Double.MAX_VALUE);
btn2.setMaxWidth(Double.MAX_VALUE);
btn3.setMaxWidth(Double.MAX_VALUE);
VBox vbox = new VBox(10, btn1, btn2, btn3);
vbox.setPadding(new Insets(10));
vbox.setAlignment(Pos.CENTERED);
```

Figure 5-4 shows how these buttons appear when the pane is added to a scene and the scene displayed in a stage. Notice that all three buttons have adopted the width of the widest button (btn3).

Figure 5-4:
Three but-
tons with
the same
width.

Using the Flow Layout

The flow layout comes in two flavors: horizontal and vertical. A horizontal flow layout arranges its child nodes in a row until the width of the pane reaches a certain size that you can specify. When that size is reached, the layout begins a new row of child nodes beneath the first row. This flow continues, starting a new row each time the size limit is reached, until all the child nodes have been placed.

A vertical flow layout works the same way except that child nodes are laid out in columns until the size limit is reached. When the size limit is reached, a new column immediately to the right of the first column is started.

You use the `FlowPane` class to create a flow layout. Table 5-6 shows the constructors and most commonly used methods for the `FlowPane` class.

Table 5-6	FlowPane Constructors and Methods
Constructor	*Description*
`FlowPane()`	Creates an empty horizontal flow layout with both the horizontal and vertical gaps set to zero.
`FlowPane(double hgap, double vgap)`	Creates an empty horizontal flow layout with the specified horizontal and vertical gaps.
`FlowPane(double hgap, double vgap, Node... children)`	Creates a horizontal flow layout with the specified horizontal and vertical gaps and populated with the specified child nodes.
`FlowPane(Node... children)`	Creates a horizontal flow layout with both the horizontal and vertical gaps set to zero and populated with the specified child nodes.
Note: In each of the following constructors, `Orientation` *can be* `Orientation.HORIZONTAL` *or* `Orientation.VERTICAL`*.*	
`FlowPane(Orientation orientation)`	Creates an empty flow layout with the specified orientation and both the horizontal and vertical gaps set to zero.
`FlowPane(Orientation orientation, double hgap, double vgap)`	Creates an empty flow layout with the specified orientation and the specified horizontal and vertical gaps.
`FlowPane(Orientation orientation, double hgap, double vgap, Node... children)`	Creates a flow layout with the specified orientation and horizontal and vertical gaps, populated with the specified children.
`FlowPane(Orientation orientation, Node... children)`	Creates a flow layout with the specified orientation and both the horizontal and vertical gaps set to zero, populated with the specified children.
Method	*Description*
`ObservableList<Node> getChildren()`	Returns the collection of all child nodes. The collection is returned as an `ObservableList` type, which includes the method `addAll`, letting you add one or more nodes to the list.

(continued)

Table 5-6 *(continued)*

Method	Description
`void setAlignment(Pos alignment)`	Sets the alignment for nodes within the rows and columns. See Table 5-5 for an explanation of the `Pos` enumeration. For more information, see the section "Aligning Nodes in a Layout Pane" earlier in this chapter.
`void setColumn Alignment(Pos alignment)`	Sets the alignment for nodes within the columns. See Table 5-5 for an explanation of the `Pos` enumeration. For more information, see the section "Aligning Nodes in a Layout Pane" earlier in this chapter.
`void setHgap(double value)`	Sets the horizontal gap. For a horizontal flow layout, this is the amount of space between nodes. For a vertical flow layout, this is the amount of space between columns.
`static void setMargin(Node child, Insets value)`	Sets the margins for a given child node. See Table 5-2 for the constructors of the `Insets` class. For more information, see the section "Adding Space with Margins" earlier in this chapter.
`void setOrientation(Orientation orientation)`	Sets the orientation of the flow layout, which can be `Orientation.HORIZONTAL` or `Orientation.VERTICAL`.
`void setPadding(Insets value)`	Sets the padding around the inside edges of the flow layout. See Table 5-2 for the constructors of the `Insets` class. For more information, see the section "Spacing Things Out" earlier in this chapter.

Method	Description
`void setPrefWrapLength (double value)`	Sets the preferred wrap length for the pane. For a horizontal flow layout, this represents the preferred width of the pane; for a vertical flow layout, it represents the preferred height.
`void setRowAlignment(Pos alignment)`	Sets the alignment for nodes within the rows. See Table 5-5 for an explanation of the `Pos` enumeration. For more information, see the section "Aligning Nodes in a Layout Pane" earlier in this chapter.
`void setSpacing(double value)`	Sets the spacing between nodes displayed within the flow layout. For more information, see the section "Spacing Things Out" earlier in this chapter.
`void setVgap(double value)`	Sets the vertical gap. For a vertical flow layout, this is the amount of space between nodes. For a horizontal flow layout, this is the amount of space between rows.

The `FlowPane` class is defined in the `javafx.scene.layout` package, so you should include the following `import` statement in any program that uses a flow layout:

```
import javafx.scene.layout.*;
```

The constructors for this class let you specify the horizontal and vertical gaps, which provide the spacing between the horizontal and vertical elements of the layout, the orientation (horizontal or vertical), and the child nodes with which to populate the layout.

To set the limit at which the flow layout wraps, you use the `setPrefWrap Length` method. The wrap length is applied to the dimension in which the pane flows its contents. Thus, for a horizontal flow layout, the wrap length specifies the preferred width of the pane; for a vertical flow layout, the wrap length specifies the pane's preferred height.

Note that regardless of the preferred wrap length, if you don't call this method, the wrap length defaults to 400 pixels.

The following example creates a horizontal layout with 10 pixels of horizontal and vertical gaps, populated by five buttons, and a preferred wrap length of 300 pixels:

```
Button btn1 = new Button("Button One");
Button btn2 = new Button("Button Two");
Button btn3 = new Button("Button Three");
Button btn4 = new Button("Button Four");
Button btn5 = new Button("Button Five");
FlowPane pane = new FlowPane(Orientation.HORIZONTAL,
        10, 10, btn1, btn2, btn3, btn4, btn5);
pane.setPrefWrapLength(300);
```

Figure 5-5 shows how these buttons appear when the layout is added to a scene and the scene displayed in a stage. This figure also shows how the buttons in the flow layout are rearranged when the user resizes the window. Notice that initially, the first three buttons appear on the first row and the next two appear on the second row. When the window is dragged a bit wider, the buttons reflow so that four fit on the first row and just one spills to the second row. Then, when the window is dragged smaller, just two buttons appear on the first two rows and a third row is created for the fifth button.

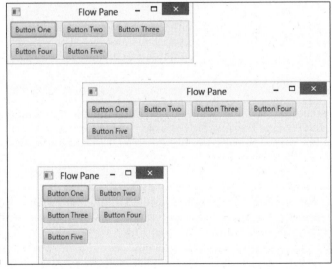

Figure 5-5: A flow layout pane with five buttons.

Using the Border Layout

The border layout is a pane that is carved into five regions: Top, Left, Center, Right, and Bottom, as shown in Figure 5-6. When you add a component to the layout, you can specify which of these regions the component goes in.

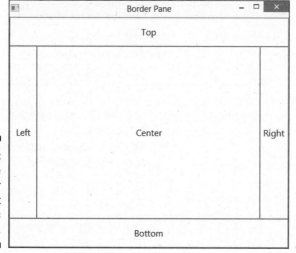

Border Pane

	Top
Left	Center	Right
	Bottom

Figure 5-6:
How the border layout carves things up.

Border layout is the ideal layout manager for applications that have a traditional window arrangement in which menus and toolbars are displayed at the top of the window, a status bar or OK and Cancel buttons are displayed at the bottom, a navigation pane is displayed on the left, various task panes are displayed on the right, and content is displayed in the middle.

You use the BorderPane class to create a border layout. Table 5-7 lists the constructors and the most commonly used methods for the BorderPane class.

Table 5-7	BorderPane Constructors and Methods
Constructor	*Description*
BorderPane ()	Creates an empty border layout.
BorderPane (Node center)	Creates a border layout with the specified center node.

(continued)

Table 5-7 *(continued)*

Constructor	Description
`BorderPane (Node center, Node top, Node right, Node bottom, Node left)`	Creates a border layout with the specified center, top, right, bottom, and left nodes.

Method	Description
`void setCenter(Node node)`	Sets the center node.
`void setTop(Node node)`	Sets the top node.
`void setRight(Node node)`	Sets the right node.
`void setBottom(Node node)`	Sets the bottom node.
`void setLeft(Node node)`	Sets the left node.
`void setAlignment(Pos alignment)`	Sets the alignment for nodes within border pane. See Table 5-5 for an explanation of the `Pos` enumeration. For more information, see the section "Aligning Nodes in a Layout Pane" earlier in this chapter.
`static void setMargin(Node child, Insets value)`	Sets the margins for a given child node. See Table 5-2 for the constructors of the `Insets` class. For more information, see the section "Adding Space with Margins" earlier in this chapter.

The `BorderPane` class is defined in the `javafx.scene.layout` package, so you should include the following `import` statement in any program that uses a border layout:

```
import javafx.scene.layout.*;
```

The default constructor for this class creates an empty border layout, to which you can add nodes later, as in this example:

```
Button btn1 = new Button("Button One");
Button btn2 = new Button("Button Two");
Button btn3 = new Button("Button Three");
VBox vbox = new VBox(btn1, btn2, btn3);

BorderPane pane = new BorderPane();
pane.setCenter(vbox);
```

Here, three buttons are created and added to a VBox. Then, a border layout is created, and the VBox is added to its center region.

Alternatively, you can add a node to the center region via the BorderPane constructor, like this:

```
BorderPane pane = new BorderPane(vbox);
```

The third constructor listed in Table 5-7 lets you add nodes to all five regions at once. The following example assumes that you have already created five panes, named centerPane, topPane, rightPane, bottomPane, and leftPane:

```
BorderPane pane = new BorderPane(centerPane,
    topPane, rightPane, bottomPane, leftPane);
```

Here are a few additional important points to know about the BorderPane class:

✔ **If you don't add a node to one of the regions, that region is not rendered.**

✔ **The border layout regions are sized according to their contents.**

Thus, if you add a VBox pane to the right region, the width of the VBox pane will determine the width of the right region.

✔ **If the user resizes the window to make it wider, the top, center, and bottom regions will expand in width — the width of the left and right regions remains unchanged.**

Similarly, if the user drags the window to make it taller, the left, center, and right regions expand in height; the height of the top and bottom regions remains the same.

✔ **The nodes you add to the regions of a border pane will themselves almost always be other layout panes.**

In Chapter 6, you see a comprehensive example that shows how to create a complex layout that uses various combinations of VBox, HBox, and FlowPane layout panes as the nodes for each region of a BorderPane.

Chapter 6

Getting Input from the User

*I*n the first five chapters of this book, I discuss how to create JavaFX programs using only two basic JavaFX input controls: labels and buttons. If all you ever want to write are programs that display text when the user clicks a button, you can put the book down now. But if you want to write programs that actually do something worthwhile, you need to use other JavaFX input controls.

In this chapter, you find out how to use some of the most common JavaFX controls. First, you read about the label and controls that get information from the user. You find out more details about the text field control, which gets a line of text, and the text area control, which gets multiple lines. Then I move on to two input controls that get either/or information from the user: radio buttons and check boxes.

Along the way, you discover an important aspect of any JavaFX program that collects input data from the user: data validation. Data validation routines are essential to ensure that the user doesn't enter bogus data. For example, you can use data validation to ensure that the user enters data into required fields or that the data the user enters into a numeric field is indeed a valid number.

Using Text Fields

A *text field* is a box into which the user can type a single text. You create text fields by using the TextField class. Table 6-1 shows some of the more interesting and useful constructors and methods of this class.

Table 6-1	Handy TextField Constructors and Methods
Constructor	**Description**
TextField()	Creates a new text field.
TextField(String text, int cols)	Creates a new text field with an initial text value.
Method	**Description**
String getText()	Gets the text value entered in the field.
void requestFocus()	Asks for the focus to be moved to this text field. Note that the field must be in a scene for the focus request to work.
void setEditable(boolean value)	If false, makes the field read-only.
void setMaxWidth(double width)	Sets the maximum width for the field.
void setMinWidth(double width)	Sets the minimum width for the field.
void setPrefColumnCount(int cols)	Sets the preferred size of the text field in columns (that is, the number of average-width text characters).
void setPrefWidth(double width)	Sets the preferred width for the field.
void setPromptText(String prompt)	Sets the field's prompt value. The prompt value will not be displayed if the field has a text value or if the field has focus.
void setText(String text)	Sets the field's text value.

The TextField class is defined in the javafx.scene.control package, so you should include the following imports statement in any program that uses a text field:

```
imports javafx.scene.control.*;
```

The most common way to create a text field is to call the constructor without arguments, like this:

```
TextField text1 = new TextField();
```

You can set the initial value to be displayed like this:

```
TextField text1 = new TextField("Initial value");
```

Or, if you need to set the value later, you can call the setText method:

```
text1.setText("Text value");
```

To retrieve the value that the user has entered into a text field, call the getText method like this:

```
String value = text1.getText();
```

As with any JavaFX control, managing the width of a text field can be a bit tricky. Ultimately, JavaFX will determine the width of the text field based on a number of factors, including the size of the window that contains the stage and scene and any size constraints placed on the pane or panes that contain the text field. You can set minimum and maximum limits for the text field size by calling the setMinWidth and setMaxWidth methods, and you can indicate the preferred width via the setPrefWidth method, as in this example:

```
TextField text1 = new TextField();
text1.setMinWidth(150);
text1.setMaxWidth(250);
text1.setPrefWidth(200);
```

Another way to set the preferred width is with the setPrefColumnCount method, which sets the width in terms of average-sized characters. For example, the following line sizes the field large enough to display approximately 50 characters:

```
text1.setPrefColumnCount(50);
```

Note that the setPrefColumnCount method does *not* limit the number of characters the user can enter into the field. Instead, it limits the number of characters the field can display at one time.

Whenever you use a text field, provide a prompt that lets the user know what data he should enter into the field. One common way to do that is to place a label control immediately to the left of the text field. For example:

```
Label lblName = new Label("Name:");
lblName.setMinWidth(75);
TextField txtName = new TextField();
txtName.setMinWidth(200);
HBox pane = new HBox(10, lblName, txtName);
```

Here, a label and a text field are created and added to an HBox pane so they will be displayed side-by-side.

JavaFX also allows you to display a prompt inside of a text field. The prompt is displayed in a lighter text color and disappears when the field receives focus. You use the setPromptText method to create such a prompt:

```
TextField txtName = new TextField();
txtName.setPromptText("Enter the customer's name");
```

Here, the text Enter the customer's name will appear inside the text field.

To retrieve the value entered by the user into a text field, you use the getText method, as in this example:

```
String lastName = textLastName.getText();
```

Here the value entered by the user in the textLastName text field is assigned to the String variable lastName.

Figure 6-1 shows the operation of a simple program that uses a text field to allow the user to enter the name of a character in a play and the name of the actor who will play the role. Assuming the user enters text in both fields, the program then displays a message box indicating who will play the role of the character. If the user omits either or both fields, a message box displays to indicate the error. (The program uses the MessageBox class that was presented in Listing 4-2 in Chapter 4 to display the message box.)

Figure 6-1 shows what the main stage for this program looks like, as well as the message box windows displayed when the user enters both names or when the user omits a name. The JavaFX code for this program is shown in Listing 6-1.

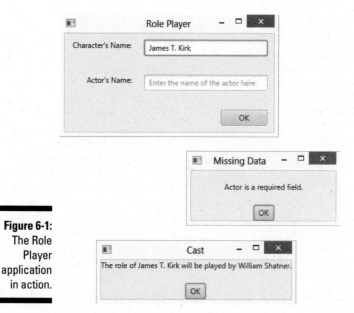

Figure 6-1:
The Role
Player
application
in action.

Listing 6-1:   The Role Player Program

```
import javafx.application.*;
import javafx.stage.*;
import javafx.scene.*;
import javafx.scene.layout.*;
import javafx.scene.control.*;
import javafx.geometry.*;

public class RolePlayer extends Application               →8
{
    public static void main(String[] args)
    {
        launch(args);
    }

    TextField txtCharacter;                               →15
    TextField txtActor;

    @Override public void start(Stage primaryStage)
    {

        // Create the Character                           →20
        Label lblCharacter = new Label("Character's Name:");
        lblCharacter.setMinWidth(100);
        lblCharacter.setAlignment(Pos.BOTTOM_RIGHT);
```

(continued)

Listing 6-1 *(continued)*

```
// Create the Character text field                          →25
txtCharacter = new TextField
txtCharacter.setMinWidth(200);
txtCharacter.setMaxWidth(200);
txtCharacter.setPromptText(
    "Enter the name of the character here.");

// Create the Actor label                                   →32
Label lblActor = new Label("Actor's Name:");
lblActor.setMinWidth(100);
lblActor.setAlignment(Pos.BOTTOM_RIGHT);

// Create the Actor text field                              →37
txtActor = new TextField();
txtActor.setMinWidth(200);
txtActor.setMaxWidth(200);
txtActor.setPromptText("Enter the name of the actor here.");

// Create the OK button                                      →43
Button btnOK = new Button("OK");
btnOK.setMinWidth(75);
btnOK.setOnAction(e -> btnOK_Click() );

// Create the Character pane                                 →48
HBox paneCharacter = new HBox(20, lblCharacter, txtCharacter);
paneCharacter.setPadding(new Insets(10));

// Create the Actor pane                                     →52
HBox paneActor = new HBox(20, lblActor, txtActor);
paneActor.setPadding(new Insets(10));

// Create the Button pane                                    →56
HBox paneButton = new HBox(20, btnOK);
paneButton.setPadding(new Insets(10));
paneButton.setAlignment(Pos.BOTTOM_RIGHT);

// Add the Character, Actor, and Button panes to a VBox      →61
VBox pane = new VBox(10, paneCharacter, paneActor, paneButton);

// Set the stage                                             →64
Scene scene = new Scene(pane);
primaryStage.setScene(scene);
primaryStage.setTitle("Role Player");
primaryStage.show();
}
```

```
public void btnOK_Click()                                       →71
{
    String errorMessage = "";                                   →73

    if (txtCharacter.getText().length() == 0)                   →75
    {
        errorMessage += "\nCharacter is a required field.";
    }

    if (txtActor.getText().length() == 0)                       →80
    {
        errorMessage += "\nActor is a required field.";
    }

    if (errorMessage.length() == 0)                             →85
    {
        String message = "The role of "
            + txtCharacter.getText()
            + " will be played by "
            + txtActor.getText()
            + ".";
        MessageBox.show(message,"Cast");
    }
    else
    {
        MessageBox.show(errorMessage, "Missing Data");          →96
    }
}
}
```

This program isn't very complicated, so the following paragraphs just hit the highlights:

→8:   The name of the program's main class is RolePlayer.

→15: These class variables allow any of the RolePlayer class methods to access the two text fields.

→20: These lines create a label to identify the Character text box. The field is set to a minimum width of 100 pixels and is right-justified so that the labels that identify the two text fields will be aligned properly.

→25: These lines create the Character text field with a minimum and maximum width of 200 pixels. The prompt text is set to Enter the name of the character here. This text will appear within the text field whenever the text field does not have focus. In Figure 6-1, the Character text field has focus so the prompt text isn't visible.

→32: These lines create a label to identify the Actor text field. Like the Character label, the Actor label's width is set to 100 pixels and it's right-aligned.

→37: These lines create the Actor text field, set its width to 200 pixels, and assign prompt text. You can see the prompt text in Figure 6-1 because the Actor text field doesn't have focus.

→43: These lines create the OK button. The `btnOK_Click` method is called when the user clicks the button.

→48: These lines create an `HBox` pane and add the Character label and text box to it.

→52: These lines create another `HBox` pane and add the Actor label and text box to it.

→56: These lines create a third `HBox` pane to hold the button.

→61: Now that all the controls are created and added to `HBox` panes, the three `HBox` panes are added to a `VBox` pane so that the text boxes with their associated labels and the button are stacked vertically.

→64: These lines create a scene to show the `VBox` pane and then add the scene to the primary stage and show the stage.

→71: The `btnOK_Click` method is called whenever the user clicks OK.

→73: The `errorMessage` variable holds any error message that might be necessary to inform the user of missing data.

→75: This `if` statement ensures that the user has entered data into the Character text box. If no data is entered, an error message is created.

→80: This `if` statement ensures that the user has entered data into the Actor text box. If no data is entered, an error message is appended to the `errorMessage` field.

→85: This `if` statement determines whether any data validation errors have occurred by testing the length of the `errorMessage` field. If the length is zero, no error has been detected, so the program assembles the `message` variable to display which actor will be playing which character. Then, the `show` method of the `MessageBox` class is called to display the message. (You can find the code for the `MessageBox` class in Listing 4-2 in Chapter 4.)

→96: This line displays the error message if the user forgets to enter data in the Character or Actor text fields.

Validating Numeric Data

You need to take special care if you're using a text field to get numeric data from the user. The `getText` method returns a string value. You can pass this value to one of the `parse` methods of the wrapper classes for the primitive numeric types. To convert the value entered in a text box to an `int`, use the `parseInt` method:

```
int count = Integer.parseInt(txtCount.getText());
```

Here the result of the `getText` method is used as the parameter of the `parseInt` method.

Table 6-2 lists the `parse` methods for the various wrapper classes. ***Note:*** Each of these methods throws `NumberFormatException` if the string can't be converted. As a result, you need to call the `parseInt` method in a `try/catch` block to catch this exception.

Table 6-2	Methods That Convert Strings to Numbers
Wrapper Class	*parse Method*
Integer	parseInt(String)
Short	parseShort(String)
Long	parseLong(String)
Byte	parseByte(String)
Float	parseFloat(String)
Double	parseDouble(String)

If your program uses more than one or two numeric-entry text fields, consider creating separate methods to validate the user's input. The following code snippet shows a method that accepts a text field and a string that provides an error message to be displayed if the data entered in the field can't be converted to an `int`. The method returns a Boolean value that indicates whether the field contains a valid integer:

```
private boolean isInt(TextField f, String msg)
{
    try
    {
        Integer.parseInt(f.getText());
        return true;
    }
    catch (NumberFormatException e)
    {
        MessageBox.show(msg, "Data Entry Error");
        return false;
    }
}
```

You can call this method whenever you need to check whether a text field has a valid integer. (The MessageBox class is the same one used in Listing 6-1; you find the code for it in Chapter 4, in Listing 4-2.)

Here's a method that gets the value entered in a txtCount text field and displays it in message box if the value entered is a valid integer:

```
public void buttonOKClick()
{
    if (isInt(textCount,
        "You must enter an integer."))
    {
        MessageBox.show("You entered " +
            Integer.parseInt(textCount.getText()),
            "Your Number");
    }
    textCount.requestFocus();
}
```

Here the isInt method is called to make sure that the text entered by the user can be converted to an int. If so, the text is converted to an int and displayed in a message box.

Using Check Boxes

A *check box* is a control that the user can click to check or clear. Check boxes let the user specify a Yes or No setting for an option. Figure 6-2 shows a window with three check boxes.

Strictly speaking, a check box can have *three* states: checked, unchecked, and undefined. The undefined state is most often used in conjunction with a `TreeView` control.

Figure 6-2:
Three check
boxes.

To create a check box, you use the `CheckBox` class. Its favorite constructors and methods are shown in Table 6-3.

Table 6-3   Notable CheckBox Constructors and Methods

Constructor	Description
`CheckBox()`	Creates a new check box that is initially unchecked.
`CheckBox(String text)`	Creates a new check box that displays the specified text.

Method	Description
`String getText()`	Gets the text displayed by the check box.
`boolean isSelected()`	Returns `true` if the check box is checked or `false` if the check box is not checked.
`void setOnAction (EventHandler<ActionEvent> value)`	Sets an `ActionEvent` listener to handle action events.
`void setSelected(boolean value)`	Checks the check box if the parameter is `true`; unchecks it if the parameter is `false`.
`void setText(String text)`	Sets the check box text.

As with any JavaFX control, if you want to refer to a check box in any method within the program, declare a class variable to reference the control:

```
CheckBox chkPepperoni, chkMushrooms, chkAnchovies;
```

Then you can use statements like these in the `start` method to create the check boxes and add them to a layout pane (in this case, `pane1`):

```
chkPepperoni = new CheckBox("Pepperoni");
pane1.add(chkPepperoni);

chkMushrooms = new CheckBox("Mushrooms");
pane1.add(chkMushrooms);

chkAnchovies = new CheckBox("Anchovies");
pane1.add(chkAnchovies);
```

Notice that I didn't specify the initial state of these check boxes in the constructor. As a result, they're initially unchecked. If you want to create a check box that's initially checked, call `setSelected` method, like this:

```
chkPepperoni.setSelected(true);
```

In an event listener, you can test the state of a check box by using the `isSelected` method, and you can set the state of a check box by calling its `setSelected` method. Here's a method that displays a message box and clears all three check boxes when the user clicks OK:

```
public void btnOK_Click()
{
    String msg = "";
    if (chkPepperoni.isSelected())
        msg += "Pepperoni\n";
    if (chkMushrooms.isSelected())
        msg += "Mushrooms\n";
    if (chkAnchovies.isSelected())
        msg += "Anchovies\n";
    if (msg.equals(""))
        msg = "You didn't order any toppings.";
    else
        msg = "You ordered these toppings:\n"
                + msg;
    MessageBox.show(msg, "Your Order");
    chkPepperoni.setSelected(false);
    chkMushrooms.setSelected(false);
    chkAnchovies.setSelected(false);
}
```

Here, the name of each pizza topping selected by the user is added to a text string. If you select pepperoni and anchovies, for example, the following message displays:

```
You ordered these toppings:
Pepperoni
Anchovies
```

If you want, you can add event listeners to check boxes to respond to events generated when the user clicks those check boxes. Suppose that your restaurant has anchovies on the menu, but you refuse to actually make pizzas with anchovies on them. Here's a method you can call in an event listener to display a message if the user tries to check the Anchovies check box; after displaying the message, the method then clears the check box:

```
public void chkAnchovies_Click(){
    MessageBox.show("We don't do anchovies here.",
        "Yuck!")
    chkAnchovies.setSelected(false);
}
```

To add this event listener to the Anchovies check box, call its `setOnAction` method, like this:

```
chkAnchovies.setOnAction(e -> chkAnchovies_Click() );
```

Add a listener to a check box only if you need to provide immediate feedback to the user when she selects or deselects the box. In most applications, you wait until the user clicks a button to examine the state of any check boxes in the frame.

Using Radio Buttons

Radio buttons are similar to check boxes, but with a crucial difference: They travel in groups, and a user can select only one radio button at a time from each group. When you click a radio button to select it, the radio button within the same group that was previously selected is deselected automatically. Figure 6-3 shows a window with three radio buttons.

Figure 6-3:
A window
with three
radio
buttons.

To work with radio buttons, you use two classes. First, you create the radio buttons themselves with the `RadioButton` class, whose constructors and methods are shown in Table 6-4. Then you create a group for the buttons with the `ToggleGroup` class and add the radio buttons to the toggle group.

A `ToggleGroup` object is simply a way of associating a set of radio buttons so that only one of the buttons can be selected. The toggle group object itself is not a control and is not displayed. To display radio buttons, you add the individual radio buttons, not the toggle group, to a layout pane.

Table 6-4   Various RadioButton Constructors and Methods

Constructor	Description
`RadioButton()`	Creates a new radio button with no text.
`RadioButton(String text)`	Creates a new radio button with the specified text.

Method	Description
`String getText()`	Gets the text displayed by the radio button.
`boolean isSelected()`	Returns `true` if the radio button is selected or `false` if the radio button is not selected.
`void setOnAction (EventHandler<ActionEvent> value)`	Sets an `ActionEvent` listener to handle action events.
`void setSelected(boolean value)`	Selects the radio button if the parameter is `true`; de-selects it if the parameter is `false`.
`void setText(String text)`	Sets the check box text.

The usual way to create a radio button is to declare a variable to refer to the button as a class variable so that it can be accessed anywhere in the class, as in this example:

```
RadioButton rdoSmall, rdoMedium, rdoLarge;
```

Then, in the `start` method, you call the `RadioButton` constructor to create the radio button:

```
rdoSmall = new RadioButton("Small");
```

Thereafter, you can add the radio button to a layout pane in the usual way.

To create a toggle group to group radio buttons that work together, call the `ToggleGroup` class constructor:

```
ToggleGroup sizeGroup = new ToggleGroup();
```

Then call the `setToggleGroup` method of each radio button:

```
rdoSmall.setToggleGroup(sizeGroup);
rdoMedium.setToggleGroup(sizeGroup);
rdoLarge.setToggleGroup(sizeGroup);
```

Toggle groups have nothing to do with how radio buttons display. To display radio buttons, you must still add them to a layout pane. And there's no rule that says that all the radio buttons within a toggle group must be added to the same layout pane. However, it is customary to display all the radio buttons in a single toggle group together on the scene so that the user can easily see that the radio buttons belong together.

If you've worked with radio buttons in Swing, you'll want to note an important distinction between the way JavaFX toggle groups work versus how button groups work in Swing. In JavaFX, radio buttons that are outside a toggle group are independent of one another. In Swing, radio buttons that are outside a button group are all part of a default group. Thus, in JavaFX, always add radio buttons to a toggle group, even if the scene has only a single toggle group.

Looking at a Pizza Order Application

To give you an idea of how to use the controls that I present in this chapter together with the layout panes that I present in Chapter 5, this section presents a fairly complicated application that lets the user order a pizza. The user enters his name, address, and phone number into text fields, selects the pizza's size and crust style using radio buttons, and chooses toppings via check boxes. Figure 6-4 shows the main window displayed by the Pizza Order application.

Figure 6-4:
The Pizza
Order
applica-
tion's main
window.

When the user enters the data for his pizza order and clicks OK, this program displays a message box summarizing the order, as shown in Figure 6-5.

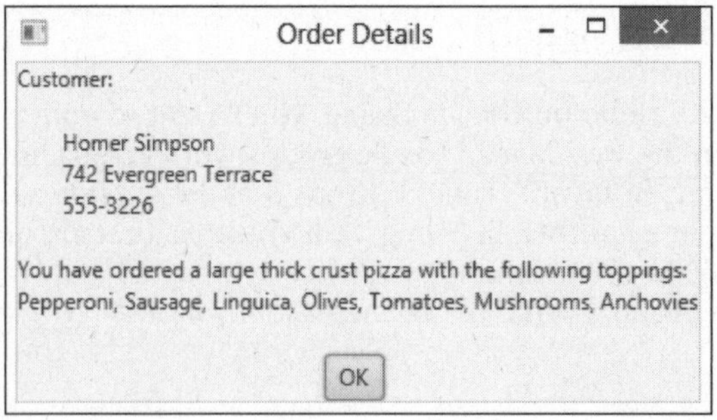

Figure 6-5:
The Pizza
Order
application
confirms the
user's order.

It may not be obvious at first glance, but the scene displayed by the Pizza Order application uses a total of 12 layout panes to govern the arrangement of its controls. The overall scene is organized with a border pane whose top region displays the title (Order Your Pizza Now!). The center region displays the text fields, radio buttons, and check boxes that let the user configure her pizza order. And the bottom region contains the OK and Cancel buttons.

For your reference, Table 6-5 lists the 12 layout panes that are used to organize this content.

Table 6-5   Layout Panes Used in the Pizza Order Application

Name	Class	Description
paneMain	BorderPane	The scene's main root pane.
paneTop	HBox	Contains the title text that's displayed in the top region of the border pane.
paneName	HBox	Contains the label and text box for the customer's name, placed side-by-side.
panePhone	HBox	Contains the label and text box for the phone number, placed side-by-side.
paneAddress	HBox	Contains the label and the text box for the address, placed side-by-side.
paneCustomer	VBox	Contains the name, phone, and address panes, stacked vertically.
paneSize	VBox	Contains a label with the text "Size" and the three radio buttons that let the user choose the pizza size, stacked vertically.
paneCrust	VBox	Contains a label with the text "Crust" and the two radio buttons that let the user choose the crust style, stacked vertically.
paneToppings	FlowPane	A flow pane that contains the check boxes for the toppings.
paneTopping	VBox	Contains a label with the text "Toppings" and the flow pane that lists the toppings, stacked vertically.
paneOrder	HBox	Contains the three VBox panes that list the sizes, crust styles, and toppings arranged side-by-side. This pane is displayed in the center region of the border pane.
paneBottom	HBox	Contains the OK and Cancel buttons arranged side-by-side. A spacer is used to force the buttons to the right margin. This pane is displayed in the bottom region of the border pane.

The source code for the Pizza Order application is shown in Listing 6-2. Note that this program makes use of the `MessageBox` class that I present in Chapter 4. The source code for that class can be found in Listing 4-2.

Listing 6-2: The Pizza Order Application

```java
import javafx.application.*;
import javafx.stage.*;
import javafx.scene.*;
import javafx.scene.layout.*;
import javafx.scene.control.*;
import javafx.geometry.*;
import javafx.scene.text.*;


public class PizzaOrder extends Application
{
    public static void main(String[] args)
    {
        launch(args);
    }

    Stage stage;

    // Customer name, phone, and address fields

    TextField txtName;
    TextField txtPhone;
    TextField txtAddress;

    // Size radio buttons

    RadioButton rdoSmall;
    RadioButton rdoMedium;
    RadioButton rdoLarge;

    // Crust style radio buttons

    RadioButton rdoThin;
    RadioButton rdoThick;

    // Topping radio buttons

    CheckBox chkPepperoni;
    CheckBox chkSausage;
```

```
CheckBox chkLinguica;
CheckBox chkOlives;
CheckBox chkMushrooms;
CheckBox chkTomatoes;
CheckBox chkAnchovies;

@Override public void start(Stage primaryStage)
{
    stage = primaryStage;


    // ----- Create the top pane -----

    Text textHeading = new Text("Order Your Pizza Now!");
    textHeading.setFont(new Font(20));
    HBox paneTop = new HBox(textHeading);
    paneTop.setPadding(new Insets(20, 10, 20, 10));


    // ---------- Create the customer pane ----------

    // Create the name label and text field

    Label lblName = new Label("Name:");
    lblName.setPrefWidth(100);
    txtName = new TextField();
    txtName.setPrefColumnCount(20);
    txtName.setPromptText("Enter the customer's name here");
    txtName.setMaxWidth(Double.MAX_VALUE);
    HBox paneName = new HBox(lblName, txtName);

    // Create the phone number label and text field

    Label lblPhone = new Label("Phone Number:");
    lblPhone.setPrefWidth(100);
    txtPhone = new TextField();
    txtPhone.setPrefColumnCount(20);
    txtPhone.setPromptText("Enter the customer's phone number here");
    HBox panePhone = new HBox(lblPhone, txtPhone);

    // Create the address label and text field

    Label lblAddress = new Label("Address:");
    lblAddress.setPrefWidth(100);
    txtAddress = new TextField();
```

(continued)

Listing 6-2 *(continued)*

```
        txtAddress.setPrefColumnCount(20);
        txtAddress.setPromptText("Enter the customer's address here");
        HBox paneAddress = new HBox(lblAddress, txtAddress);

        // Create the customer pane

        VBox paneCustomer = new VBox(10, paneName,
            panePhone, paneAddress);


        // ---------- Create the order pane ----------

        // Create the size pane

        Label lblSize = new Label("Size");
        rdoSmall = new RadioButton("Small");
        rdoMedium = new RadioButton("Medium");
        rdoLarge = new RadioButton("Large");
        rdoMedium.setSelected(true);
        ToggleGroup groupSize = new ToggleGroup();
        rdoSmall.setToggleGroup(groupSize);
        rdoMedium.setToggleGroup(groupSize);
        rdoLarge.setToggleGroup(groupSize);

        VBox paneSize = new VBox(lblSize, rdoSmall, rdoMedium, rdoLarge);
        paneSize.setSpacing(10);

        // Create the crust pane

        Label lblCrust = new Label("Crust");
        rdoThin = new RadioButton("Thin");
        rdoThick = new RadioButton("Thick");
        rdoThin.setSelected(true);
        ToggleGroup groupCrust = new ToggleGroup();
        rdoThin.setToggleGroup(groupCrust);
        rdoThick.setToggleGroup(groupCrust);

        VBox paneCrust = new VBox(lblCrust, rdoThin, rdoThick);
        paneCrust.setSpacing(10);

        // Create the toppings pane

        Label lblToppings = new Label("Toppings");
        chkPepperoni = new CheckBox("Pepperoni");
        chkSausage = new CheckBox("Sausage");
        chkLinguica = new CheckBox("Linguica");
        chkOlives = new CheckBox("Olives");
```

```
chkMushrooms = new CheckBox("Mushrooms");
chkTomatoes = new CheckBox("Tomatoes");
chkAnchovies = new CheckBox("Anchovies");

FlowPane paneToppings = new FlowPane(Orientation.VERTICAL,
    chkPepperoni, chkSausage, chkLinguica, chkOlives,
    chkMushrooms, chkTomatoes, chkAnchovies);
paneToppings.setPadding(new Insets(10, 0, 10, 0));
paneToppings.setHgap(20);
paneToppings.setVgap(10);
paneToppings.setPrefWrapLength(100);

VBox paneTopping = new VBox(lblToppings, paneToppings);

// Add the size, crust, and toppings pane to the order pane

HBox paneOrder = new HBox(50, paneSize, paneCrust, paneTopping);

// Create the center pane

VBox paneCenter = new VBox(20, paneCustomer, paneOrder);
paneCenter.setPadding(new Insets(0,10, 0, 10));


// ---------- Create the bottom pane ----------

Button btnOK = new Button("OK");
btnOK.setPrefWidth(80);
btnOK.setOnAction(e -> btnOK_Click() );

Button btnCancel = new Button("Cancel");
btnCancel.setPrefWidth(80);
btnCancel.setOnAction(e -> btnCancel_Click() );

Region spacer = new Region();

HBox paneBottom = new HBox(10, spacer, btnOK, btnCancel);
paneBottom.setHgrow(spacer, Priority.ALWAYS);
paneBottom.setPadding(new Insets(20, 10, 20, 10));

// ---------- Finish the scene ----------

BorderPane paneMain = new BorderPane();
paneMain.setTop(paneTop);
paneMain.setCenter(paneCenter);
paneMain.setBottom(paneBottom);
```

(continued)

Listing 6-2 *(continued)*

```java
        // Create the scene and the stage

        Scene scene = new Scene(paneMain);
        primaryStage.setScene(scene);
        primaryStage.setTitle("Pizza Order");
        primaryStage.show();
    }

    public void btnOK_Click()
    {

        // Create a message string with the customer information

        String msg = "Customer:\n\n";
        msg += "\t" + txtName.getText() + "\n";
        msg += "\t" + txtAddress.getText() + "\n";
        msg += "\t" + txtPhone.getText() + "\n\n";
        msg += "You have ordered a ";

        // Add the pizza size

        if (rdoSmall.isSelected())
            msg += "small ";
        if (rdoMedium.isSelected())
            msg += "medium ";
        if (rdoLarge.isSelected())
            msg += "large ";

        // Add the crust style

        if (rdoThin.isSelected())
            msg += "thin crust pizza with ";
        if (rdoThick.isSelected())
            msg += "thick crust pizza with ";

        // Add the toppings

        String toppings = "";
        toppings = buildToppings(chkPepperoni, toppings);
        toppings = buildToppings(chkSausage, toppings);
        toppings = buildToppings(chkLinguica, toppings);
        toppings = buildToppings(chkOlives, toppings);
        toppings = buildToppings(chkTomatoes, toppings);
        toppings = buildToppings(chkMushrooms, toppings);
        toppings = buildToppings(chkAnchovies, toppings);
```

```
        if (toppings.equals(""))
            msg += "no toppings.";
        else
            msg += "the following toppings:\n"
                + toppings;

        // Display the message

        MessageBox.show(msg, "Order Details");
    }

    public String buildToppings(CheckBox chk, String msg)
    {
        // Helper method for displaying the list of toppings
        if (chk.isSelected())
        {
            if (!msg.equals(""))
            {
                msg += ", ";
            }
            msg += chk.getText();
        }
        return msg;
    }

    public void btnCancel_Click()
    {
        stage.close();
    }
}
```

Part II
JavaFX Controls

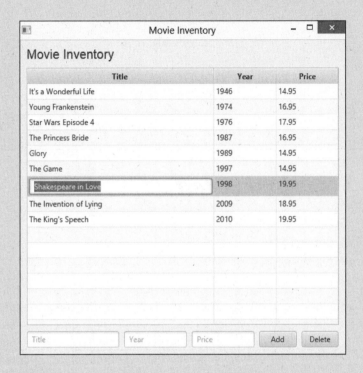

In this part . . .

- ✔ Controlling controls
- ✔ Organizing lists
- ✔ Building tables
- ✔ Creating menus
- ✔ Visit www.dummies.com/extras/javafx for great Dummies content online.

Chapter 7

Introducing the JavaFX Node Hierarchy

In This Chapter

▶ Introducing the most important packages and classes that make up JavaFX

▶ Looking at the important methods that all controls inherit via the `Node`, `Parent`, and `Region` classes

The simplest definition of a JavaFX control is this: A *control* is an object created from a class that directly or indirectly inherits the JavaFX `Control` class. The `Control` class provides all the basic functions that are required for a JavaFX object to be considered a control. For example, any class that inherits the `Control` class has a visual representation in a scene, can be added to a layout pane, can automatically adjust its size within parameters you set by calling methods such as `setMaxWidth` or `setMinHeight`, and can have a tooltip that pops up when the user hovers the mouse over the control.

Although all controls have those features in common, not all those features are provided directly by the `Control` class. That's because the `Control` class itself inherits the `Region` class, which in turn, inherits the `Parent` class, which in turn inherits the `Node` class. Each of these classes along this inheritance chain contributes features to every JavaFX control.

In this chapter, you read about some of the more important features that are common to every JavaFX control by virtue of the fact that every control inherits the `Control` class, which in turn inherits the `Region`, `Parent`, and `Node` classes.

An Overview of JavaFX Packages

Before I look at the classes that make up the Node class hierarchy, I want to briefly discuss the various packages that make up JavaFX. JavaFX itself consists of a total of 665 classes that are spread out over 36 distinct packages, which all begin with the root name javafx.

So far in this book, you've seen JavaFX classes from the following seven packages:

✔ **javafx.application:** The most important class in this package is Application, which provides the basic lifecycle functions of a JavaFX application.

As I discuss in Chapter 2, all JavaFX programs extend the Application class and implement the start method, which is called to initiate the application. The Application class also creates the application's primary stage and passes it to the start method via the primaryStage parameter. This allows the program to display a scene in the application's window.

✔ **javafx.stage:** The most important class in this package is Stage, which represents a window in which a user interface can be displayed. You read about the Stage class in Chapter 4. There are other classes in this class that may occasionally be useful, such as FileChooser and DirectoryChooser, which display dialog boxes that let you select files and directories.

✔ **javafx.scene:** This package contains several important classes that deal with creating user-interface scenes that can then be displayed in a stage. The two most important classes in this package are

• Scene, which creates a scene object.

You can read about the Scene class in Chapter 4.

• Node, which is the base class for all objects contained in a scene, including controls and layout panes.

For more information about the Node class, see the section "The Node Class" later in this chapter.

✔ **javafx.scene.control:** This package contains most of JavaFX's user-interface control classes, including Button, Label, CheckBox, and RadioButton. Also included in this package is Control, the base class from which all user-interface controls are derived. For more information about the Control class, see the section "The Control Class" later in this chapter. (***Note:*** There are a few JavaFX controls that are defined in other packages, including `javafx.scene.control.cell` and `javafx.scene.web`.)

✔ **`javafx.scene.layout`:** This package contains the layout pane classes, such as `HBox`, `VBox`, and `BorderPane`. Two other important classes defined in this package are `Pane` and `Region`. All the layout pane classes are based on the `Pane` class, and both the `Pane` class in this package and the `Control` class in the `javafx.scene.control` class are based on the `Region` class. For more information about the `Region` class, see the section "The Region Class" later in this chapter.

✔ **`javafx.geometry`:** This is a relatively small package that defines several classes and enumerations that are related to the geometry of JavaFX nodes. In Chapter 5, you figure out how to use the `Insets` class to control spacing within a layout pane as well as the `Pos` enumeration to specify alignments.

✔ **`javafx.collections`:** This package defines the `ObservableList` class, which is used by the `getChildren` method of the `Pane` class. You also encounter several control classes in the next few chapters that require this package.

Because these seven packages contain most of the JavaFX classes you'll use in applications that work mostly with controls (as opposed to classes that work with other user-interface objects such as graphs, shapes, or animations), I recommend you import all the classes in these seven packages in all your programs:

```
import javafx.application.*;
import javafx.stage.*;
import javafx.scene.*;
import javafx.scene.control.*;
import javafx.scene.layout.*;
import javafx.scene.geometry.*;
import javafx.collections.*;
```

Although you don't need all the classes in all these packages in every program, including these entire packages every time eliminates the need to keep track of which programs need which specific classes.

In the rest of this chapter, I take a closer look at the classes that are inherited by all JavaFX controls: `Node`, `Parent`, `Region`, and `Control`.

The Node Class

The JavaFX `Control` class hierarchy begins at the `Node` class, which represents an object that can be added to the JavaFX scene. Well, actually, the topmost class in the `Control` class hierarchy is the `Object` class, but that's hardly worth mentioning here because *all* Java class hierarchies begin with the `Object` class — `Object` is the mother of all Java classes.

All objects that are a part of a scene belong to a *scene graph,* which is a tree structure that contains all the nodes that make up a user interface. To be a part of a scene graph, an object must inherit the `Node` class. Thus, the `Node` class is the base class for all classes that can be added to a JavaFX scene.

Like any other tree structure, a scene graph begins with a single node — the *root node* — which can have one or more child nodes, each of which in turn can have one or more child nodes. A node that has at least one child node is a *branch node;* a node that has no children is a *leaf node.* A scene can have only one root node, but it can have many branch and leaf nodes.

The `Node` class is an abstract class, which means that you can't directly create an instance of it. In other words, the following code results in a compiler error:

```
Node myNode = new Node();
```

However, you can use the `Node` class to hold nodes whose type you are uncertain of or don't care about. For example:

```
Node myNode = new Button();
```

In this case, the `myNode` variable is of type `Node`, but it's used to hold a reference to a `Button` control.

Many methods of classes up and down the `Node` hierarchy accept or return objects of type `Node`. For example, the `getChildren` method used with layout panes, such as `HBox` and `FlowPane`, returns list of `Node` objects. And the `add` method used to add an object to a layout pane's node list accepts a `Node` object as a parameter. In other words, any `Node` object can be added to a layout pane.

Table 7-1 lists just a few of the methods you're likely to use in most JavaFX programs. Note that this table drastically simplifies the complexity of the `Node` class. There are actually more than 300 methods defined by this class. More than one third of them are related to event handling: The `Node` class is the class that's responsible for most event handling for all nodes, including events that handle mouse, keyboard, and touchscreen interaction with the node.

Table 7-1	Commonly Used Methods of the Node Class
Method	*Explanation*
`Parent getParent()`	Returns this node's `Parent` node.
`String getId()`	Returns the ID of this node.
`void setId(String id)`	Sets the ID of this node. The ID should be unique within the scene graph.
`Node lookup(String id)`	Searches the node's children for a node whose ID matches the parameter.
`String getStyle()`	Returns the CSS style string for the node.
`Void setStyle(String style)`	Sets the CSS style string for the node.

The `getParent` method returns a node's parent node. This method returns an object of type `Parent`, which is a node that can have children (as you discover in the following section). Every node in a scene graph except the root node must have a parent node, and that parent node will always be of type `Parent`. If you call this method on the root node, null will be returned.

Notice that every node can have a unique string identifier, which makes it easy to distinguish nodes from one another in complicated scene graphs and can also be helpful when you use CSS to format your scenes. You can set the string identifier by calling the `setID` method, which accepts a string argument like this:

```
myNode.setId("LBL3");
```

Here, the string `LBL3` is associated with the node.

You can later find this node by calling the `lookup` method. This method is a little quirky in that you must preface the ID you're looking for with a hash symbol (#). For example, here's how you might search an entire scene graph for a control whose ID is `LBL3`:

```
Node myNode = scene.getRoot().lookup("#LBL3");
```

Here, the getRoot method of the scene variable (which I assume to be of type Scene) is called to get the root node of the scene. Then, the lookup method is called to return the node whose ID is LBL3.

There are many other methods of the Node class that let you apply common formatting or other features for all types of nodes. For example, the setStyle method lets you apply CSS-style formatting to any type of node. And the setRotate method lets you rotate any node. You can read about these and other Node methods in later chapters of this book.

The Parent Class

Although ten different classes directly inherit the Node class, the only one you need to be concerned with when working with JavaFX controls is the Parent class. For an explanation of all ten of the subclasses of Node, see the sidebar "Ten Different Kinds of Nodes" in this chapter.

The Parent class has all the capabilities of the Node class, plus the added ability to have child nodes. Its main job is to manage a collection of child nodes, which is represented as a standard Java list. You can access this list by calling the getChildren method.

You've seen this method in action in layout panes, such as HBox and VBox. For example, the following code creates an HBox pane and then adds two controls to it:

```
Label lblAddress = new Label("Address:");
TextField txtAddress = new TextField();
HBox hbox = new HBox();
hbox.getChildren().addAll(lblAddress, txtAddress);
```

The getChildren method returns an object of type ObservableList, which in turn extends the List interface. Between them, these two interfaces define a few dozen methods that you can use to manipulate the parent's child nodes. Table 7-2 lists a few of the more commonly used of these methods.

Interestingly, the getParent method is defined in the Parent class with protected access. That means that although the getParent method is available to any class that inherits the Parent class, the getParent method is *not* accessible to the outside world. For the getParent method to become public, a class that inherits the Parent class must override the getParent method with public access.

Table 7-2   Commonly Used ObservableList Methods

Method	Explanation
void add(Node node)	Adds a single child node to the existing list of children.
void addAll(Node nodes...)	Adds multiple child nodes.
void remove(Node node)	Removes the specified node from the list of children.
void clear()	Removes all child nodes.
int size()	Returns the number of child nodes.

That's precisely what the Pane class does. The Pane class is the base class of all layout panes; it inherits the Parent class and then overrides the getParent method. Here's a snippet of the actual code from the Pane class:

```
@Override public ObservableList<Node> getChildren()
{
    return super.getChildren();
}
```

As you can see, the getChildren method in the Pane class simply calls the getChildren method of its superclass (Parent) and returns the result.

One class derived from the Parent class which you may use on occasion is the Group class. The Group class is a bit like a layout pane such as HBox or FlowPane, except that it doesn't provide any actual layout for the child nodes it contains. When you create a Group, you can pass the child nodes to the constructor, like this:

```
Group group = new Group(Node1, Node2, Node3);
```

Or, you can use the default constructor and add child nodes via the getChildren method, like this:

```
Group group = new Group();
group.getChildren().addAll(Node1, Node2, Node3);
```

You'll see examples of Group nodes occasionally throughout this book.

Ten Different Kinds of Nodes

In all, ten different classes directly inherit the Node class, creating ten distinct inheritance branches beneath Node. The only one of these ten I discuss in the chapters that make up this part of the book is the Parent class because all JavaFX controls and layout panes are derived from the Parent class. However, to give you a general idea of what other types of objects besides controls and layout panes can be added to a scene graph, the following paragraphs give a brief summary of what each of the ten subclasses of Node provide:

✔ **Camera:** An object that's used to graphically render a three-dimensional screen on a flat display.

A camera is a node because in scene graphs that represent 3D layout, the camera can be positioned at a specific location within that layout, thus rendering the flat image of the 3D layout from a specific perspective.

✔ **Canvas:** A node that you can draw on using drawing commands, much like an artist can draw on a canvas to create a painting.

A canvas is a two-dimensional object that has a height and a width.

✔ **ImageView:** Represents an image viewer, used to display a two-dimensional image.

✔ **LightBase:** An abstract class that serves as the base class for lighting sources that illuminate a scene rendered by a camera.

Like a camera, a light source is a node so that you can position it at a specific location within a scene to create realistic lighting effects.

✔ **MediaView:** Represents a media viewer that can play media, such as sound or video.

✔ **Parent:** A node that can contain child nodes. All controls and layout panes inherit the Parent class.

✔ **Shape:** A two-dimensional shape such as a rectangle or a circle.

The Text class also inherits the Shape class, providing an easy way to display text within a scene.

✔ **Shape3D:** A three-dimensional shape such as a box, cylinder, or sphere.

✔ **Subscene:** Marks a branch of a scene that can be rendered with its own camera.

✔ **SwingNode:** Allows you to incorporate Swing objects into a JavaFX scene graph.

The Region Class

Next in line in the Node class hierarchy is the Region class. Region is the last common ancestor class shared by both the Control class and the Pane class. Thus, the Region class is the last class from which controls and layout panes share common features.

As its name implies, the Region class defines a visible area of the scene that has a physical size — that is, a height and a width. The size of a region depends on a number of factors, but by default will be determined by the size of the content it contains. You can set minimum, maximum, and pre-ferred size constraints that the region will honor, and you can specify a fixed amount of padding that provides a margin between the region's content and its outer edges. In addition, the visual style of a region can be set by a Cascading Style Sheet.

Table 7-3 shows the most commonly used methods provided by the Region class, which are all related to setting the size of the region.

Table 7-3	Common Methods of the Region Class
Method	*Explanation*
void setMaxHeight(double height)	Sets the maximum height for the region.
void setMinHeight(double height)	Sets the minimum height for the region.
void setPrefHeight(double height)	Sets the preferred height for the region.
void setMaxWidth(double width)	Sets the maximum width for the region.
void setMinWidth(double width)	Sets the minimum width for the region.
void setPrefWidth(double width)	Sets the preferred width for the region.
double getHeight()	Gets the actual height of the region.
double getWidth()	Gets the actual width of the region.
void setPadding(Insets value)	Sets the padding around the inside edges of the Hbox.

The Region class provides three distinct parameters that let you control the height and width of the region. For both the height and the width, you can set a minimum value, a preferred value, and a maximum value. As their names imply, JavaFX will not make the control smaller than the minimum size or larger than the maximum size, and, if possible, will shoot for the preferred size.

Within these parameters, JavaFX will determine the ideal height and width for the region based on the content it contains. For a control, such as a label or a button, the content is the text that's displayed by the label or the button. For more complex controls, the content is more complex. And for layout panes, the content consists of the aggregate of all the nodes that are added to the pane.

If you don't specify any height or width constraints, all three — minimum, preferred, and maximum — default to the actual computed size of the control's contents.

Note: In many cases, the contents of a region will resize automatically to fill whatever space is available to it. Thus, if the user dynamically resizes the window that contains the scene, the size of all the regions contained within the scene may expand or contract to fill the available space.

If you want to set an exact value for a region's width or height, set all three parameters (minimum, preferred, and maximum) to the same value. For example:

```
lbl.setMinWidth(150);
lbl.setPrefWidth(150);
lbl.setMaxWidth(150);
```

You might, in this case, prefer to create a constant:

```
final static int LABEL_WIDTH = 150;
lbl.setMinWidth(LABEL_WIDTH);
lbl.setPrefWidth(LABEL_WIDTH);
lbl.setMaxWidth(LABEL_WIDTH);
```

That way, if you change your mind about the width of the label, you have to change the value in only one place.

One other setting affects the height or width of a region: the amount of padding you specify. *Padding* provides margins around the edges of the region to prevent crowded-looking scenes. *Note:* You're more likely to use padding with layout panes than with controls.

To specify padding, use the `Insets` class, which is defined in the `javafx.geometry` package. `Insets` provides two constructors. The first lets you set even margins around all four sides of a region:

```
pane.setPadding(new Insets(10));
```

Or, you can set different values for the top, right, bottom, and left edges:

```
pane.setPadding(new Insets(10,0,10,0);
```

In this example, the top and bottom margins are set to 10 pixels, but the right and left margins are set to 0.

For more information about padding, flip to Chapter 5.

The Control Class

The ultimate purpose of this chapter is to give you an overview of the features that are common to all JavaFX controls by virtue of the fact that all controls inherit the `Control` class. Now that you've finally made it to a discussion of the `Control` class itself, brace yourself for a little disappointment: The `Control` class itself isn't all that interesting. As Table 7-4 reveals, there are really only three methods of interest. It turns out that most of the features that are common to all controls are actually provided by the `Region`, `Parent`, and `Node` controls.

Table 7-4	Methods of the Control Class
Method	*Explanation*
`void setTooltip(Tooltip value)`	Sets a tooltip for the control.
`void setContextmenu(Contextmenu value)`	Sets a context menu for the control. For more information, see Chapter 10.
`void setSkin(Skin value)`	Sets a skin for the control. For more information, see Chapter 12.

The `Control` adds three main features to the `Region` class: the ability to add tooltips, context menus, and CSS skins. You can read about context menus in Chapter 10, and you see how CSS skins work in Chapter 12. So for now, I just look at tooltips.

A *tooltip* is a pop-up balloon that provides an explanation of a control's function. Creating a tooltip couldn't be easier: You call the `Tooltip` constructor, passing the text of the tooltip as an argument, and then assign the tooltip to a control by calling the control's `setTooltip` method. Here's an example:

```
btnSave.setTooltip(new Tooltip("Saves the file"));
```

Then, when the user hovers the mouse over the button, the tooltip appears.

Congratulations! You now know about the most important methods that are available to all JavaFX controls by virtue of the fact that they all inherit the `Control` class, which in turn inherits `Region`, which inherits `Parent`, which inherits `Node`.

Now, in the remaining chapters of this Part, you discover how to use some of the most commonly used and useful JavaFX controls, including radio buttons, check boxes, choice boxes, lists, tree views, tables, and menus.

Chapter 8

Choosing from a List

. . . .

In This Chapter

▶ Using the `ChoiceBox` control

▶ Working with the `ObservableList` interface

▶ Listening for changes to the user's selection

▶ Using the `ComboBox` and `ListView` controls

▶ Using the `TreeView` control

. . . .

An entire category of JavaFX controls are designed to let the user choose one or more items from a list. This chapter presents three such controls: choice boxes, combo boxes, and lists. Along the way, you discover how to use the `ObservableList` interface, which is used to manage the list of items displayed by a choice box, combo box, or a list view control.

Actually, if you've read along so far, you've already been briefly introduced to the `ObservableList` interface, as it's also used to manage the list of controls that are displayed in a layout pane. In Chapter 5, you read about how to use the `addAll` method of this interface. In this chapter, you read about the additional capabilities of this interface.

You also discover how to add an event listener that can respond when the user changes the current selection.

Using Choice Boxes

A *choice box* is a control that lets the user choose an item from a drop-down list. Initially, the choice box shows just the item that's currently selected. When the user clicks the choice box, the list of choices reveals. The user can change the selection by clicking any of the items in the list. Figure 8-1 shows a scene with a simple choice box.

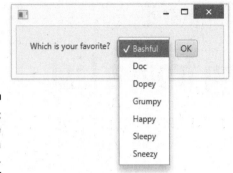

You use the ChoiceBox class to create choice boxes. Table 8-1 lists the most frequently used constructors and methods of this class.

Table 8-1   Common ChoiceBox Constructors and Methods

Constructor	Description
ChoiceBox<T>()	Creates an empty choice list of the specified type.
ChoiceBox<T>(Observable List<T> items)	Creates a choice list and fills it with the values in the specified list.

Method	Description
ObservableList<T> getItems()	Gets the list of items.
void setItems (ObservableList<T> items)	Sets the list of items.
T getValue()	Returns the currently selected item.
void setValue(T value)	Sets the currently selected item.
void show()	Shows the list of items.
void hide()	Hides the list of items.
boolean isShowing()	Indicates whether the list of items is currently visible.

Creating a choice box

Creating a choice box is easy. The `ChoiceBox` class is generic, so specify a type for the list that will be associated with the choice box. For example:

```
ChoiceBox<String> choice = new ChoiceBox<String>();
```

Here, a choice box that displays strings is created.

The next step is to add items to the choice box. You can do that by calling the `getItems` method to access the list of items and then calling the `add` method to add an item:

```
choice.getItems().add("Bashful");
choice.getItems().add("Doc");
choice.getItems().add("Dopey");
choice.getItems().add("Grumpy");
choice.getItems().add("Happy");
choice.getItems().add("Sleepy");
choice.getItems().add("Sneezy");
```

Alternatively, you could call the `addAll` method and add all the strings at once, like this:

```
choice.getItems().addAll("Bashful", "Doc", "Dopey",
                         "Grumpy", "Happy", "Sleepy",
                         "Sneezy");
```

The `getItems` method returns an object of type `ObservableList`, which offers a number of methods that let you work with the list. For more information, see the section "Working with Observable Lists" later in this chapter.

The `ChoiceBox` class also includes a constructor that lets you add an `ObservableList` object when you create the choice box. This lets you create the list before you create the choice box. You see an example of this constructor in action in the section "Working with Observable Lists" in this chapter.

You can add any kind of object you want to a choice box. The choice box calls the `toString` method of each item to determine the text to display in the choice list. Suppose you have a class named `Astronaut` that represents an astronaut on a space mission:

```
class Astronaut
{
    private String firstName;
    private String lastName;

    public Astronaut(String FirstName, String LastName)
    {
        firstName = FirstName;
        lastName = LastName;
    }

    public String toString()
    {
        return firstName + " " + lastName;
    }
}
```

Then, you could create a choice box listing the crew of Apollo 13 like this:

```
ChoiceBox<Astronaut> apollo13;
Apollo13 = new ChoiceBox<Astronaut>();
apollo13.getItems().add(new Astronaut("Jim", "Lovell"));
apollo13.getItems().add(new Astronaut(
    "John", "Swigert"));
apollo13.getItems().add(new Astronaut("Fred", "Haise"));
```

If you wish, you can display the contents of a choice box without waiting for the user to click the box. To do that, call the show method, like this:

```
apollo13.show();
```

To hide the list, call the hide method:

```
apollo13.hide();
```

Setting a default value

By default, a choice box has no initial selection when it's first displayed. To set an initial value, call the setValue method, passing it the list object that you want to make the initial selection.

If the choice box contains strings, you can set the initial value by passing the desired string value to the `setValue` method:

```
choice.setValue("Dopey");
```

If the specified string doesn't exist in the list, the initial value will remain unspecified.

If the choice box contains objects, such as the `Astronaut` objects, illustrated in the preceding section, you must pass a reference to the object you want to be the default choice. For example:

```
Astronaut lovell = new Astronaut("Jim", "Lovell");
Astronaut swigert = new Astronaut("John", "Swigert");
Astronaut haise = new Astronaut("Fred", "Haise");
ChoiceBox apollo13 = new ChoiceBox<Astronaut>();
apollo13.getItems().addAll(lovell, swigert, haise);
apollo13.setValue(lovell);
```

Here, Jim Lovell is set as the default astronaut.

Getting the selected item

You can call the `getValue` method to get the item selected by the user. The type of the value returned depends on the type specified when you created the choice box. For example, if you specified type `String`, the `getValue` method returns strings. If you specified type `Astronauts` for the choice box, the `getValue` method returns astronauts.

The `getValue` method is often used in the action event handler for a button. For example:

```
public void btnOK_Click()
{
    String message = "You chose ";
    message += apollo13.getValue();
    MessageBox.show(message, "Your Favorite Astronaut");
}
```

The `MessageBox` class used in this example can be found in Chapter 4.

Working with Observable Lists

As you saw in the previous section, the ChoiceBox class does not include methods that let you directly add or remove items from the list displayed by the choice box. Instead, it includes a method named getItems that returns an object of type ObservableList. The object returned by this method is an *observable list;* it represents the list displayed by the choice box.

To work with the items displayed by a choice box, you must first access the observable list and then use methods of the ObservableList class to access the individual items in the list.

Observable lists are used not only by the ChoiceBox class, but also by other control classes that display list items, such as ComboBox and List, which you can read about later in this chapter. Both of those classes also have a getItems method that returns an ObservableList.

Observable lists are also used by layout panes, such as HBox and VBox, which you can read about in Chapter 5. The getChildren method that's common to all layout classes returns an ObservableList.

So far in this book, I've discussed just two methods of the ObservableList interface: add and addAll, which lets you add items to the observable list. Here's an example of the add method from earlier in this chapter:

```
cbox.getItems().add("Bashful");
```

And here's an example from Chapter 5, which uses the addAll method to add buttons to a layout pane:

```
pane.getChildren().addAll(btnOK, btnCancel);
```

The ObservableList interface has many other methods besides add and addAll. Table 8-2 shows the methods you're most likely to use.

Table 8-2	Commonly Used ObservableList Methods
Method	*Description*
void add(E element)	Adds the specified element to the end of the list.
void add(int *index*, E *element*)	Adds the specified object to the list at the specified index position.
void addAll(E...elements)	Adds all the specified elements to the end of the list.

Method	Description
`void addAll(Collection<E> c)`	Adds all the elements of the specified collection to the end of the list.
`E set(int index, E elem)`	Sets the specified element to the specified object. The element that was previously at that position is returned as the method's return value.
`void clear()`	Deletes all elements from the array list.
`void remove(int fromIndex, int toIndex)`	Removes all objects whose index values are between the values specified.
`void removeAll(E...elements)`	Removes all objects whose index values are between the values specified.
`boolean contains(Object elem)`	Returns a `boolean` that indicates whether the specified object is in the list.
`E get(int index)`	Returns the object at the specified position in the list.
`int indexOf(Object elem)`	Returns the index position of the first occurrence of the specified object in the list. If the object isn't in the list, it returns -1.
`boolean isEmpty()`	Returns a `boolean` value that indicates whether the list is empty.
`E remove(int index)`	Removes the object at the specified index and returns the element that was removed.
`boolean remove(Object elem)`	Removes an object from the list. **Note:** More than one element refers to the object; this method removes only one of them. It returns a `boolean` that indicates whether the object was in the list.
`int size()`	Returns the number of elements in the list.
`void addListener(ListChange Listener listener)`	Adds a `ListChangeListener` that's called whenever the list changes.

If you're familiar with Java collection classes, such as `ArrayList`, you may have noticed that many of the methods listed in Table 8-2 are familiar. That's because the `ObservableList` class extends the `List` class, which is implemented by classes, such as `ArrayList` and `Vector`. As a result, any method that can be used with an `ArrayList` can also be used with an `ObservableList`.

For example, you can clear the contents of a choice box in the same way you'd clear the contents of an array list:

```
cbox.getItems().clear();
```

If you need to know how many items are in a choice box, call the `size` method:

```
int count = cbox.getItems().size();
```

To remove a specific item from the list, use the `remove` method:

```
cbox.getItems().remove("Grumpy");
```

This method succeeds whether or not the string `"Grumpy"` appears in the list.

You can easily insert items from an existing Java collection, such as an array list, into a choice box by specifying the collection in the `addAll` method. For example, suppose you already have an array list named `list` that contains the items you want to display in the choice box. You can add the items like this:

```
cbox.getItems().addAll(list);
```

You might be wondering why an observable list is required for the items displayed by list-based JavaFX controls. Why not just use the existing collection classes? The reason is that for list-based controls to work efficiently, the controls themselves need to monitor any changes you might make to the list of items so that the control can automatically update the displayed items. The last method listed in Table 8-2 (`addListener`) provides this capability by allowing you to add a listener that's called whenever the contents of the list changes. You will rarely call this method directly. But the controls that use observable lists *do* call this method to create event listeners that automatically update the control whenever the contents of the list changes.

Note: You do *not* use the addListener method to respond when the user selects an item in a choice box or other type of list control. Instead, you use an interesting construct called a *selection model* to respond to changes in the selected item, as described in the next section.

Listening for Selection Changes

It's not uncommon to want your program to respond immediately when the user changes the selection of a choice box or other list control, without waiting for the user to click a button to submit the data. For example, you might have a label whose value you want to update immediately whenever the user changes the selection. You might even want to show or hide different controls based on the selection.

Unfortunately, the choice box and other list controls don't generate an action event when the user changes the selection. As a result, the ChoiceBox class doesn't have a setOnAction method. Instead, you must use a complicated sequence of method calls to set up a different type of event listener, called a *change listener*.

Here's the sequence:

1. **Get the selection model by calling the getSelectionModel method on the choice box.**

   The getSelectionModel method returns the control's *selection model,* which is an object that manages how the user can select items from the list. The selection model is an object that implements one of several classes that extend the abstract SelectionModel class. For a choice box, the selection model is always of type SingleSelectionMode, which implements a selection model that allows the user to select just one item from the list at a time.

2. **Get the selectedItem property by calling the selectedItem Property method on the selection model.**

   The SelectionModel class has a method named selectedItem Property that accesses a property named selectedItem, which represents the item currently selected. (A *property* is a special type of JavaFX object that I discuss more about in Chapter 19. For now, just assume that a property is an object whose value can be monitored by a listener that's called whenever the value of the property changes.)

3. **Add a change listener by calling the `addListener` method on the `selectedItem` property.**

   The listener will be called whenever the value of the `selectedItem` property changes. The change listener implements a functional interface called, naturally, `ChangeListener`. Because `ChangeListener` is a functional interface (that is, it has just one method), you can use a Lambda expression to implement the change listener.

You normally do all three of these steps in a single statement, as in this example:

```
choice.getSelectionModel().selectedItemProperty()
    .addListener( (v, oldValue, newValue) ->
        lbl.setText(newValue); );
```

In the preceding example, the change listener sets the value displayed by a label control to the new value selected by the user.

Being a functional interface, `ChangeListerner` defines a single function named `changed`, which is called whenever the value of the property changes. The `changed` method receives three arguments:

✔ **`observable`:** The property whose value has changed

✔ **`oldValue`:** The previous value of the property

✔ **`newValue`:** The new value of the property

These three parameters are specified in the parentheses at the beginning of the Lambda expression. In the body of the Lambda expression, the `newValue` parameter is assigned to the text of a label. Thus, the value selected by the user will be displayed by the label, and the label will be updated automatically whenever the user changes the choice box selection.

Using Combo Boxes

A *combo box* is a more advanced sibling to the choice box control. The main improvements you get with a combo box are

✔ **A combo box includes the ability to limit the number of items displayed when the list is shown.**

   If the number of items in the list exceeds the limit, a scroll bar is added automatically to allow the user to scroll through the entire list.

✔ **A combo box includes a text field that lets the user enter a value directly rather than select the value from a list.**

The text field is optional and is not shown by default, but you can add it with a single method call.

Figure 8-2 shows a combo box with the text field shown.

✔ **A combo box fires an action event whenever the user changes the selection.**

Thus, setting up an event handler to respond to the user's selection change is easier with a combo box than it is with a choice box.

Figure 8-2:
A combo
box.

You use the ComboBox class to create combo boxes. Table 8-3 lists the most frequently used constructors and methods of this class.

Table 8-3   Common ComboBox Constructors and Methods

Constructor	Description
ComboBox<T>()	Creates an empty combo box of the specified type.
ComboBox<T> (ObservableList<T> items)	Creates a combo box and fills it with the values in the specified list.

Method	Description
void setEditable(boolean value)	If true, a text field is displayed to allow the user to directly edit the selection.
void setVisibleRowCount(int value)	Sets the number of items to display.

(continued)

Table 8-3 *(continued)*

Method	Description
`void setPromptText(String text)`	Sets the prompt text initially displayed in the text field.
`ObservableList<T> getItems()`	Gets the list of items.
`void setItems (ObservableList<T> items)`	Sets the list of items.
`T getValue()`	Returns the currently selected item.
`void setValue(T value)`	Sets the currently selected item.
`void show()`	Shows the list of items.
`void hide()`	Hides the list of items.
`void setOnAction(Event Handler<ActionEvent> handler)`	Sets an event handler that's called whenever the selection changes.
`boolean isShowing()`	Indicates whether the list of items is currently visible.

Creating combo boxes

Creating a combo box is much like creating a choice box. Because the `ComboBox` is generic, specify a type for the items it will contain, as in this example:

```
ComboBox<String> cbox = new ComboBox<String>();
```

Then you can use the `getItems` method to access the `ObservableList` object that contains the content of the list displayed by the combo box. For example, you can add items to the list like this:

```
cbox.getItems().addAll("Bashful", "Doc", "Dopey",
                       "Grumpy", "Happy", "Sleepy",
                       "Sneezy");
```

For more information about working with the `ObservableList` interface, flip to the section "Working with Observable Lists" earlier in this chapter.

By default, the user isn't allowed to edit the data in the text field portion of the combo box. If you want to allow the user to edit the text field, use the `setEditable` method, like this:

```
cbo.setEditable(true);
```

Then the user can type a value that's not in the combo box.

If you want, you can limit the number of items displayed by the list by calling the `setVisibleRows` method:

```
cbo.setVisibleRows(10);
```

Here, the list displays a maximum of ten items. If the list contains more than ten items, a scroll is added automatically so the user can scroll through the entire list.

You can also specify a prompt text to display in the text field component of a combo box by calling the `setPromptText` method:

```
cbo.setPromptText("Make a choice");
```

Here, the text `Make a choice` displays in the text field.

Getting the selected item

To get the item selected by the user, use the `getValue` method, just as you do for a choice box. You typically do that in an action event handler that responds to a button click. For example:

```
public void btnOK_Click()
{
    String message = "You chose ";
    message += cbo.getValue();
    MessageBox.show(message, "Your Choice ");
}
```

The `MessageBox` class used in this example can be found in Chapter 4.

Bear in mind that the value returned by the `getValue` method may not be one of the values in the combo box's list. That's because the user can enter anything he wishes to in the text field of an editable combo box. If you want to know whether the user selected an item from the list or entered a different item via the text field, use the `contains` method of the `ObservableList` class, like this:

```
if (!cbo.getItems().contains(cbo.getValue()))
{
    MessageBox.show("You chose outside the box",
        "Good Thinking!");
}
```

Here, the message box displays if the user enters an item that's not in the list.

Handling combo box events

When the user selects an item from a combo box, an action event is generated. In most applications, you simply ignore this event because you usually don't need to do anything immediately when the user selects an item. Instead, the selected item is processed when the user clicks a button.

If you want to provide immediate feedback when the user selects an item, you can set up an event handler by calling the combo box's `setOnAction` method. In most cases, the easiest way to do that is to create a method that contains the code you want to execute when the user selects an item and then pass this method to the `setOnAction` method via a Lambda expression.

For example, the following method displays a message box that says He's my favorite too! if the user picks Dopey:

```
Public void cbo_Changed()
{
    if (if cbo.getValue().equals("Dopey"))
    {
        MessageBox.show("He's my favorite too!",
            "Good Choice");
    }
}
```

Here's the code to call this method whenever the user changes the combo box selection:

```
cbo.setOnAction (e -> cbo_Changed() );
```

Using List Views

A *list view* is a powerful JavaFX control that displays a list of objects within a box. Depending on how the list is configured, the user can select one item in the list or multiple items. In addition, you have amazing control over how the items in the list display. Figure 8-3 shows a sample scene with a list view.

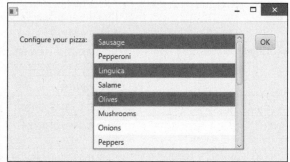

Figure 8-3:
A list view
control.

List views and combo boxes have several important differences:

- ✔ **A list view doesn't have a text field that lets the user edit the selected item.** Instead, the user must select items directly from the list view.

- ✔ **The list view doesn't drop down.** Instead, the list items display in a box whose size you can specify.

- ✔ **The items in a list view can be arranged vertically (the default) or horizontally.** Figure 8-4 shows a horizontal list box.

- ✔ **List views allow users to select more than one item.** By default, a list view lets users select just one item, but you can easily configure it to allow for multiple selections.

    To select multiple items in a list, hold down the Ctrl key and click the items you want to select. To select a range of items, click the first item, hold down the Shift key, and click the last item.

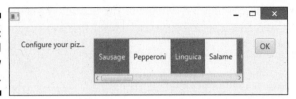

Figure 8-4:
A horizontal
list view
control.

You use the `ListView` class to create a list view control. Table 8-4 lists the most frequently used constructors and methods of this class.

Table 8-4   Common ListView Constructors and Methods

Constructor	Description
`ListView<T>()`	Creates an empty list view of the specified type.
`ListView<T>(ObservableList<T> items)`	Creates a list view and fills it with the values in the specified list.

Method	Description
`ObservableList<T> getItems()`	Gets the list of items.
`void setItems (ObservableList<T> items)`	Sets the list of items.
`void setOrientation (Orientation o)`	Sets the orientation of the list. The orientation can be `Orientation.HORIZONTAL` or `Orientation.VERTICAL`.
`MultipleSelectionModel<T> getSelectionModel()`	Returns the selection model for the list view control. You can use the selection model to get an observable list of selected items by calling its `getSelectedItems` method. You can also retrieve the most recently selected item by calling `getSelectedItem`.

Creating a list view

Creating a list view control is similar to creating a combo box. Here's an example that creates the list view that's shown in Figure 8-3:

```
ListView list = new ListView();
list.getItems().addAll("Sausage", "Pepperoni",
    "Linguica", "Salame", "Olives", "Mushrooms",
    "Onions", "Peppers", "Pineapple", "Spinach",
    "Canadian Bacon", "Tomatoes", "Kiwi",
    "Anchovies", "Gummy Bears");
```

Notice that the list view shown in Figure 8-3 shows only the first eight items in the list. As with a combo box, a scroll bar is automatically added to a list view if the total number of items in the items collection cannot be displayed.

By default, the list view control allows only a single selection to be made. To allow multiple selections, add this line:

```
list.getSelectionModel().setSelectionMode(SelectionMode.MULTIPLE);
```

To arrange the list view horizontally rather than vertically, add this line:

```
list.setOrientation(Orientation.HORIZONTAL);
```

Getting the selected items

Getting the selected items from a list view control is a bit tricky. First, you must get the selection model object by calling the getSelectionModel. Then, you call the selection model's getSelectedItems method. This returns a read-only observable list that contains just the items that have been selected.

Here's an example that builds a string that lists all the items selected by the user for the pizza toppings list view that is shown in Figure 8-3:

```
String tops = "";
ObservableList<String> toppings;
toppings = list.getSelectionModel().getSelectedItems();
for(String topping : toppings)
{
    tops += topping + "\n";
}
```

In the preceding example, the `tops` string will contain all the toppings selected by the user, separated by new line characters.

Using Tree Views

A *tree view* is a fancy JavaFX control that displays hierarchical data in outline form, which we computer nerds refer to as a tree. Tree structures are very common in the world of computers. The folder structure of your disk drive is a tree, as is a JavaFX scene graph.

Figure 8-5 shows a JavaFX scene that has a tree view control in it. In this example, I use a tree control to represent a few of my favorite TV series, along with series that were spun off from them.

Figure 8-5:
A tree view
control.

Before I get into the mechanics of how to create a tree control, you need to know a few terms that describe the elements in the tree itself:

- ✔ **Node:** Each element in the tree is a *node*. Each node in a tree is created from `TreeItem` class. The `TreeItem` class is a generic class, so you can associate a type with it. Thus, you can create a tree using objects of any type you wish, including types you create yourself.

- ✔ **Root node:** A *root node* is the starting node for a tree. Every tree must have one — and only one — root node. When you create a tree component, you pass the root node to the `TreeView` constructor.

- ✔ **Child node:** The nodes that appear immediately below a given node are that node's *child nodes.* A node can have more than one child.

- ✔ **Parent node:** The node immediately above a given node is that node's *parent node.* Every node except the root node must have one — and only one — parent.

- ✔ **Sibling nodes:** *Sibling nodes* are children of the same parent.

- ✔ **Leaf node:** A *leaf node* is one that doesn't have any children.

- ✔ **Path:** A path contains the node and all its ancestors — that is, its parent, its parent's parent, and so on — all the way back to the root.

- ✔ **Expanded node:** An *expanded node* is one whose children are visible.

- ✔ **Collapsed node:** A *collapsed node* is one whose children are hidden.

Building a tree

Before you can actually create a tree view, you must first build the tree it displays. To do that, use the `TreeItem` class, the details of which I discuss in Table 8-5.

Table 8-5	The TreeItem Class
Constructor	*Description*
`TreeItem<T> ()`	Creates an empty tree node.
`TreeItem<T>(T value)`	Creates a tree node with the specified value.

(continued)

Table 8-5 (continued)

Method	Description
`T getValue()`	Returns the tree item's value.
`void setValue(T value)`	Sets the tree item's value.
`ObservableList getChildren()`	Returns an `ObservableList` that represents the children of this tree item.
`TreeItem getParent()`	Gets this node's parent.
`void setExpanded(boolean expanded)`	Specify `true` to expand the node.
`boolean isExpanded()`	Returns a `boolean` that indicates whether the tree item is expanded.
`boolean isLeaf()`	Returns a `boolean` that indicates whether the tree item is a leaf node (that is, has no children). A leaf node can't be expanded.
`TreeItem nextSibling()`	Returns the next sibling of this tree item. If there is no next sibling, returns `null`.
`TreeItem prevSibling()`	Returns the previous sibling of this tree item. If there is no previous sibling, returns `null`.

The `TreeItem` class provides three basic characteristics for each node:

✔ **The value,** which contains the data represented by the node.

In my example, I use strings for the user objects, but you can use objects of any type you want for the user object. The tree control calls the user object's `toString` method to determine what text to display for each node. The easiest way to set the user object is to pass it via the `TreeItem` constructor.

✔ **The parent of this node,** unless the node happens to be the root.

✔ **The children of this node,** represented as an `ObservableList`.

> The list will be empty if the node happens to be a leaf node. You
> can create or retrieve child nodes using the familiar methods of the
> `ObservableList` interface. For more information, refer to the section
> "Working with Observable Lists" earlier in this chapter.

In this section, I build a tree that lists spinoff shows from three popular television shows of the past:

- ✔ *The Andy Griffith Show,* which had two spinoffs: *Gomer Pyle, U.S.M.C.,* and *Mayberry R.F.D.*

- ✔ *All in the Family,* which directly spawned four spinoffs: *The Jeffersons, Maude, Gloria,* and *Archie Bunker's Place.*

  In addition, two of these spinoffs had spinoffs of their own involving the maids: The Jeffersons' maid became the topic of a short-lived show called *Checking In,* and Maude's maid became the main character in *Good Times.*

- ✔ *Happy Days,* which spun off *Mork and Mindy, Laverne and Shirley,* and *Joanie Loves Chachi.*

You can take many approaches to building trees, most of which involve some recursive programming. I'm going to avoid recursive programming in this section to keep things simple, but my avoidance means that you have to hard-code some of the details of the tree into the program. Most real programs that work with trees need some type of recursive programming to build the tree.

The first step in creating a tree is declaring a `TreeItem` variable for each node that isn't a leaf node. For my TV series example, I start with the following code:

```
TreeItem andy, archie, happy,
        george, maude;
```

These variables can be local variables within the `start` method because once you get the tree set up, you won't need these variables anymore. You see why you don't need variables for the leaf nodes in a moment.

Next, I create the root node and set its expanded status to `true` so that it will be expanded when the tree displays initially:

```
TreeItem root = new TreeItem("Spin Offs ");
root.setExpanded(true);
```

To simplify the task of creating all the other nodes, I use the following helper method, `makeShow`:

```
public TreeItem<String> makeShow(String title,
    TreeItem<String> parent)
{

    TreeItem<String> show = new TreeItem<String>(title);
    show.setExpanded(true);
    parent.getChildren().add(show);
    return show;
}
```

This method accepts a string and another node as parameters, and returns a node whose user object is set to the `String` parameter. The returned node is also added to the parent node as a child, and the node is expanded. Thus you can call this method to both create a new node and place the node in the tree.

The next step is creating some nodes. Continuing my example, I start with the nodes for *The Andy Griffith Show* and its spinoffs:

```
andy = makeShow("The Andy Griffith Show", root);
makeShow("Gomer Pyle, U.S.M.C.", andy);
makeShow("Mayberry R.F.D.", andy);
```

Here, `makeShow` is called to create a node for *The Andy Griffith Show,* with the root node specified as its parent. The node returned by this method is saved in the `andy` variable. Then `makeShow` is called twice to create the spinoff shows, this time specifying `andy` as the parent node.

Because neither *Gomer Pyle, U.S.M.C.,* nor *Mayberry R.F.D.* had a spinoff show, I don't have to pass these nodes as the parent parameter to the `makeShow` method. That's why I don't bother to create a variable to reference these nodes.

Next in my example, I create nodes for *All in the Family* and its spinoffs:

```
archie = makeShow("All in the Family", root);
george = makeShow("The Jeffersons", archie);
makeShow("Checking In", george);
maude = makeShow("Maude", archie);
makeShow("Good Times", maude);
makeShow("Gloria", archie);
makeShow("Archie Bunker's Place", archie);
```

In this case, *The Jeffersons* and *Maude* have child nodes of their own. As a result, variables are required for these two shows so that they can be passed as the parent parameter to `makeShow` when I create the nodes for *Checking In* and *Good Times*.

Finally, here's the code that creates the nodes for *Happy Days* and its spinoffs:

```
happy = makeShow("Happy Days", root);
makeShow("Mork and Mindy", happy);
makeShow("Laverne and Shirley", happy);
makeShow("Joanie Loves Chachi", happy);
```

The complete tree is successfully created in memory, so I can get on with the task of creating a `TreeView` control to show off the tree.

Creating a TreeView control

You use the `TreeView` class to create a tree component that displays the nodes of a tree. Table 8-6 shows the key constructors and methods of this class.

Table 8-6	The TreeView Class
Constructor	**Description**
`TreeView<T>()`	Creates an empty tree (not very useful, if you ask me).
`TreeView<T>(TreeItem root)`	Creates a tree that displays the tree that starts at the specified node.
Method	**Description**
`TreeItem getRoot()`	Gets the root node.
`void setRoot(TreeItem root)`	Sets the root node.
`MultipleSelectionModel<T> getSelectionModel()`	Returns the selection model for the list view control. You can use the selection model to get an observable list of selected items by calling its `getSelectedItems` method. You can also retrieve the most recently selected item by calling `getSelectedItem`.
`void setRootVisible (boolean visible)`	Determines whether the root node should be visible.

The first step in creating a `TreeView` control is declaring a `TreeView` variable as a class instance variable so that you can access it in any method within your program, as follows:

```
TreeView tree;
```

Then, in the application's `start` method, you call the `TreeView` constructor to create the tree view control, passing the root node of the tree you want it to display as a parameter:

```
tree = new TreeView(root);
```

By default, the user can select just one node from the tree. To allow the user to select multiple nodes, use this strange incantation:

```
tree.getSelectionModel().setSelectionMode(
    SelectionModel.MULTIPLE);
```

Here the `getSelectionModel` method is called to get the selection model that manages the selection of nodes within the tree. This method returns an object of type `MultipleSelectionModel`, which includes a method named `setSelectionMode` that lets you set the selection mode. To allow multiple items to be selected, you must pass this method the `SelectionModel.MULTIPLE`.

That's it! You now have a `TreeView` control that you can add to a layout pane and display in your scene.

 Although the tree displayed by a tree view control must begin with a root node, in many cases the root node is superfluous. For example, in the example you've been looking at, what's the point of showing the root node? The `TreeView` control lets you suppress the display of the root node if you don't want it to be shown. To hide the root node, just call this method:

```
tree.setShowRoot(false);
```

Figure 8-6 shows how the tree appears with the root node hidden.

Figure 8-6:
A tree view
control
with the
root node
hidden.

Getting the selected node

There are several ways to determine which node or nodes are currently selected in a tree view. One way is to access the tree's selection model by calling the getSelectionModel. Then, you can call the selection model's getSelectedItems method to return a read-only observable list that contains the items that have been selected.

For example:

```
String msg = "";
ObservableList<TreeItem<String>> shows =
    tree.getSelectionModel().getSelectedItems();
for(TreeItem show : shows)
{
    msg += show.getValue() + "\n";
}
```

In the preceding example, the `msg` string will contain all the shows that the user has selected from the tree, separated by new line characters.

An alternative is to add an event handler that's called whenever the selection changes. You can do that like this:

```
tree.getSelectionModel().selectedItemProperty()
    .addListener( (v, oldValue, newValue) ->
            tree_SelectionChanged(newValue) );
```

Here, the `getSelectionModel` method is called to retrieve the selection model. Then, the `selectedItemProperty` is called to retrieve the selected item property. Finally, an event listener is created for this property by using a Lambda expression that calls a method named `tree_SelectionChanged`. The value of the new selection is passed as a parameter.

Here's what the `tree_SelectionChanged` method looks like:

```
public void tree_SelectionChanged(TreeItem<String> item)
{
    if (item != null)
    {
        lblShowName.setText(item.getValue());
    }
}
```

Here, a label named `lblShowName` is updated to display the value of the newly selected item. *Note:* An `if` statement is used to ensure that the item is not null. That's necessary because if the user deselects an item, the `tree_SelectionChanged` method will be called with a `null` value as its `item` parameter.

Looking at a complete program that uses a tree view

Whew! That was a lot of information to digest. In this section, I put it all together.

Listing 8-1 shows the complete program that creates the scene shown in Figure 8-6. This program lets the user select a show from the tree and displays the title of the selected show in a label below the tree.

Listing 8-1:   The Spinoff Program

```
import javafx.application.*;
import javafx.stage.*;
import javafx.scene.*;
import javafx.scene.layout.*;
import javafx.scene.control.*;
import javafx.geometry.*;

public class SpinOffs extends Application
{
    public static void main(String[] args)
    {
        launch(args);
    }

    TreeView<String> tree;                                      →15
    Label lblShowName;

    @Override public void start(Stage primaryStage)
    {
        TreeItem<String>  root, andy, archie,                   →20
                      happy, george, maude;

        root = new TreeItem<String>("Spin Offs");               →23
        root.setExpanded(true);

        andy = makeShow(                                        →26
            "The Andy Griffith Show", root);
        makeShow("Gomer Pyle, U.S.M.C.", andy);
        makeShow("Mayberry R.F.D", andy);

        archie = makeShow("All in the Family", root);           →31
        george = makeShow("The Jeffersons", archie);
        makeShow("Checking In", george);
        maude = makeShow("Maude", archie);
        makeShow("Good Times", maude);
        makeShow("Gloria", archie);
        makeShow("Archie Bunker's Place", archie);

        happy = makeShow("Happy Days", root);                   →39
        makeShow("Mork and Mindy", happy);
        makeShow("Laverne and Shirley", happy);
        makeShow("Joanie Loves Chachi", happy);

        tree = new TreeView<String>(root);                      →44
        tree.setShowRoot(false);
        tree.getSelectionModel().selectedItemProperty()         →46
            .addListener( (v, oldValue, newValue) ->
                tree_SelectionChanged(newValue) );
```

(continued)

Listing 8-1 *(continued)*

```
        lblShowName = new Label();

        VBox pane = new VBox(10);
        pane.setPadding(new Insets(20,20,20,20));
        pane.getChildren().addAll(tree, lblShowName);          →54

        Scene scene = new Scene(pane);

        primaryStage.setScene(scene);
        primaryStage.setTitle("My Favorite Spin Offs");
        primaryStage.show();

    }

    public TreeItem<String> makeShow(String title,
            TreeItem<String> parent)                           →64
    {
        TreeItem<String> show = new TreeItem<String>(title);
        show.setExpanded(true);
        parent.getChildren().add(show);
        return show;
    }

    public void tree_SelectionChanged(TreeItem<String> item)   →73
    {
        if (item != null)
        {
            lblShowName.setText(item.getValue());
        }
    }

}
```

All the code in this program has already been shown in this chapter, so I just point out the highlights here:

→**15:** The tree and list models are defined as class instance variables.

→**20:** `TreeItem` variables are defined for the root node and each show that has spinoff shows.

→**23:** The root node is created with the text `Spin-Offs`.

→**26:** These lines create the nodes for *The Andy Griffith Show* and its spinoffs.

→**31:** These lines create the nodes for *All in the Family* and its spinoffs.

→**39:**   These lines create the nodes for *Happy Days* and its spinoffs.

→**44:**   This line creates the `TreeView` control, specifying `root` as the root node for the tree. The next line hides the root node.

→**46:**   This line creates the event listener for the selected item property. The Lambda expression causes the method named `tree_SelectionChanged` to be called whenever the selection status of the `TreeView` control changes.

→**54:**   The `TreeView` control and the label are added to a `VBox` layout pane, which is then added to the scene just before the stage is shown.

→**64:**   The `makeShow` method creates a node from a string and adds the node to the node passed as the parent parameter.

→**73:**   The `tree_SelectionChanged` method is called whenever the selected node changes. It simply displays the title of the selected show in the `lblShowName` label, provided the passed `TreeItem` is not `null`.

Chapter 9

Working with Tables

In This Chapter

▶ Creating rows and columns with the `TableView` control

▶ Using the `TableColumn` class to format the individual columns of a table

▶ Building a simple items list for a `TableView`

▶ Editing the contents of a `TableView` control

A JavaFX table is one of JavaFX's most flexible and powerful controls; it lets you display data in a spreadsheet-like format, with rows of data aligned in neat columns. Both horizontal and vertical scrolling is provided automatically, and you can configure the table control to allow the user to edit the contents of the table's cells.

In this chapter, you discover several classes that work together to create a table. The first is the `TableView` class, which renders the table within a scene. A table consists of one or more columns that are created using the `TableColumn` class. Thus, to create a table, you must first create one or more table columns using the `TableColumn` class, and then use the `TableView` class to create a table, and finally add the columns to the table.

Because a table control is inextricably bound to an underlying items list, this chapter begins by showing you how to create the items list required to support a table. The sample data used for this chapter is a DVD movie collection that lists each movie's title, the year it was made, and the price paid for the movie.

Next, you figure out how to display this data in a simple table that shows one row for each movie in the collection. After you know how to do that, I explore how to make the table editable so that the user can correct errors in the data or add new movies to the collection.

Along the way, I discuss how to work with a variety of classes and interfaces that are required to support the workings of a table. It's going to be a fun ride, so hang on!

Creating the Data for a Table

The underlying data for a table control is an `ObservableList`, just as for a list view, combo box, or choice box. However, the nature of a table control lends itself to more complicated data structures than can be displayed by a list view or other simple list-based controls. List views, combo boxes, and choice boxes can display just one data value for each item in the underlying list. In contrast, a table can display multiple values from the underlying list, each in its own column.

The most common way to create the items list for a table is to create a custom class that defines the objects that will display in the table. Then, the table can extract the data for each column by calling various methods of the custom data class.

For example, Table 9-1 shows the constructors and methods of a `Movie` class that will serve as the data model for all the examples shown in this chapter. This class keeps track of three values associated with each movie: title, year, and price. Methods are provided to set or get these values.

Table 9-1	The Movie class
Constructor	*Description*
`Movie()`	Creates an empty Movie object.
`Movie(String title, int year, double price)`	Creates a Movie object with the specified title, year, and price.
Method	*Description*
`String getTitle()`	Gets the title.
`void setTitle(String title)`	Sets the title.
`int getYear()`	Gets the year.
`void setYear(int year)`	Sets the year.
`double getPrice()`	Gets the price.
`void setPrice(double price)`	Sets the price.

Notice that the names of these methods all either include the word `get` or `set`. That's required for the class to work as the items list for a table control. In JavaFX parlance, the values these methods access are *properties*. The name of the property must follow the word `get` or `set`; thus, the name of the property accessed by the `getTitle` and `setTitle` methods is `title`. (Notice that the name of the property begins with a lowercase letter, but is capitalized in the `get` or `set` method.)

JavaFX properties are actually much more than a naming convention for creating methods to `get` and `set` values. Properties have other advanced features as well, such as the ability to automatically bind them together so that when the value of a property in one object changes, the corresponding property value in another object automatically changes as well. And you can create listeners for properties so that code is executed automatically whenever the value of a property changes.

To create a property, you must use one of several predefined classes that implements the `Property` interface (or create your own class that implements `Property`). Because working with the `Property` interface is a complicated topic of its own, I devote an entire chapter to it. Thus, you discover how to create proper properties in Chapter 15. For my purposes here, I use fake properties (I like to call them *sham properties*), which are simply class fields that can be accessed with `get` and `set` methods that follow the same naming conventions actual properties use. As long as the `Movie` class conforms to these naming standards, it will work as an items list for a table control.

Listing 9-1 shows the source code for the `Movie` class.

Listing 9-1:   The Movie Class

```
public class Movie
{
    private String title;                                        →3
    private int year;
    private double price;

    public Movie()                                               →7
    {
        this.title = "";
        this.year = 0;
        this.price = 0.0;
    }

    public Movie(String title, int year, double price)           →14
    {
        this.title = title;
        this.year = year;
        this.price = price;
    }
```

(continued)

Listing 9-1 *(continued)*

```java
    public String getTitle()                                    →21
    {
        return this.title;
    }

    public void setTitle(String title)                          →26
    {
        this.title = title;
    }

    public int getYear()                                        →31
    {
        return this.year;
    }

    public void setYear(int year)                               →36
    {
        this.year = year;
    }

    public double getPrice()                                    →41
    {
        return this.price;
    }

    public void setPrice(double price)                          →46
    {
        this.price = price;
    }

}
```

The code for this class is pretty straightforward, so I just point out the highlights here:

→ **3:**   These three private class fields are used internally to hold the title, year, and price for each movie.

→ **7:**   The default constructor creates a `Movie` object with no data.

→ **14:**   This constructor lets the user specify data for the movie's title, year, and price.

→ **21:**   The `getTitle` method retrieves the value of the `title` property.

→ **26:**   The `setTitle` method sets the value of the `title` property.

→ **31:**   The `getYear` method retrieves the value of the `year` property.

→ **36:**   The `setYear` method sets the value of the `year` property.

→ **41:** The `getPrice` method retrieves the value of the `price` property.

→ **46:** The `setPrice` method sets the value of the `price` property.

With this class, you can easily create a `Movie` object:

```
Movie m = new Movie("The King's Speech", 2010, 19.95);
```

Or, if you prefer, you could do it this way:

```
Movie m = new Movie();
m.setTitle("The King's Speech");
m.setYear(2010);
m.setPrice(19.95);
```

After you create a `Movie` object, you must add it to an `ObservableList` that can be used as the items list for a `TableView`. The easiest way to do that is to first create the `TableView` and then use its `getItems` methods to access the observable list:

```
TableView<Movie> table = new TableView<Movie>();
table.getItems().add(m);
```

Notice that `TableView` is a generic class, so specify the data type when you create it.

In a real-life program, the data displayed by a table will almost certainly come from a file or a database. Thus, you need to write Java code to read the data from the file or database, create an object for each record, and add that record to the list. You probably want to isolate this code into a separate method with a name such as `loadData`. Then, you can pass the observable list to this method as a parameter.

Reading data from a file or database is beyond the scope of this book, but if you want to figure out how to do it, I recommend you pick up a copy of my book, *Java All-In-One For Dummies,* 4th Edition (John Wiley & Sons). That book contains several sample programs that read and write this very data to and from various types of files and databases.

For now, rely on the following method to load the data for the table:

```
public void loadData(ObservableList<Movie> data)
{
    data.add(new Movie("It's a Wonderful Life",
        1946, 14.95));
    data.add(new Movie("Young Frankenstein",
        1974, 16.95));
```

```
    data.add(new Movie("Star Wars Episode 4",
        1976, 17.95));
    data.add(new Movie("The Princess Bride",
        1987, 16.95));
    data.add(new Movie("Glory",
        1989, 14.95));
    data.add(new Movie("The Game",
        1997, 14.95));
    data.add(new Movie("Shakespeare in Love",
        1998, 19.95));
    data.add(new Movie("The Invention of Lying",
        2009, 18.95));
    data.add(new Movie("The King's Speech",
        2010, 19.95));
}
```

Then, you can call this method whenever you need to load data into the table.

If you prefer, you can create an `ObservableList` object without first creating a `TableView`. JavaFX provides a class named `FXCollections` that contains several static methods that can create various types of observable lists. One of the most common is an *observable array list*, which is simply an observable list that's backed by an `ArrayList`. Here's an example of how you could use it in a method that creates an observable array list, populates it with movie data, and returns the observable array list back to the caller:

```
public ObservableList<Movie> loadData()
{
    ObservableList<Movie> data =
        FXCollections.observableArrayList();

    data.add(new Movie("It's a Wonderful Life",
        1946, 14.95));
    data.add(new Movie("Young Frankenstein",
        1974, 16.95));
    data.add(new Movie("Star Wars Episode 4",
        1976, 17.95));
    data.add(new Movie("The Princess Bride",
        1987, 16.95));
    data.add(new Movie("Glory",
        1989, 14.95));
    data.add(new Movie("The Game",
        1997, 14.95));
    data.add(new Movie("Shakespeare in Love",
        1998, 19.95));
    data.add(new Movie("The Invention of Lying",
        2009, 18.95));
```

```
     data.add(new Movie("The King's Speech",
        2010, 19.95));

     return data;
}
```

Then, you could call the table's `setItems` method to load the data, like this:

```
TableView<Movies> table = new TableView<Movies>();
table.setItems(loadData());
```

Creating a Read-Only Table

Now that you know how to create the underlying data for a table, time to get to the fun part. In this section, you read about how to create a simple read-only table that displays the movie data with one row per movie and separate columns for the title, year, and price of each movie. Figure 9-1 shows the table that you're after.

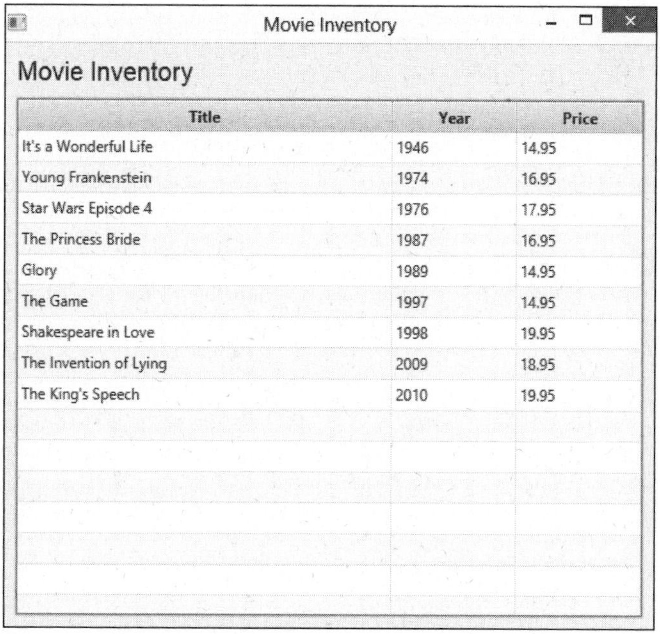

Figure 9-1: A simple read-only table.

Title	Year	Price
It's a Wonderful Life	1946	14.95
Young Frankenstein	1974	16.95
Star Wars Episode 4	1976	17.95
The Princess Bride	1987	16.95
Glory	1989	14.95
The Game	1997	14.95
Shakespeare in Love	1998	19.95
The Invention of Lying	2009	18.95
The King's Speech	2010	19.95

You use two main classes to create this table: `TableView`, which represents the entire table, and `TableColumn`, which represents an individual column. The next two sections show you how to work first with the `TableColumn` class to create the three table columns, as shown in Figure 9-1, and then with the `TableView` class to assemble the columns into a table. After that, you see the source code for the program that created the table shown in Figure 9-1.

Using the TableColumn class

The `TableColumn` class represents a single column in a table. This class allows you to bind the column to a property in the table's items list so that cell values are retrieved automatically from the correct property. Table 9-2 lists the most important constructors and methods of this class.

Table 9-2	The TableColumn class
Constructor	**Description**
`TableColumn<S, T>()`	Creates an empty table column. The type `S` should correspond to the type that's associated with the `TableView` and its `ObservableList`. The type `T` indicates the type of data displayed in the column.
`TableColumn<S, T>(String heading)`	Creates an empty table column with the specified heading text.
Method	**Description**
`void setMinWidth(double width)`	Sets the minimum width for the column. The table column may expand the width if necessary to display the column's data.
`void setMaxWidth(double width)`	Sets the maximum width for the column.
`void setPrefWidth(double width)`	Sets the preferred width for the column.
`void setText(String title)`	Sets the heading text.
`void setSortable(boolean sortable)`	If `true`, the user can sort data on this column. (The default is `true`.)
`void setCellValueFactory (PropertyValueFactory f)`	Specifies a factory class that provides values for the cells in this column. Usually specified as an instance of the `PropertyValueFactory` class.

To create a table column, first call the constructor. Typically, you specify the text to appear in the column heading when you call the constructor. You need to specify two types for the table column. The first is the type that's associated with the table itself, which is also the type associated with the table's items collection. In the example shown throughout this chapter, this type is Movie because the table will display data from an observable list of Movie objects.

The second type is the data type of the property that displays in this column. For the Title property, the type is String. Thus, the constructor for the Title column is:

```
TableColumn<Movie, String> colTitle =
    new TableColumn<Movie, String>("Title");
```

You also want to set the width of the column, like this:

```
colTitle.setMinWidth(300);
```

Here, the column will be at least 300 pixels wide. That should be wide enough to display most movie titles.

Next, you need to associate a property from the table's item collection with the column. To do that, call the setCellFactory method and supply a cell factory. A *cell factory* is a special type of object that supplies cell values to the table column. The easiest way to provide a cell factory is to use the PropertyValueFactory class, which lets you create a cell factory that returns a named property from the table's item collection.

Here's the code to accomplish that for the Title column:

```
colTitle.setCellValueFactory(
    new PropertyValueFactory<Movie, String>("Title"));
```

This statement calls the constructor of the PropertyValueFactory class, specifying Movie as the type of object that the property will be retrieved from and String as the property's value type, and passing the property's name (Title) as the sole argument for the constructor. The net effect of this statement is that the property value factory will call the getTitle method of the Movie class to populate the cells of this column.

For the sake of clarity, I simplified the signature of the setCellValueFactory method in Table 9-2. The actual signature is this:

```
void setCellValueFactory(
        Callback<TableColumn.CellDataFeatures<S,T>,
        ObservableValue<T>> value)
```

Whew! That's a mess. What it means is that the cell value factory must implement the `Callback` interface with the correct data types. The `PropertyValueFactory` class is designed specifically to work with the `setCellValueFactory` method, so it does indeed implement the `Callback` interface.

The code necessary to create the other two columns is only slightly different because rather than string values, they deal with integer and double values. Here's the code to create the Year column:

```
TableColumn<Movie, Integer> colYear =
    new TableColumn("Year");
colYear.setMinWidth(100);
colYear.setCellValueFactory(
    new PropertyValueFactory<Movie, Integer>("Year"));
```

And here's the code for the Price column:

```
TableColumn<Movie, Double> colPrice =
    new TableColumn("Price");
colPrice.setMinWidth(100);
colPrice.setCellValueFactory(
    new PropertyValueFactory<Movie, Double>("Price"));
```

Notice in both cases that the `T` type specifies the wrapper `Integer` and `Double` classes rather than the native `int` and `double` types.

Using the TableView class

After you create the table columns, the next step is to create a table and add the columns to the table. To do that, use the `TableView` class, which I discuss in Table 9-3.

Creating a table view control requires several steps, which do not necessarily have to be done in this order:

✔ **Call the `TableView` constructor to create the table view control.**

✔ **Add the table columns to the table view.**

The easiest way to do that is to call the `getColumns` method, which returns the list of columns as an observable list. Then, use the `addAll` method to add the columns.

✔ **Add data to the items list.**

I discuss several ways to do that in the earlier section "Creating the Data for a Table."

Table 9-3	The TableView class
Constructor	**Description**
`TableView<S>()`	Creates a new table view. The type `S` specifies the type of the objects contained in the items list.
`TableValue<S>(ObservableList list)`	Creates a new table view using the specified list as its items list.
Method	**Description**
`ObservableList getColumns()`	Gets the list of columns that are displayed by the table.
`ObservableList getItems()`	Gets the list of items that serves as the data source for the table.
`void setItems(ObservableList list)`	Sets the list of items used as the data source to the table.
`TableViewSelectionModel getSelectionModel()`	Gets the selection model, which allows you to work with rows selected by the user.

Here's one way to accomplish these steps for the example you've been looking at throughout this chapter:

```
TableView<Movie> table = new TableView<Movie>();
table.getColumns().addAll(colTitle, colYear, colPrice);
table.setItems(loadData());
```

The `loadData` method used here is the one that was shown right at the end of the section "Creating the Data for a Table." It returns an `ObservableList` that contains the `Movie` objects to be displayed.

You could alternatively create the table and load its data in one statement by passing the `loadData` method to the `TableView` constructor, like this:

```
TableView<Movie> table =
    new TableView<Movie>(loadData());
```

After you create a table and add columns and data items, you can display the table in a scene by adding it to a layout pane, adding the pane to the scene, and then setting the stage with the scene and showing the stage. The following section presents the code for a complete program that does precisely that.

A Program That Creates a Read-Only Table

Listing 9-2 shows the complete source code for a program that creates a read-only `TableView` control. The scene displayed by this program was shown earlier in Figure 9-1. (*Note:* To run, this program requires that the `Movie` class, which was shown in Listing 9-1, exist in the same folder.)

Listing 9-2:   The MovieInventory Program

```
import javafx.application.*;
import javafx.stage.*;
import javafx.scene.*;
import javafx.scene.control.*;
import javafx.scene.layout.*;
import javafx.scene.text.*;
import javafx.scene.control.cell.*;
import javafx.collections.*;
import javafx.geometry.*;

public class MovieInventory extends Application
{

    public static void main(String[] args)
    {
        launch(args);
    }

    @Override public void start(Stage primaryStage) {

        Label lblHeading = new Label("Movie Inventory");          →20
        lblHeading.setFont(new Font("Arial", 20));

        TableView<Movie> table = new TableView<Movie>();          →23
        table.setItems(loadData());                               →24

        TableColumn<Movie, String> colTitle = new TableColumn("Title");    →26
        colTitle.setMinWidth(300);
        colTitle.setCellValueFactory(
            new PropertyValueFactory<Movie, String>("Title"));

        TableColumn<Movie, Integer> colYear = new TableColumn("Year");     →31
        colYear.setMinWidth(100);
        colYear.setCellValueFactory(
            new PropertyValueFactory<Movie, Integer>("Year"));
```

```
    TableColumn<Movie, Double> colPrice = new TableColumn("Price");      →36
    colPrice.setMinWidth(100);
    colPrice.setCellValueFactory(
        new PropertyValueFactory<Movie, Double>("Price"));

    table.getColumns().addAll(colTitle, colYear, colPrice);              →40

    VBox paneMain = new VBox();                                          →42
    paneMain.setSpacing(10);
    paneMain.setPadding(new Insets(10, 10, 10, 10));
    paneMain.getChildren().addAll(lblHeading, table);

    Scene scene = new Scene(paneMain);                                   →47
    primaryStage.setScene(scene);
    primaryStage.setTitle("Movie Inventory");
    primaryStage.show();
}

public ObservableList<Movie> loadData()                                  →53
{
    ObservableList<Movie> data =
        FXCollections.observableArrayList();

    data.add(new Movie("It's a Wonderful Life",
        1946, 14.95));
    data.add(new Movie("Young Frankenstein",
        1974, 16.95));
    data.add(new Movie("Star Wars Episode 4",
        1976, 17.95));
    data.add(new Movie("The Princess Bride",
        1987, 16.95));
    data.add(new Movie("Glory",
        1989, 14.95));
    data.add(new Movie("The Game",
        1997, 14.95));
    data.add(new Movie("Shakespeare in Love",
        1998, 19.95));
    data.add(new Movie("The Invention of Lying",
        2009, 18.95));
    data.add(new Movie("The King's Speech",
        2010, 19.95));

    return data;     }

}
```

I've already shown and explained most of the code in this program earlier in this chapter, so I just point out a few of the highlights here:

→ **20:** These two lines create the label that appears above the table view control.

→ **23:** This line calls the `TableView` constructor to create a new `TableView` object, specifying `Movie` as the underlying data type.

→ **24:** The items list is created by calling the `loadData` method, which appears later in the program at line 53.

→ **26:** These lines create the first column, which displays the `Title` property from the `Movie` class. The width of the column is set to a minimum of 300 pixels.

→ **31:** These lines create the second column, which displays the `Year` property from the `Movie` class. The minimum width is set to 100 pixels.

→ **36:** These lines create the third column, which displays the `Price` property from the `Movie` class. The minimum width for this column is also set to 100 pixels.

→ **40:** The three columns are added to the table view control.

→ **42:** A `VBox` layout pane is created and the heading label and table view controls are added to it.

→ **47:** The scene and stage are constructed and shown.

→ **53:** The `loadData` method creates the item list, loading it with data for nine movies. The value returned from this method is used as the item list for the table view control.

Creating an Editable Table

Now that you know how to create a read-only table, the next step is to add the ability to add and remove rows from the table or edit the cells within an existing row. The following sections show you how to do that.

Adding table rows

To allow the user to add a row, you need to provide text boxes within which the user can enter data and an Add button the user can click to create a new row using the data entered by the user. In the `OnAction` event for the button, you simply create a new object using the data the user entered into the text field and then add the object to the table's items collection.

Assuming you have created text fields named `txtTitle`, `txtYear`, and `txtPrice`, here's a method you can call from the event handler for the Add button to add a new `Movie` item to the items collection:

```
public void btnAdd_Clicked()
{
    Movie m = new Movie();
    m.setTitle(txtTitle.getText());
    m.setYear(Integer.parseInt(txtYear.getText()));
    m.setPrice(Double.parseDouble(txtPrice.getText()));
    table.getItems().add(m);
    txtTitle.clear();
    txtYear.clear();
    txtPrice.clear();
}
```

This method starts by creating a new `Movie` object and setting the `Title`, `Year`, and `Price` properties to the values entered by the user. Then, the method adds the new `Movie` object to the items collection. Finally, the method clears the three text boxes.

Notice that the static `parse` methods of the `Integer` and `Double` wrapper classes are used to convert the string values entered into the text fields into valid integer and double values. Unfortunately, these methods do not do any reasonable amount of data validation; if the user enters a value that can't be converted to an integer or a double, the `parse` method will throw an exception, which this method doesn't handle. I leave it to you to figure out how to add data validation and error messages to this code.

Deleting table rows

Deleting an item from a table view requires simply that you add a Delete button to the scene. The user can then delete one or more rows by selecting the rows and then pressing the Delete button. Here's a method you could call from the `OnAction` handler for a Delete button:

```
public void btnDelete_Clicked()()
{
    ObservableList<Movie> sel, items;
    items = table.getItems();
    sel = table.getSelectionModel().getSelectedItems();
    for (Movie m : sel)
    {
        items.remove(m);
    }
}
```

This method accesses both the items collection of the table and the selectedItems collection of the table's selection model. Then, a for-each loop is used to delete every item in the selectedItems collection from the items collection.

This method does not verify that the user really wants to remove the selected rows. In a more realistic program, you'd want to first display an alert box asking the user whether she really wants to delete the rows. Then, you'd delete the rows only if the user clicks Yes.

Editing table cells

To allow users to edit individual table cells, you need to do three things:

- **Mark the table as editable by calling the setEditable method, passing a value of true.**

- **Create a cell factory for each column that you want to allow the user to edit.**

  You do that by calling the setCellFactory method of the TableColumn class.

- **Add an event listener that's called whenever the user finishes editing a table cell.**

  This listener is responsible for updating the items collection with the data entered by the user.

To allow the user to edit the contents of a column, you must set a cell factory for the column. A *cell factory* is an object that renders the content of a cell. By default, the cell factory renders the content as a text object. To enable editing, provide a cell factory that renders the content as a text field.

The easiest way to create a text field in a table column is to use the TextFieldTableCell. This class includes a static method named forTableColumn that returns a cell factory suitable for editing data with a text box. Here's how you use it:

```
colTitle.setCellFactory(
    TextFieldTableCell.forTableColumn());
```

It's as simple as that. After the cell factory is set up, the cell will turn into a text field whenever the user clicks it. The user can then edit the data in the text field. When the user presses Enter or Tab or clicks outside the field, the text field is replaced once again with a simple text object.

The only problem remaining is that although the cell factory lets the user edit the contents of a cell via the text field, the cell factory does not automatically update the table's items collection to reflect any changes the user might make when editing the cell. To do that, you must set up an action listener that responds when the user finishes editing the cell. Then, in that listener, you can update the items collection.

Here's how you can use a Lambda expression to set up a listener for the `onEditComit` event:

```
colTitle.setOnEditCommit(
    e -> colTitle_OnEditCommit(e) );
```

In this example, the method `colTitle_OnEditCommit` will be called whenever the user finishes editing the contents of a cell in the Title column.

Writing the event handler for the `OnEditCommit` event is a little tricky. The `OnEditCommit` event generates an event object of type `CellEditEvent`, which contains important information you need to access in the event handler. Table 9-4 lists the methods of this class.

Table 9-4	The CellEditEvent class
Method	*Description*
`T getNewValue()`	Gets the new value entered by the user.
`T getOldValue()`	Gets the previous value of the cell.
`S getRowValue()`	Gets the data object for the row edited by the user.
`TableColumn<S, T> get TableColumn()`	Gets the table column on which this event occurred.
`TableView<S>`	Gets the table view on which this event occurred.
`TableValue<S> (ObservableList list)`	Creates a new table view using the specified list as its items list.

The CellEditEvent class contains information you can use to update the items collection with the new data entered by the user. Specifically, the getRowValue method returns the items collection object for the row that's being edited, and the getNewValue method contains the updated value entered by the user. After you get the row object, you can update the appropriate property with the new value.

Unfortunately, the CellEditEvent class has more than one method, which disqualifies it as a functional class that can be used in a Lambda expression. So in the preceding example, the e parameter that's passed into the Lambda function is passed as a generic Event rather than as the more specific CellEditEvent. The Lambda function, in turn, passes this argument to the colTitle_OnEditCommit method, which must receive it as an Event. This method then casts it to a CellEditEvent so that it can access the getRowValue and getNewValue methods.

```
public void colTitle_OnEditCommit(Event e)
{
    TableColumn.CellEditEvent<Movie, String> ce;
    ce = (TableColumn.CellEditEvent<Movie, String>) e;
    Movie m = ce.getRowValue()
    m.setTitle(ce.getNewValue());
}
```

With this event handler in place, the user can update the title of any movie by double-clicking the title, typing a new value, and pressing Enter.

A Program That Creates an Editable Table

Listing 9-3 shows a refined version of the movie inventory program that was written in Listing 9-2. This program adds the ability to edit existing movies as well as the ability to add and delete movies. The scene displayed by this program is shown in Figure 9-2. (***Note:*** To run, this program requires that the Movie class, which was discussed in Listing 9-1, exist in the same folder.)

Figure 9-2:
The Movie-
Inventory-
Editor
program in
action.

Listing 9-3:   The MovieInventoryEditor Program

```
import javafx.application.*;
import javafx.stage.*;
import javafx.scene.*;
import javafx.scene.control.*;
import javafx.scene.layout.*;
import javafx.scene.text.*;
import javafx.event.*;
import javafx.scene.control.cell.*;
import javafx.beans.property.*;
import javafx.collections.*;
import javafx.geometry.*;
import javafx.util.converter.*;

public class MovieInventoryEditor extends Application
{
    public static void main(String[] args)
    {
        launch(args);
    }
```

(continued)

Listing 9-3 *(continued)*

```
private TableView<Movie> table;
private TextField txtTitle, txtYear, txtPrice;

@Override public void start(Stage primaryStage) {

    Label lblHeading = new Label("Movie Inventory");
    lblHeading.setFont(new Font("Arial", 20));

    table =  new TableView<Movie>();
    table.setEditable(true);
    table.setItems(loadData());

    TableColumn colTitle = new TableColumn("Title");
    colTitle.setMinWidth(300);
    colTitle.setCellValueFactory(
        new PropertyValueFactory<Movie, String>("Title"));
    colTitle.setCellFactory(                                          →37
        TextFieldTableCell.forTableColumn());
    colTitle.setOnEditCommit( e -> colTitle_OnEditCommit(e) );        →39

    TableColumn colYear = new TableColumn("Year");
    colYear.setMinWidth(100);
    colYear.setCellValueFactory(
        new PropertyValueFactory<Movie, Integer>("Year"));
    colYear.setCellFactory(                                           →45
        TextFieldTableCell.forTableColumn(
            new IntegerStringConverter()));
    colYear.setOnEditCommit( e -> colYear_OnEditCommit(e) );          →48

    TableColumn colPrice = new TableColumn("Price");
    colPrice.setMinWidth(100);
    colPrice.setCellValueFactory(
        new PropertyValueFactory<Movie, Double>("Price"));
    colPrice.setCellFactory(                                          →54
        TextFieldTableCell.forTableColumn(
            new DoubleStringConverter()));
    colPrice.setOnEditCommit( e -> colPrice_OnEditCommit(e) );        →57

    table.getColumns().addAll(colTitle, colYear, colPrice);

    txtTitle = new TextField();                                       →61
    txtTitle.setPromptText("Title");
    txtTitle.setMinWidth(100);

    txtYear = new TextField();                                        →65
    txtYear.setMaxWidth(100);
    txtYear.setPromptText("Year");
```

```
        txtPrice = new TextField();                              →69
        txtPrice.setMaxWidth(100);
        txtPrice.setPromptText("Price");

        Button btnAdd = new Button("Add");                       →73
        btnAdd.setMinWidth(60);
        btnAdd.setOnAction(e -> btnAdd_Clicked() );

        Button btnDelete = new Button("Delete");                 →77
        btnDelete.setMinWidth(60);
        btnDelete.setOnAction(e -> btnDelete_Clicked() );

        HBox paneAdd = new HBox();                               →81
        paneAdd.setSpacing(8);
        paneAdd.getChildren().addAll(txtTitle, txtYear, txtPrice,
            btnAdd, btnDelete);

        VBox paneMain = new VBox();
        paneMain.setSpacing(10);
        paneMain.setPadding(new Insets(10, 10, 10, 10));
        paneMain.getChildren().addAll(lblHeading, table, paneAdd);

        Scene scene = new Scene(paneMain);

        primaryStage.setScene(scene);
        primaryStage.setTitle("Movie Inventory");
        primaryStage.show();
    }

    public ObservableList<Movie> loadData()
    {
        ObservableList<Movie> data =
            FXCollections.observableArrayList();

        data.add(new Movie("It's a Wonderful Life",
            1946, 14.95));
        data.add(new Movie("Young Frankenstein",
            1974, 16.95));
        data.add(new Movie("Star Wars Episode 4",
            1976, 17.95));
        data.add(new Movie("The Princess Bride",
            1987, 16.95));
        data.add(new Movie("Glory",
            1989, 14.95));
        data.add(new Movie("The Game",
            1997, 14.95));
        data.add(new Movie("Shakespeare in Love",
            1998, 19.95));
```

(continued)

Listing 9-3 *(continued)*

```
      data.add(new Movie("The Invention of Lying",
         2009, 18.95));
      data.add(new Movie("The King's Speech",
         2010, 19.95));

    return data;
}

public void colTitle_OnEditCommit(Event e)                      →125
{
    TableColumn.CellEditEvent<Movie, String> ce;
    ce = (TableColumn.CellEditEvent<Movie, String>) e;
    Movie m = ce.getRowValue();
    m.setTitle(ce.getNewValue());
    }

public void colYear_OnEditCommit(Event e)                       →133
{
    TableColumn.CellEditEvent<Movie, Integer> ce;
    ce = (TableColumn.CellEditEvent<Movie, Integer>) e;
    Movie m = ce.getRowValue();
    m.setYear(ce.getNewValue());
    }

public void colPrice_OnEditCommit(Event e)                      →141
{
    TableColumn.CellEditEvent<Movie, Double> ce;
    ce = (TableColumn.CellEditEvent<Movie, Double>) e;
    Movie m = ce.getRowValue();
    m.setPrice(ce.getNewValue());
    }

public void btnAdd_Clicked()                                    →149
{
    Movie m = new Movie();
              m.setTitle(txtTitle.getText());
              m.setYear(Integer.parseInt(txtYear.getText()));
              m.setPrice(Double.parseDouble(txtPrice.getText()));
              table.getItems().add(m);
              txtTitle.clear();
              txtYear.clear();
              txtPrice.clear();
}


public void btnDelete_Clicked()                                 →161
```

```
{
    ObservableList<Movie> sel, items;
    items = table.getItems();
    sel = table.getSelectionModel().getSelectedItems();

    for (Movie m : sel)
        items.remove(m);
}
}
```

Because this program builds on the program that was written in Listing 9-2, I just point out the important differences here:

→ **37:** This line creates the cell factory for the Title column.

→ **39:** This line creates the `OnEditCommit` event listener for the Title column. The event handler calls the `colTitle_OnEditCommit` method, passing the `Event` object e as an argument.

→ **45:** This line creates the cell factory for the Year column.

→ **48:** This line creates the `OnEditCommit` event listener for the Year column. The event handler calls the `colYear_OnEditCommit` method, passing the `Event` object e as an argument.

→ **54:** This line creates the cell factory for the Price column.

→ **57:** This line creates the `OnEditCommit` event listener for the Price column. The event handler calls the `colPrice_OnEditCommit` method, passing the `Event` object e as an argument.

→ **61:** These lines create the `txtTitle` text field in which the user can enter the title for a new movie.

→ **65:** These lines create the `txtYear` text field in which the user can enter the year for a new movie.

→ **69:** These lines create the `txtPrice` text field in which the user can enter the price for a new movie.

→ **73:** These lines create the Add button. The event handler calls the `btnAdd_Clicked` method.

→ **77:** These lines create the Delete button. The event handler calls the `btnDelete_Clicked` method.

→ **81:** These lines create an `HBox` layout pane and add the three text fields and the two buttons to it.

→ **125:** The `colTitle_OnEditCommit` method is called when the user commits an edit for a Title cell. It updates the `Movie` item from the items list with the new value entered by the user.

→ **133:** The `colYear_OnEditCommit` method is called when the user commits an edit for a Year cell. It updates the `Movie` item from the items list with the new value entered by the user.

→ **141:** The `colPrice_OnEditCommit` method is called when the user commits an edit for a Price cell. It updates the `Movie` item from the items list with the new value entered by the user.

→ **149:** The `btnAdd_Clicked` method is called when the user clicks the Add button. This method creates a new `Movie` object using data from the text fields and then adds the new object to the items list. It then clears the text fields.

→ **161:** The `btnDelete_Clicked` method is called when the user clicks the Delete button. It gets the list of selected items from the selection model and then uses that list to remove all the selected items from the items list.

Chapter 10

Making Menus

. . . .

In This Chapter

▶ Creating basic and dynamic menus

▶ Working with separators and action listeners

▶ Constructing menus with check boxes and radio buttons

▶ Creating submenus and custom menu items

. . . .

*I*n this chapter, you find out how to adorn your programs with menus. You work with menus in applications, so you're probably already familiar with what menus are and how they work. I don't review those basics in this chapter. Instead, I jump right into the details of how to create a menu and add it to a scene.

Introducing Classes for Creating Menus

The following paragraphs describe the classes you use most often when you create menus:

✔ **MenuBar:** This class is the top-level container for menus that appear in the menu bar at the top of a scene.

✔ **Menu:** Each menu in the menu bar is represented by a Menu object. The menu bar, as shown in Figure 10-1, has two Menu objects: one for the Game menu and the other for the Options menu. A Menu object contains a collection of MenuItem objects that display when the user clicks the menu.

✔ **MenuItem:** Menu items are represented by the MenuItem class or one of its subclasses. The Game menu shown in Figure 10-1 has four MenuItem objects: New Game, Pause Game, Quit Game, and Exit. It also includes one SeparatorMenuItem object; SeparatorMenuItem is a subclass of the MenuItem class.

Interestingly, the `Menu` class is actually a subclass of `MenuItem`. That means that the items collection of a menu can contain other submenus. When the user clicks the submenu, the submenu's collection of menu items displays.

✔ **`CheckMenuItem`:** This special type of menu item has a check box associated with it. Although they're not shown in Figure 10-1, the Options menu has two `CheckMenuItem` objects in it. This class extends `MenuItem`.

✔ **`RadioMenuItem`:** This special type of menu item has a radio button associated with it. The `RadioMenuItem` class extends `MenuItem`.

✔ **`CustomMenuItem`:** A custom menu item can have any JavaFX `Node` object associated with it. With a custom menu item, you can add controls, such as text fields or list boxes, to a menu.

✔ **`SeparatorMenuItem`:** A separator menu item simply displays a separator line in a menu. You use this class to create visual groupings with a menu.

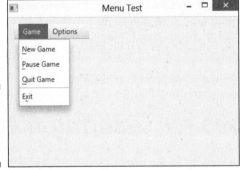

Figure 10-1:
A scene
with a menu
bar.

Creating a Basic Menu Bar

The basics of creating menus are pretty straightforward. First, you create a menu bar by calling the `MenuBar` constructor:

```
MenuBar menuBar = new MenuBar();
```

Then you create one or more menus and add it or them to the menu bar. When the menu bar is finished, you add it to a layout pane just as you would add any other node:

```
pane.getChildren().add(menuBar);
```

For your reference, Table 10-1 lists the most useful constructors and methods of the MenuBar class.

Table 10-1	The MenuBar Class
Constructor	**Description**
MenuBar()	Creates a menu bar.
Method	**Description**
ObservableList getMenus()	Returns the list of menus contained in this menu bar. You can use any of the methods of the ObservableList interface to add or remove menus from the menu bar.

Creating Menus

To create each menu, you use the Menu and MenuItem classes, whose constructors and methods I discuss in the next two tables in this chapter. Start by calling the Menu constructor and giving a name to the menu:

```
Menu menuGame = new Menu("_Game");
```

Here, the underline in the text string marks the mnemonic shortcut key that the user can use to get at the menu without touching the mouse. In this case, the letter *G* is the mnemonic.

The mnemonic character allows the user to open the menu by pressing the mnemonic character while holding down the Alt key. When the user presses the Alt key, all the visible mnemonic characters will be underlined so the user can determine which characters are the mnemonics.

Table 10-2 lists the most important constructors and methods of the Menu class for your reference.

Table 10-2	The Menu Class
Constructor	**Description**
`Menu(String name)`	Creates a menu with the specified name.
Method	**Description**
`ObservableList getItems()`	Returns an `ObservableList` collection that represents the menu items in this menu. You can then use any method of the `ObservableList` interface to add or remove menu items.
`String getText()`	Gets the menu's text.
`void setText(String text)`	Sets the menu's text.

Creating Menu Items

After you create a menu, the next step is creating menu items and adding them to the menu. To create a menu item, simply call the `MenuItem` constructor, passing the text to be displayed as a parameter:

```
MenuItem menuItemNewGame = new MenuItem("_New Game");
```

Once again, the underscore identifies the mnemonic shortcut for the menu item. Thus, the user can select this menu item by pressing Alt+N.

To add an event handler to a menu, use the `setOnAction` method. For example:

```
menuItemNewGame.setOnAction(e -> StartNewGame());
```

Here, the method `StartNewGame` will be called when the user chooses the New Game menu item.

Here's a short sequence that creates the four menu items shown in Figure 10-1, assigning an action event handler to each item:

```
MenuItem menuItemNewGame =
    new MenuItem("_New Game");
menuItemNewGame.setOnAction(e -> StartNewGame());

MenuItem menuItemPauseGame =
    new MenuItem("_Pause Game");
menuItemNewGame.setOnAction(e -> PauseGame());
```

```
MenuItem menuItemQuitGame =
    new MenuItem("_Quit Game");
menuItemNewGame.setOnAction(e -> QuitGame());

MenuItem menuItemExit =
    new MenuItem("E_xit");
menuItemExit.setOnAction(e -> ExitProgram());
```

After you create your menu items, you can add them to the menu like this:

```
menuGame.getChildren().add(menuItemNewGame);
menuGame.getChildren().add(menuItemPauseGame);
menuGame.getChildren().add(menuItemQuitGame);
menuGame.getChildren().add(menuItemExit);
```

Alternatively, you could use the addAll method to add the menu items all at once:

```
menuGame.getChildren().addAll(menuItemNewGame,
    menuItemPauseGame, menuItemQuitGame, menuItemExit);
```

Table 10-3 lists some constructors and methods of the MenuItem class in case you want to look them up quickly later.

Table 10-3	The MenuItem Class
Constructor	*Description*
MenuItem(String name)	Creates a menu item with the specified name.
Method	*Description*
String getText()	Gets the menu item's text.
void setText(String text)	Sets the menu item's text.
boolean isDisable()	Returns true if the menu item is disabled.
void setDisable()	Disables the menu item.
void setDisable(boolean value)	If value is true, disables the menu item. Otherwise, enables the menu item.
setOnAction(EventHandler <ActionEvent> value)	Sets an action event handler that is called when the user selects this menu item.

Using Separators

A *menu separator* is a menu item whose only purpose is to create visual separation within a menu so that items appear grouped logically. The menu that was shown in Figure 10-1 includes a separator that divides the three menu items that start, pause, or end games from the item that exits the program.

To create a separator, you use the `SeparatorMenuItem` class. Usually, you create the separator in the same statement you use to add the separator to the menu, like this:

```
menuGame.getItems().add(new SeparatorMenuItem());
```

Here's an example that adds a separator between the Quit Game menu item and the Exit menu item:

```
menuGame.getChildren().add(menuItemNewGame);
menuGame.getChildren().add(menuItemPauseGame);
menuGame.getChildren().add(menuItemQuitGame);
menuGame.getChildren().add(new SeparatorMenuItem());
menuGame.getChildren().add(menuItemExit);
```

Using Action Listeners

Menu items generate action events when selected by the user. As with any other action event, you handle the action events for menus by creating an action event handler that is called when the action event is generated. The easiest way to do that is by creating a method to call when the action event occurs, and then using a Lambda expression with the menu item's `setOnAction` method to call the method you created.

Here's a simple method that you might associate with an Exit menu item. This method simply exits the program by calling the `close` method of the primary stage:

```
private void menuItemExit_OnClick()
{
    stage.close();
}
```

Note: For this method to work, `stage` must be a class field that's been assigned to the primary stage in the program's `start` method.

To use this listener, pass it via a Lambda expression to the Exit menu item's `setOnAction` method, as follows:

```
menuItemExit.setOnAction(e -> exitMenuAction() );
```

If you prefer, you can eliminate the separate method altogether and call `stage.close()` directly in the `setOnAction` method, like this:

```
exitItem.addActionListener(e -> stage.close());
```

However, I prefer to create separate methods to handle each menu item. This practice makes it easier to add code (for example, to ensure that the user has saved her work before exiting).

A common way to handle action events for a menu is to use a single method to handle events for all the menu items in the menu. To do that, you must pass the `ActionEvent` object to the event handler method via the Lambda expression when you call the `setOnAction` method, as in this example:

```
menuItemExit.setOnAction(e -> menuAction(e) );
```

Then the `menuAction` method can use nested `if` statements to determine which menu item was chosen by the user, as in this example:

```
public void menuAction(ActionEvent e)
{
    if (e.getSource() == newItem)
        newGame();
    else if (e.getSource() == pauseItem)
        pauseGame();
    else if (e.getSource() == quitItem)
        quitGame();
    // and so on
}
```

Here's a sample action listener that you may want to use while you're figuring out how to work with menus. This action listener simply displays the text of each menu item on the console whenever the user chooses a menu command. That way, you can be certain you're setting up your menus and action listeners properly:

```
public void menuAction(ActionEvent e)
    {
        MenuItem item = (MenuItem)e.getSource();
        System.out.println(item.getText());
    }
}
```

Creating Menus That Change

In many applications, menu items change as you work with the program. Some items may be disabled in certain situations, and the text of a menu item may change depending on the context in which the command could be used.

For example, you may want the Pause Game menu item in the Game menu to change to Resume Game when the user pauses the game. Then, if the user resumes the game, this menu item reverts to Pause Game. You could do that in several ways. The easiest is to just look at the text in the menu item. If the text is _Pause Game, change it to _Resume Game; if the text is _Resume Game, change it to _Pause Game. Here's a snippet of code that does the job:

```
if (menuItemPauseGame.getText().equals("_Pause Game"))
{
    menuItemPauseGame.setText("_Resume Game");
}
else
{
    menuItemPauseGame.setText("_Pause Game");
}
```

In a real program, of course, this code also pauses and resumes the game.

Enabling or disabling menu items depending on what's happening in the program is also common. Suppose that you don't want to allow users to quit the game while the game is paused. In that case, you disable the Quit Game menu item when the user chooses Pause Game and enable it again if the user chooses Resume Game, like this:

```
if (menuItemPauseGame.getText().equals("_Pause Game"))
{
    menuItemPauseGame.setText("_Resume Game");
    menuItemQuitGame.setDisable(true);
}
else
{
    menuItemPauseGame.setText("_Pause Game");
    menuItemQuitGame.setDisable(false);
}
```

Using Check and Radio Menu Items

A *check menu item* is a menu item that resembles a check box that the user can click to check or uncheck. Check menu's ideal for menu items that allow users to select program options.

A *radio menu item* is similar to a check menu item except that it can be grouped with other radio menu items, much like a radio button. As with radio buttons, only one item in a group of radio menu items can be selected at a time. So when the user clicks a radio menu item, any other radio items in the same group are automatically unchecked.

Figure 10-2 shows an Options menu that contains two check menu items and three radio items. A separator is used to separate the check items from the radio items.

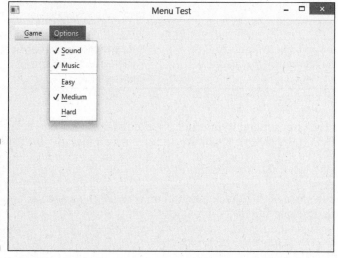

Figure 10-2:
A menu with check menu items and radio menu items.

To create a check menu item, use the `CheckMenuItem` class, whose constructors and methods are listed in Table 10-4. This class inherits the `MenuItem` class, so most of its methods are the same.

Table 10-4	The CheckMenuItem Class
Constructor	**Description**
CheckMenuItem(String name)	Creates a check menu item with the specified name.
Method	**Description**
boolean isSelected()	Returns true if the item is checked.
void setSelected(boolean value)	Specify true to check the item or false to uncheck the item.
String getText()	Gets the menu item's text.
void setText(String text)	Sets the menu item's text.
boolean isDisable()	Returns true if the menu item is disabled.
void setDisable()	Disables the menu item.
void setDisable(boolean value)	If value is true, disables the menu item. Otherwise, enables the menu item.
setOnAction(EventHandler <ActionEvent> value)	Sets an action event handler that's called when the user selects this menu item.

Initially, the check menu item is not checked. If you want the default setting for the item to be checked, call the setSelected method, like this:

```
menuItemMusic.setSelected(true);
```

To test the state of the check menu item, you use the isSelected method, as in this example:

```
if (menuItemMusic.isSelected() == true)
    System.out.println(
        "Your mamma can't dance.");
else
    System.out.println(
        "Your daddy can't rock and roll.");
```

Here two different messages display on the console, depending on the setting of the check box for the musicItem menu item.

To create a radio menu item, use the RadioMenuItem class shown in Table 10-5.

Table 10-5	The RadioMenuItem Class
Constructor	**Description**
`RadioMenuItem(String name)`	Creates a radio menu item with the specified name.
Method	**Description**
`void setToggleGroup(ToggleGroup group)`	Assigns this radio menu item to a toggle group.
`ToggleGroup getToggleGroup()`	Retrieves the toggle group that this radio menu item is a member of.
`boolean isSelected()`	Returns `true` if the item is checked.
`void setSelected(boolean value)`	Specify `true` to check the item or `false` to uncheck the item.
`String getText()`	Gets the menu item's text.
`void setText(String text)`	Sets the menu item's text.
`boolean isDisable()`	Returns `true` if the menu item is disabled.
`void setDisable()`	Disables the menu item.
`void setDisable(boolean value)`	If `value` is `true`, disables the menu item. Otherwise, enables the menu item.
`setOnAction(EventHandler <ActionEvent> value)`	Sets an action event handler that's called when the user selects this menu item.

As you can see, this class is almost the same as the `CheckMenuItem` class. The only significant difference is the addition of the `setToggleGroup` method, which lets you add a radio menu item to a toggle group. Here's a snippet of code that creates three radio menu items, then creates a toggle group and adds the three radio menu items to the group:

```
RadioMenuItem menuItemEasy =
    new RadioMenuItem("_Easy");
RadioMenuItem menuItemMedium =
    new RadioMenuItem("_Medium");
RadioMenuItem menuItemHard =
    new RadioMenuItem("_Hard");

ToggleGroup groupDifficulty = new ToggleGroup();
```

```
menuItemEasy.setToggleGroup(groupDifficulty);
menuItemMedium.setToggleGroup(groupDifficulty);
menuItemHard.setToggleGroup(groupDifficulty);
```

Creating Submenus

A *submenu* is a menu within a menu. Submenus are possible because the Menu class is itself a subclass of the MenuItem class, which means that any item in a menu can itself be another menu. When the user clicks a submenu, the submenu opens to reveal its menu items. Submenus can be created within submenus, as many levels deep as you wish. But few menus are nested more than two or three levels deep.

The following example creates a version of the Options menu that isolates the three difficulty choices into a separate submenu named Difficulty:

```
// Create the check menu items
CheckMenuItem menuItemSound =
    new CheckMenuItem("_Sound");
CheckMenuItem menuItemMusic =
    new CheckMenuItem("_Music");

// Create the radio menu items
RadioMenuItem menuItemEasy =
    new RadioMenuItem("_Easy");
RadioMenuItem menuItemMedium =
    new RadioMenuItem("_Medium");
RadioMenuItem menuItemHard =
    new RadioMenuItem("_Hard");
ToggleGroup difficultyGroup = new ToggleGroup();
menuItemEasy.setToggleGroup(difficultyGroup);
menuItemMedium.setToggleGroup(difficultyGroup);
menuItemHard.setToggleGroup(difficultyGroup);

// Create the Difficulty submenu
Menu menuDifficulty = new Menu("_Difficulty");
menuDifficulty.getItems().add(menuItemEasy);
menuDifficulty.getItems().add(menuItemMedium);
menuDifficulty.getItems().add(menuItemHard);

// Create the Options menu
Menu menuOptions = new Menu("_Options");
menuOptions.getItems().add(menuItemSound);
menuOptions.getItems().add(menuItemMusic);
menuOptions.getItems().add(menuDifficulty);
```

Figure 10-3 shows this menu in action.

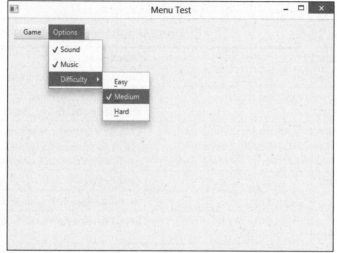

Figure 10-3:
A menu with
a submenu.

Creating Custom Menu Items

A *custom menu item* is a menu item that can contain any JavaFX node. This allows you to easily convert any JavaFX node into a menu item. For example, you can turn a text field, choice box, or combo box into a menu item by adding it to a custom menu item and then adding the custom menu item to a menu. Figure 10-4 shows an example of a custom menu item that contains a text field.

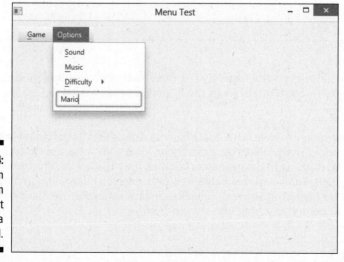

Figure 10-4:
A custom
menu item
that
contains a
text field.

To create a custom menu item, use the CustomMenuItem class. Table 10-6 shows the details of this class.

Table 10-6	The CustomMenuItem Class
Constructor	*Description*
CustomMenuItem()	Creates an empty custom menu item.
CustomMenuItem(Node content)	Creates a custom menu item with the specified node as its content.
CustomMenuItem(Node content, boolean value)	Creates a custom menu item with the specified node as its content and the specified hideOnClick setting.
Method	*Description*
Node getContent()	Gets the menu item's content.
void setContent(Node content)	Sets the menu item's content.
void setHideOnClick(boolean value)	Sets the HideOnClick property. This property should be set to false for most custom menu items.
boolean isHideOnClick()	Indicates the HideOnClick setting.
boolean isDisable()	Returns true if the menu item is disabled.
void setDisable()	Disables the menu item.
void setDisable(boolean value)	If value is true, disables the menu item. Otherwise, enables the menu item.
setOnAction(EventHandler <ActionEvent> value)	Sets an action event handler that's called when the user selects this menu item.

As you can see, you can specify the node that you want to add as the custom menu item's content either in the constructor or via the setContent method.

One common problem with custom menu items is that they have a tendency to disappear when the user clicks them. That's because the default behavior for menu items is to disappear as soon as they're clicked. For most custom menu items, that's not desirable. For example, if a custom menu item contains a text field but the text field disappears whenever the user clicks it, the user can't enter anything into the text field.

To avoid that, you can call the `setHideOnClick` method with a value of `false` as its parameter. This suppresses the hide-on-click behavior, allowing the user to click the custom menu item to select it. Then, the user can enter data into the field. ***Note:*** You can also set the hide-on-click behavior via the class constructor.

The following example shows how to create a text field custom menu item and add it to a menu:

```
TextField txtName = new TextField();
txtName.setPromptText("Player Name");
CustomMenuItem menuItemName =
    new CustomMenuItem(txtName);
menuItemName.setHideOnClick(false);
menuOptions.getItems().add(menuItemName);
```

Part III

Enhancing Your Scenic Design

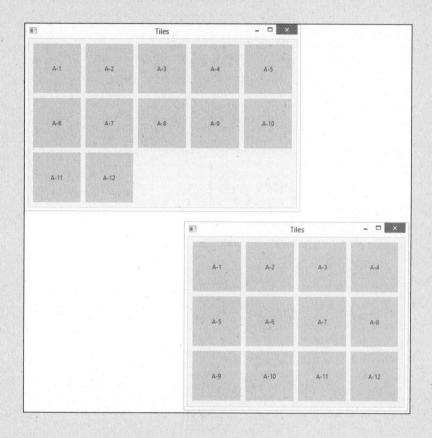

In this part . . .

- ↵ Arranging elements
- ↵ Managing themes and style sheets
- ↵ Customizing shapes
- ↵ Making shapes look more realistic
- ↵ Visit `www.dummies.com/extras/javafx` for great Dummies content online.

Chapter 11

More about Layout Panes for Precise Scene Design

*I*n Chapter 5, you can read about how to work with four basic layout pane classes that let you control the arrangement of controls in a scene: HBox, which arranges nodes horizontally; VBox, which arranges nodes vertically; FlowPane, which arranges nodes both horizontally and vertically; and BorderPane, which divides the scene into five regions: Top, Right, Bottom, Left, and Center.

In this chapter, you discover four additional layout panes that give you additional ways to arrange the elements in a scene. Specifically, you discover how to use the following five layout pane classes:

✔ **StackPane:** The StackPane class is a bit different than the other layout panes in that it doesn't visually separate nodes from one another. Instead, it displays nodes directly on top of each other. For example, if you add a rectangle shape and a text shape to a stack pane, the text will appear directly over the rectangle.

✔ **AnchorPane:** This layout lets you anchor nodes to the top, right, bottom, left, or center of the pane. As the pane resizes, the nodes are repositioned but remain tied to their anchor points. *Note:* A node can be anchored to more than one position. For example, you might anchor a node to the top and the right. Then, when you resize the pane, the node will remain near the top-right corner of the pane.

✔ `GridPane`: Arranges nodes in a grid of rows and columns. The grid does not have to be uniformly sized like a chess board. Instead, the width of each column and the height of each row can vary according to its content. In addition, content can span columns or rows. `GridPane` is an ideal layout type for forms that gather information from the user via user interface controls such as text boxes, list boxes, and so on.

✔ `TilePane`: If you want a layout that resembles a chess board, in which each cell in a grid is the same size, `TilePane` is the layout pane you're looking for. `TilePane` is ideal for organizing thumbnails of image files or other objects of the same size.

✔ `ScrollPane`: Technically, the `ScrollPane` class is not a layout pane at all; it inherits the `Control` class, not the `Pane` class. However, it's primary use is to create layouts that are too large to display all at once and so require a scroll bar to allow the user to pan left and right or up and down (or both) to see all its contents.

Keep in mind that layout panes are typically used in combinations to create the complete layout for your scene. For example, you might use a `GridPane` to organize user input controls and then place the `GridPane` in the center section of a `BorderPane` to place it in the middle of the scene. Or, you might use `VBox` panes to display labels beneath image thumbnails and then add the `VBox` panes to a tile pane to display the labeled images in a tiled arrangement.

Using the StackPane Layout

A *stack pane* layout is unusual in that it does not arrange its nodes by spreading them out so that you can see them all. Instead, it stacks its nodes one on top of the other so that they overlap. The first node you add to a stack pane at the bottom of the stack; the last node is on the top.

You will most often use a stack pane layout with shapes rather than controls. Because I haven't yet covered shapes, I limit the examples in this section to simple rectangles created with the `Rectangle` class. You can read more about this class in Chapter 13. For now, just realize that you can create a rectangle like this:

```
Rectangle r1 = new Rectangle(100,100);
```

To add a fill color, call the `setFill` method, like this:

```
r1.setFill(Color.RED);
```

The `Color` class defines a number of constants for commonly used colors. In this section, I use just three: `LIGHTGRAY`, `DARKGRAY`, and `DIMGRAY`.

The `Rectangle` class is in the `javafx.scene.shape` package, and the `Color` class is in `javafx.scene.paint`. Thus, you need to include the following import statements to use these classes:

```
import javafx.scene.shapes.*;
import javafx.scene.paint.*;
```

To create a stack pane, you use the `StackPane` class, whose constructors and methods are shown in Table 11-1.

Table 11-1	StackPane Constructors and Methods
Constructor	**Description**
`StackPane()`	Creates an empty stack pane.
`StackPane(Node... children)`	Creates a stack pane with the specified child nodes. This constructor lets you create a stack pane and add child nodes to it at the same time.
Method	**Description**
`ObservableList<Node> getChildren()`	Returns the collection of all child nodes that have been added to the stack pane. The collection is returned as an `ObservableList` type, which includes the methods `add` and `addAll`, which lets you add one or more nodes to the list.

(continued)

Table 11-1 *(continued)*

Method	Description
`static void setAlignment (Pos alignment)`	Sets the alignment for child nodes within the stack pane. See Table 5-5 in Chapter 5 for an explanation of the `Pos` enumeration.
`static void setMargin(Node child, Insets value)`	Sets the margins for a given child node. See Table 5-2 in Chapter 5.
`void setPadding(Insets value)`	Sets the padding around the inside edges of the stack pane. See Table 5-2 in Chapter 5 for an explanation of the `Insets` class.

The simplest way to create a stack pane is to first create the nodes that you will place in the pane and then call the `StackPane` constructor, passing the child nodes as parameters. For example:

```
Rectangle r1 = new Rectangle(100,100);
r1.setFill(Color.DARKGRAY);
Rectangle r2 = new Rectangle(50,50);
r2.setFill(Color.LIGHTGRAY);
StackPane stack = new StackPane(r1, r2);
```

Here, I first create a pair of rectangles, one 100x100, the other 50x50. The larger rectangle is filled dark gray, the smaller one light gray. Then, I create a stack pane that holds the two rectangles. Figure 11-1 shows how this pane appears when displayed. As you can see, the smaller rectangle is displayed within the larger one.

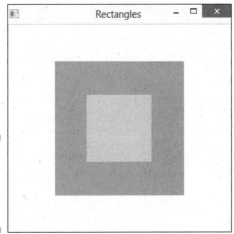

Figure 11-1:
Two rectangles displayed in a StackPane.

If you prefer, you can call the getChildren method to add nodes to the stack pane, like this:

```
stack.getChildren().add(r1);
stack.getChildren().add(r2);
```

Or like this:

```
stack.getChildren().addAll(r1,r2);
```

Note: The order in which you add nodes to a stack pane has a major impact on how the child nodes are displayed. For example, suppose you reversed the order in which the two rectangles are added:

```
stack.getChildren().addAll(r2,r1);
```

Then, the larger rectangle will be displayed over the top of the smaller one. The result is that the user will see only the larger rectangle. (Unless, of course, the larger rectangle is transparent. I discuss how to create transparent shapes in Chapter 13.)

By default, the objects in a stack pane are centered on top of one another. You can change that by using the setAlignment method. The argument for this method is of type Pos, the same as for other layout panes that have a setAlignment method. If you need a refresher on the Pos enumeration, flip to Table 5-5 in Chapter 5. Here's an example that displays three rectangles of various sizes aligned at the top left of the stack pane:

```
Rectangle r1 = new Rectangle(400,150);
r1.setFill(Color.DARKGRAY);

Rectangle r2 = new Rectangle(200, 400);
r2.setFill(Color.LIGHTGRAY);

Rectangle r3 = new Rectangle(150,150);
r3.setFill(Color.DIMGRAY);

StackPane stack = new StackPane(r1, r2, r3);
stack.setAlignment(Pos.TOP_CENTER);
```

Figure 11-2 shows how this pane appears when displayed in a scene.

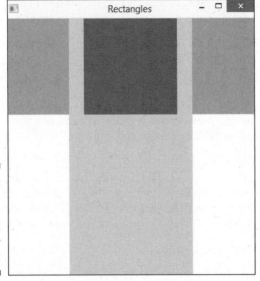

Figure 11-2:
Three rect-
angles dis-
played with
top-center
alignment.

As with other layout panes, you can use the `setPadding` method to add padding around the perimeter of the pane. For example, the following line creates
a 50-pixel buffer around the edge of the pane:

```
stack.setPadding(new Insets(50));
```

The `setPadding` method accepts an argument of type `Insets`. For more
information about the `Insets` class, flip to Table 5-2 in Chapter 5.

You can also add margins to individual nodes within a stack pane. To do so,
call the `setMargin` method, passing both the node and an `Insets` object
that describes the margin:

```
stack.setMargin(r1, new Insets(25));
```

Using the TilePane layout

The *tile pane layout* is similar to the flow pane layout: It arranges nodes in neat
rows and columns, either horizontally or vertically. The crucial difference is
that in a tile pane layout, all the cells are the same size. The tile pane layout

calculates the size of the largest node in its child node collection and then uses that size as the size for each cell. This creates a nice grid-like appearance, as shown in Figure 11-3.

By default, a tile pane shows five nodes in each row, using as many rows as necessary to display all its nodes. Thus, the tile pane in Figure 11-3 displays its 12 rectangles in two rows of five and a third row of just two.

If you adjust the size of the tile pane, the number of nodes per row adjusts automatically. For example, Figure 11-4 shows the same tile pane resized so that the 12 rectangles are displayed in three rows of four.

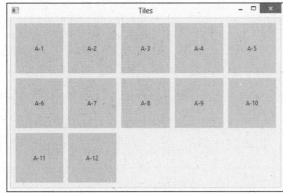

Figure 11-3:
A dozen rectangles displayed in a tile pane.

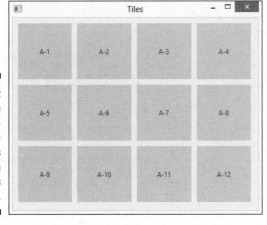

Figure 11-4:
A tile pane automatically rearranges its tiles when the pane is resized.

To create a tile pane, you use the `TilePane` class, as I describe in Table 11-2.

Table 11-2	TilePane Constructors and Methods
Constructor	**Description**
`TilePane()`	Creates an empty tile pane.
`TilePane(Node. . . children)`	Creates a tile pane with the specified child nodes.
`TilePane(double hgap, double vgap)`	Creates an empty tile pane with the specified gaps between rows and columns.
`TilePane(Orientation orientation)`	Creates an empty tile pane with the specified orientation. You can specify `Orientation.HORIZONTAL` or `Orientation.VERTICAL`.
`TilePane(double hgap, double vgap, Node. . .children)`	
`TilePane(Orientation orientation, double hgap, double vgap)`	
`TilePane(Orientation orientation, Node. . . children)`	
`TilePane(Orientation orientation, double hgap, double vgap, Node. . . children)`	
Method	**Description**
`ObservableList<Node> getChildren()`	Returns the collection of all child nodes that have been added to the tile pane. The collection is returned as an `ObservableList` type, which includes the methods `add` and `addAll`, which lets you add one or more nodes to the list.

Method	Description
`void setHgap(double value)`	Sets the size of the gap that appears between columns.
`void setVgap(double value)`	Sets the size of the gap that appears between rows.
`void setOrientation(Orientation orientation)`	Sets the orientation. Allowable values are `Orientation.HORIZONTAL` and `Orientation.VERTICAL`.
`void setPrefColumns(int value)`	Sets the number of columns preferred for this tile pane.
`void setPrefRows(int value)`	Sets the number of rows preferred for this tile pane.
`void setPrefTileWidth(double value)`	Sets the preferred width for each cell.
`void setPrefTileHeight(double value)`	Sets the preferred height for each cell.
`static void setMargin(Node node, Insets value)`	Sets the margin for a particular node. See Table 5-2 in Chapter 5 for an explanation of the `Insets` class.
`void setMinHeight(double value)`	Sets the minimum height of the tile pane.
`void setMaxHeight(double value)`	Sets the maximum height of the tile pane.
`void setPrefHeight(double value)`	Sets the preferred height of the tile pane.
`void setMinWidth(double value)`	Sets the minimum width of the tile pane.
`void setMaxWidth(double value)`	Sets the maximum width of the tile pane.

(continued)

Table 11-2 *(continued)*

Method	Description
void setPrefWidth(double value)	Sets the preferred width of the tile pane.
void setPadding(Insets value)	Sets the padding around the inside edges of the tile pane. See Table 5-2 in Chapter 5 for an explanation of the Insets class.

Here's the code that creates the tile pane shown in Figures 11-3 and 11-4:

```
TilePane tile1 = new TilePane();
tile1.setHgap(10);
tile1.setVgap(10);
tile1.setPadding(new Insets(10,10,10,10));
for (int i=1; i<13; i++)
{
    Rectangle r = new Rectangle(100, 100);
    r.setFill(Color.LIGHTGRAY);
    Label l = new Label("A-" + i);
    StackPane s = new StackPane(r, l);
    tile1.getChildren().add(s);
}
```

As you can see, a for loop is used to create 12 labeled rectangles, which are added to the tile pane. In the for loop, I first create a 100x100-pixel rectangle and set its color to light gray. Then, I create a label and assign it a text value that consists of the string "A-" followed by an integer value. Finally, I create a stack pane and add the rectangle and the label to it. The result is that the label appears on top of the rectangle. I then add the stack pane to the tile pane.

Using the ScrollPane Layout

When a layout is too large to fit in a window, you want to provide horizontal or vertical scroll bars (or both) so the user can scroll to see the entire layout. The easiest way to do that is with a scroll pane. A *scroll pane* envelops a single node with an area that automatically displays horizontal or vertical scroll bars whenever necessary. Thus, the scroll bars are not displayed if the entire layout fits within the scroll pane. If the layout is taller than the scroll pane, a vertical scroll bar appears. And if the layout is wider than the scroll pane, a horizontal scroll bar appears.

Technically, a scroll pane is not really a layout pane. The ScrollPane class is a descendant of the Control class, not the Pane class. Even so, scroll panes are typically used in conjunction with layout panes to accommodate layouts that are too large to fit onscreen.

Figure 11-5 shows a tile pane similar to the ones shown in the preceding section contained within a scroll pane. As you can see, the tile pane in this example displays two tiles per row, and a vertical scroll bar is visible, allowing the user to scroll to see all the tiles. To create margins around the scroll pane, I added the scroll pane to a stack pane and then set margins on the stack pane.

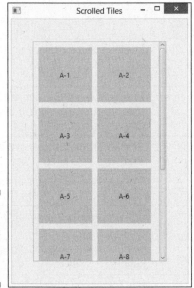

Figure 11-5:
A tile pane
contained
within a
scroll pane.

To create a scroll pane, use the `ScrollPane` class depicted in Table 11-3.

Table 11-3   ScrollPane Constructors and Methods

Constructor	Description
`ScrollPane()`	Creates an empty scroll pane.
`ScrollPane(Node node)`	Creates a scroll pane with the specified child node.

Method	Description
`void getContent(Node node)`	Sets the node contained within this scroll pane.
Note: The allowable values for the following two methods are shown at the end of this table.	
`void setHbarPolicy(ScrollPane. ScrollBarPolicy value)`	Sets the policy for the horizontal scroll bar.
`void setVbarPolicy(ScrollPane. ScrollBarPolicy value)`	Sets the policy for the vertical scroll bar.
`void setPannable(boolean value)`	If `true`, the user can pan the contents of the scroll pane using the mouse. The default is `false`.
`void setMinHeight(double value)`	Sets the minimum height of the tile pane.
`void setMaxHeight(double value)`	Sets the maximum height of the tile pane.
`void setPrefHeight(double value)`	Sets the preferred height of the tile pane.
`void setMinWidth(double value)`	Sets the minimum width of the tile pane.
`void setMaxWidth(double value)`	Sets the maximum width of the tile pane.
`void setPrefWidth(double value)`	Sets the preferred width of the tile pane.
`void setPadding(Insets value)`	Sets the padding around the inside edges of the tile pane. See Table 5-2 in Chapter 5 for an explanation of the `Insets` class.

ScrollBarPolicy Enumeration	Description
ScrollPane. ScrollBarPolicy.ALWAYS	Always show a scroll bar.
ScrollPane. ScrollBarPolicy.NEVER	Never show a scroll bar.
ScrollPane. ScrollBarPolicy.AS_NEEDED	Show a scroll bar only when it's needed.

The easiest way to create a scroll pane is to call the `ScrollPane` constructor and pass the node you want scrolled as a parameter, like this:

```
ScrollPane spane = new ScrollPane(tile1);
```

You will most likely also want to set the size constraints for the scroll pane. The following code fixes the width at 250 and allows the layout to determine the height, with a preferred height of 400:

```
spane.setMaxWidth(250);
spane.setMinWidth(250);
spane.setPrefWidth(250);
spane.setPrefHeight(400);
```

If you want, you can set a policy for the vertical and horizontal scroll bars. By default, the scroll bars appear only if necessary. If you want a scroll bar to always appear, even when it isn't necessary, set the policy to ALWAYS as in this example:

```
spane.setVBarPolicy(ScrollBarPolicy.ALWAYS);
```

The complete program used to create the scroll pane shown in Figure 11-5 is shown in Listing 11-1.

Listing 11-1: The ScrolledTile Program

```
import javafx.application.*;
import javafx.stage.*;
import javafx.scene.*;
import javafx.scene.layout.*;
import javafx.scene.control.*;
import javafx.scene.shape.*;
import javafx.scene.paint.*;
import javafx.geometry.*;
```

(continued)

Listing 11-1 *(continued)*

```
public class ScrolledTile extends Application
{
    public static void main(String[] args)
    {
        launch(args);
    }

    @Override public void start(Stage primaryStage)
    {

        TilePane tile1 = new TilePane();                              →20
        tile1.setHgap(10);
        tile1.setVgap(10);
        tile1.setPrefColumns(2);
        tile1.setPadding(new Insets(10,10,10,10));
        for (int i=1; i<13; i++)                                       →25
        {
            Rectangle r = new Rectangle(100, 100);
            r.setFill(Color.LIGHTGRAY);
            Label l = new Label("A-" + i);
            StackPane s = new StackPane(r, l);
            tile1.getChildren().add(s);
        }

        ScrollPane spane = new ScrollPane(tile1);                     →34
        spane.setMinWidth(250);
        spane.setPrefWidth(250);
        spane.setMaxWidth(250);
        spane.setPrefHeight(400);
        spane.setVbarPolicy(ScrollPane.ScrollBarPolicy.ALWAYS);       →39

        StackPane stack = new StackPane(spane);                       →41
        stack.setMargin(spane, new Insets(40,40,40,40));

        Scene scene = new Scene(stack);                               →44
        primaryStage.setScene(scene);
        primaryStage.setTitle("Scrolled Tiles");
        primaryStage.show();
    }
}
```

The following paragraphs describe the highlights of this program:

→ **20:** This line and the four lines that follow it create the tile pane, set the horizontal and vertical gaps to 10 pixels, set the preferred width to two columns, and set the padding.

→ **25:** A `for` loop is used to create 12 labeled rectangles and add them to the tile pane.

→ **34:** These lines create the scroll pane and set its size. The width is fixed at 250 pixels. The preferred height is 400 pixels, but the scroll pane's height can grow or shrink as needed to fill the scene.

→ **39:** The vertical scroll bar will always be displayed, even if it isn't necessary.

→ **41:** A stack pane is used here for the sole purpose of providing 40 pixels of margin around the scroll pane.

→ **44:** The stack pane is added to the scene, and the scene is finalized and displayed.

Using the GridPane Layout

The grid pane layout manager lets you arrange GUI elements in a grid of rows and columns. Unlike a tile pane, the rows and columns of a grid pane do not have to be the same size. Instead, the grid pane layout automatically adjusts the width of each column and the height of each row based on the components you add to the panel.

Here are some important features of the grid pane layout manager:

✔ You can specify which cell you want each component to go in, and you can control each component's position in the panel.

✔ You can create components that span multiple rows or columns, such as a button two columns wide or a list box four rows high.

✔ You can tell `GridPane` to stretch a component to fill the entire space allotted to it if the component isn't already big enough to fill the entire area. You can specify that this stretching be done horizontally, vertically, or both.

✔ If a component doesn't fill its allotted area, you can tell the grid pane layout manager how you want the component to be positioned within the area — for example, left- or right-aligned.

The following sections describe the ins and outs of working with grid pane layouts.

Sketching out a plan

Before you create a grid pane layout, draw a sketch showing how you want the components to appear in the panel. Then slice the panel into rows and columns, and number the rows and columns starting with zero in the top-left corner. Figure 11-6 shows such a sketch for an application that lets a user order a pizza.

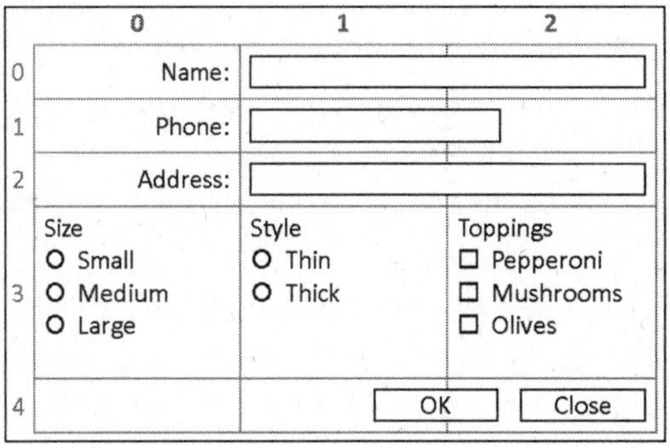

Figure 11-6: Sketching out a panel.

After you have the panel sketched out, list the components, their *x* and *y* coordinates on the grid, their alignment, and whether each component spans more than one row or column. Here's an example:

Component	x	y	Alignment	Spans
Label "Name"	0	0	Right	
Label "Phone"	0	1	Right	
Label "Address"	0	2	Right	
Name text field	1	0	Left	2
Phone text field	1	1	Left	2
Address text field	1	2	Left	2
Size radio buttons	0	3	Left	
Style radio buttons	1	3	Left	
Toppings check boxes	2	3	Left	
OK and Close buttons	2	4	Right	

After you lay out the grid, you can write the code to put each component in its proper place.

Creating a grid pane

Table 11-4 shows the most frequently used constructors and methods of the GridPane class, which you use to create a grid pane.

Table 11-4	GridPane Constructors and Methods
Constructor	**Description**
GridPane()	Creates an empty grid pane.
Method	**Description**
void add(Node node, int col, int row)	Adds a node at the specified column and row index.
void add(Node node, int col, int row, int colspan, int rowspan)	Adds a node at the specified column and row index with the specified column and row spans.
void addColumn(int col, Node... nodes)	Adds an entire column of nodes.
void addRow(int row, Node... nodes)	Adds an entire row of nodes.
<ObservableList> getColumnConstraints()	Returns the column constraints. For more information, see to Table 11-5.
<ObservableList> getRowConstraints()	Returns the row constraints. For more information, see Table 11-6.
void setColumnSpan(Node node, int colspan)	Sets the column span for the specified node.
void setRowSpan(Node node, int colspan)	Sets the row span for the specified node.
void setHalignment(Node node, HPos value)	Sets the horizontal alignment for the node. Allowable values are HPos.LEFT, HPos.CENTER, and HPos.RIGHT.
void setValignment(Node node, VPos value)	Sets the vertical alignment for the node. Allowable values are HPos.BOTTOM, HPos.CENTER, and HPos.TOP.

(continued)

Table 11-4 (continued)

Method	Description
void setHgap(double value)	Sets the size of the gap that appears between columns.
void setVgap(double value)	Sets the size of the gap that appears between rows.
static void setMargin(Node node, Insets value)	Sets the margin for a particular node. See Table 5-2 in Chapter 5 for an explanation of the Insets class.
void setPadding(Insets value)	Sets the padding around the inside edges of the grid pane. See Table 5-2 in Chapter 5 for an explanation of the Insets class.
void setMinHeight(double value)	Sets the minimum height of the grid pane.
void setMaxHeight(double value)	Sets the maximum height of the grid pane.
void setPrefHeight(double value)	Sets the preferred height of the grid pane.
void setMinWidth(double value)	Sets the minimum width of the grid pane.
void setMaxWidth(double value)	Sets the maximum width of the grid pane.
void setPrefWidth(double value)	Sets the preferred width of the grid pane.

To create a basic grid pane, you first call the GridPane constructor. Then, you use the add method to add nodes to the grid pane's cells. The parameters of the add method specify the node to be added, the node's column index, and the node's row index. For example, the following code snippet creates a label, and then creates a grid pane and adds the label to the cell at column 0, row 0:

```
Label lblName = new Label("Name");
GridPane grid = new GridPane();
grid.add(lblName, 0, 0);
```

The typical way to fill a grid pane with nodes is to call the `add` method for each node. However, if you prefer, you can add an entire column or row of nodes with a single call to either `addColumn` or `addRow`. For example, this example creates a label and a text field, and then creates a grid pane and adds the label and the text field to the first row:

```
Label lblName = new Label("Name");
TextField txtName = new TextField();
GridPane grid = new GridPane();
grid.addRow(0, lblName, txtName);
```

If a node should span more than one column, you can call the `setColumnSpan` method to specify the number of columns the node should span. For example:

```
grid.setColumnSpan(txtName, 2);
```

Here, the `txtName` node will span two columns. You use the `setRowSpan` in a similar way if you need to configure a node to span multiple rows.

To control the horizontal alignment of a node, use the `setHalignment` method as in this example:

```
grid.setHalignment(lblName, HPos.RIGHT);
```

Here, the `lblName` node is right-aligned within its column. The `setValignment` method works in a similar way.

Like other layout panes, the `GridPane` class has a host of methods for setting spacing and alignment details. You can use the `setHgap` and `setVgap` methods to set the spacing between rows and columns so that your layouts won't look so cluttered. You can use the `setPadding` and `setMargins` methods to set padding and margins, which work just as they do with other layout panes. And you can set the minimum, maximum, and preferred width and height for the grid pane.

Working with grid pane constraints

You can control most aspects of a grid pane's layouts using methods of the `GridPane` class, but unfortunately, you can't control the size of individual columns or rows. To do that, you must use the `ColumnConstraints` or `RowConstraints` class, as described in Tables 11-5 and 11-6.

Table 11-5   **The ColumnConstraints Class**

Constructor	Description
`ColumnConstraints()`	Creates an empty column constraints object.
`ColumnConstraints(double width)`	Creates a column constraint with a fixed width.
`ColumnConstraints(double min, double pref, double max)`	Creates a column constraint with the specified minimum, preferred, and maximum widths.

Method	Description
`void setMinWidth(double value)`	Sets the minimum width of the column.
`void setMaxWidth(double value)`	Sets the maximum width of the column.
`void setPrefWidth(double value)`	Sets the preferred width of the column.
`void setPercentWidth(double value)`	Sets the width as a percentage of the total width of the grid pane.
`void setHgrow(Priority value)`	Determines whether the width of the column should grow if the grid pane's overall width increases. Allowable values are `Priority.ALWAYS`, `Priority.NEVER`, and `Priority.SOMETIMES`.
`void setFillWidth(boolean value)`	If true, the grid pane will expand the nodes within this column to fill empty space.
`void setHalignment(HPos value)`	Sets the horizontal alignment for the entire column. Allowable values are `HPos.LEFT`, `HPos.CENTER`, and `HPos.RIGHT`.

Table 11-6	The RowConstraints Class
Constructor	**Description**
`RowConstraints()`	Creates an empty row constraints object.
`RowConstraints(double height)`	Creates a row constraint with a fixed height.
`RowConstraints(double min, double pref, double max)`	Creates a row constraint with the specified minimum, preferred, and maximum heights.
Method	**Description**
`void setMinHeight(double value)`	Sets the minimum height of the row.
`void setMaxHeight(double value)`	Sets the maximum height of the row.
`void setPrefHeight(double value)`	Sets the preferred height of the row.
`void setPercentHeight (double value)`	Sets the height as a percentage of the total height of the grid pane.
`void setVgrow(Priority value)`	Determines whether the height of the row should grow if the grid pane's overall height increases. Allowable values are `Priority.ALWAYS`, `Priority.NEVER`, and `Priority.SOMETIMES`.
`void setFillHeight(boolean value)`	If `true`, the grid pane will expand the nodes within this row to fill empty space.
`void setValignment(VPos value)`	Sets the vertical alignment for the entire row. Allowable values are `VPos.TOP`, `VPos.CENTER`, and `VPos.BOTTOM`.

To use column constraints to set a fixed width for each column in a grid pane, first create a constraint for each column. Then, add the constraints to the grid pane's constraints collection. Here's an example:

```
ColumnConstriants col1 = new ColumnConstraints(200);
ColumnConstriants col2 = new ColumnConstraints(200);
ColumnConstriants col3 = new ColumnConstraints(200);
GridPane grid = new GridPane();
grid.getColumnConstraints().addAll(col1, col2, col3);
```

One of the most useful features of column constraints is their ability to distribute the width of a grid pane's columns as a percentage of the overall width of the grid pane. For example, suppose the grid pane will consist of three columns and you want them to all be of the same width regardless of the width of the grid pane. The following code accomplishes this:

```
ColumnConstriants col1 = new ColumnConstraints();
col1.setPercentWidth(33);
ColumnConstriants col2 = new ColumnConstraints();
col2.setPercentWidth(33);
ColumnConstriants col3 = new ColumnConstraints();
col3.setPercentWidth(33);
GridPane grid = new GridPane();
grid.getColumnConstraints().addAll(col1, col2, col3);
```

In this example, each column will fill 33 percent of the grid.

Several of the attributes that can be set with column or row constraints mirror attributes you can set for individual nodes via the `GridPane` class. For example, you can set the horizontal alignment of an individual node by calling the `setHalignment` method on the grid pane. Or, you can set the horizontal alignment of an entire column by creating a column constraint, setting its horizontal alignment, and then applying the column constraint to a column in the grid pane.

Examining a grid pane example

Listing 11-2 shows the code for a program that displays the scene I drew for Figure 11-6, and Figure 11-7 shows how this scene appears when the program is run. Figure 11-7 shows that the final appearance of this scene is pretty close to the way I sketched it.

Figure 11-7:
The Pizza
Order appli-
cation in
action.

Listing 11-2: The Pizza Order Application

```
import javafx.application.*;
import javafx.stage.*;
import javafx.scene.*;
import javafx.scene.layout.*;
import javafx.scene.control.*;
import javafx.geometry.*;

public class PizzaOrder extends Application
{
    public static void main(String[] args)
    {
        launch(args);
    }

    Stage stage;
    TextField txtName;
    TextField txtPhone;
    TextField txtAddress;
    RadioButton rdoSmall;
    RadioButton rdoMedium;
    RadioButton rdoLarge;
    RadioButton rdoThin;
    RadioButton rdoThick;
    CheckBox chkPepperoni;
    CheckBox chkMushrooms;
    CheckBox chkAnchovies;
```

(continued)

Listing 11-2 *(continued)*

```
@Override public void start(Stage primaryStage)
{
    stage = primaryStage;

    // Create the name label and text field              →32
    Label lblName = new Label("Name:");
    txtName = new TextField();
    txtName.setMinWidth(100);
    txtName.setPrefWidth(200);
    txtName.setMaxWidth(300);
    txtName.setPromptText("Enter the name here");

    // Create the phone number label and text field      →40
    Label lblPhone = new Label("Phone Number:");
    txtPhone = new TextField();
    txtPhone.setMinWidth(60);
    txtPhone.setPrefWidth(120);
    txtPhone.setMaxWidth(180);
    txtPhone.setPromptText("Enter the phone number here");

    // Create the address label and text field           →48
    Label lblAddress = new Label("Address:");
    txtAddress = new TextField();
    txtAddress.setMinWidth(100);
    txtAddress.setPrefWidth(200);
    txtAddress.setMaxWidth(300);
    txtAddress.setPromptText("Enter the address here");

    // Create the size pane                               →56
    Label lblSize = new Label("Size");
    rdoSmall = new RadioButton("Small");
    rdoMedium = new RadioButton("Medium");
    rdoLarge = new RadioButton("Large");
    rdoMedium.setSelected(true);
    ToggleGroup groupSize = new ToggleGroup();
    rdoSmall.setToggleGroup(groupSize);
    rdoMedium.setToggleGroup(groupSize);
    rdoLarge.setToggleGroup(groupSize);

    VBox paneSize = new VBox(lblSize, rdoSmall, rdoMedium, rdoLarge);
    paneSize.setSpacing(10);
```

```
    // Create the crust pane                                        →70
    Label lblCrust = new Label("Crust");
    rdoThin = new RadioButton("Thin");
    rdoThick = new RadioButton("Thick");
    rdoThin.setSelected(true);
    ToggleGroup groupCrust = new ToggleGroup();
    rdoThin.setToggleGroup(groupCrust);
    rdoThick.setToggleGroup(groupCrust);

    VBox paneCrust = new VBox(lblCrust, rdoThin, rdoThick);
    paneCrust.setSpacing(10);

    // Create the toppings pane                                     →82
    Label lblToppings = new Label("Toppings");
    chkPepperoni = new CheckBox("Pepperoni");
    chkMushrooms = new CheckBox("Mushrooms");
    chkAnchovies = new CheckBox("Anchovies");

    VBox paneToppings = new VBox(lblToppings, chkPepperoni,
        chkMushrooms, chkAnchovies);
    paneToppings.setSpacing(10);

    // Create the buttons                                           →92
    Button btnOK = new Button("OK");
    btnOK.setPrefWidth(80);
    btnOK.setOnAction(e -> btnOK_Click() );

    Button btnCancel = new Button("Cancel");
    btnCancel.setPrefWidth(80);
    btnCancel.setOnAction(e -> btnCancel_Click() );

    HBox paneButtons = new HBox(10, btnOK, btnCancel);

    // Create the GridPane layout                                   →103
    GridPane grid = new GridPane();
    grid.setPadding(new Insets(10));
    grid.setHgap(10);
    grid.setVgap(10);
    grid.setMinWidth(500);
    grid.setPrefWidth(500);
    grid.setMaxWidth(800);

    // Add the nodes to the pane                                    →112
    grid.addRow(0, lblName, txtName);
    grid.addRow(1, lblPhone, txtPhone);
    grid.addRow(2, lblAddress, txtAddress);
    grid.addRow(3, paneSize, paneCrust, paneToppings);
    grid.add(paneButtons,2,4);
```

(continued)

Listing 11-2 *(continued)*

```
    // Set alignments and spanning                          →119
    grid.setHalignment(lblName, HPos.RIGHT);
    grid.setHalignment(lblPhone, HPos.RIGHT);
    grid.setHalignment(lblAddress, HPos.RIGHT);
    grid.setColumnSpan(txtName,2);
    grid.setColumnSpan(txtPhone,2);
    grid.setColumnSpan(txtAddress,2);


    // Set column widths                                     →127
    ColumnConstraints col1 = new ColumnConstraints();
    col1.setPercentWidth(33);
    ColumnConstraints col2 = new ColumnConstraints();
    col2.setPercentWidth(33);
    ColumnConstraints col3 = new ColumnConstraints();
    col3.setPercentWidth(33);
    grid.getColumnConstraints().addAll(col1, col2, col3);


    // Create the scene and the stage                        →136
    Scene scene = new Scene(grid);
    primaryStage.setScene(scene);
    primaryStage.setTitle("Pizza Order");
    primaryStage.setMinWidth(500);
    primaryStage.setMaxWidth(900);
    primaryStage.show();

}

public void btnOK_Click()                                   →146
{

    // Create a message string with the customer information
    String msg = "Customer:\n\n";
    msg += "\t" + txtName.getText() + "\n";
    msg += "\t" + txtPhone.getText() + "\n\n";
    msg += "\t" + txtAddress.getText() + "\n";
    msg += "You have ordered a ";

    // Add the pizza size
    if (rdoSmall.isSelected())
        msg += "small ";
    if (rdoMedium.isSelected())
        msg += "medium ";
    if (rdoLarge.isSelected())
        msg += "large ";
```

```
        // Add the crust style
        if (rdoThin.isSelected())
            msg += "thin crust pizza with ";
        if (rdoThick.isSelected())
            msg += "thick crust pizza with ";

        // Add the toppings
        String toppings = "";
        toppings = buildToppings(chkPepperoni, toppings);
        toppings = buildToppings(chkMushrooms, toppings);
        toppings = buildToppings(chkAnchovies, toppings);
        if (toppings.equals(""))
            msg += "no toppings.";
        else
            msg += "the following toppings:\n"
                + toppings;

        // Display the message
        MessageBox.show(msg, "Order Details");
    }

    public String buildToppings(CheckBox chk, String msg)          →185
    {
        // Helper method for displaying the list of toppings
        if (chk.isSelected())
        {
            if (!msg.equals(""))
            {
                msg += ", ";
            }
            msg += chk.getText();
        }
        return msg;
    }

    public void btnCancel_Click()                                  →199
    {
        stage.close();
    }

}
```

The following paragraphs point out the highlights of this program:

→ **32:** A label and text field are created for the customer's name.

→ **40:** A label and text field are created for the customer's phone number.

→ **48:** A label and text field are created for the customer's address.

→ **56:** A label and three radio buttons are created for the pizza's size. The label and radio buttons are added to a VBox named `paneSize`.

→ **70:** A label and two radio buttons are created for the pizza's crust style. The label and radio buttons are added to a VBox named `paneStyle`.

→ **82:** A label and three check boxes are created for the pizza's toppings. The label and check boxes are added to a VBox named `paneToppings`.

→ **92:** The OK and Cancel buttons are created and added to an HBox named `paneButton`.

→ **103:** The grid pane layout is created. The padding and horizontal and vertical gaps are set to 10, and the width is set to range from 500 to 800.

→ **112:** The nodes are added to the pane. The name, phone number, and address labels and text fields are added to rows 0, 1, and 2. Then, the size, crust, and toppings VBox panes are added to row 3. Finally, the HBox that contains the buttons is added to column 2 of row 4. (***Remember:*** Row and column indexes are numbered from 0, not from 1.)

→ **119:** The column alignment and spanning options are set.

→ **127:** Column constraints are created to distribute the column widths evenly.

→ **136:** The scene is created, and the stage is displayed.

→ **146:** The `btnOK_Click` method is called when the user clicks OK. This method creates a summary of the customer's order and displays it using the `MessageBox` class.

→ **185:** `buildToppings` is simply a helper method that assists in the construction of the message string.

→ **199:** The stage is closed when the user clicks the Close button.

Chapter 12

Skinning Your Application with CSS

*O*ne of the most powerful features of JavaFX is its ability to use CSS (which stands for *Cascading Style Sheets*) to control the visual appearance of your user interface. With CSS, you can change the look and feel of your application without actually changing any of the Java code that powers your application. CSS essentially disconnects the visual aspects of your program from the application logic.

The terms *theme* and *skin* are used somewhat interchangeably to refer to the look and feel of an application. A theme or skin governs many aspects of visual appearance, including the font used for text, background fills, border styles and colors, how items react when the mouse is hovered over them, and many more.

In this chapter, I first discuss how to switch an entire application between two of the default themes provided with JavaFX. Then, you discover how to craft your own style sheets and apply them to your scenes.

Using Default Style Sheets

JavaFX comes with two built-in themes: Modena and Caspian. Modena is a new theme that was introduced with JavaFX 8; Caspian is an older theme that was used with previous versions of JavaFX.

Figure 12-1 shows a version of the Pizza Order application that I present in Chapter 11; it includes a pair of radio buttons to allow the user to switch between the Modena and Caspian themes. The window on the left side of the figure shows the Modena theme; the Caspian theme is shown on the right.

Figure 12-1:
A JavaFX application shown in the Modena and Caspian themes.

To switch the theme of an application, use the setUserAgentStylesheet method of the Application class. The Application class defines two static fields that you can use to reference the built-in styles: STYLESHEET_ MODENA and STYLESHEET_CASPIAN. Thus, to set Caspian as the style sheet, use this statement:

```
Application.setUserAgentStylesheet(
    STYLESHEET_CASPIAN);
```

Because the program used to create the screens shown in Figure 12-1 is long and identical to the Pizza Order application presented in Listing 11-2 in Chapter 11, I don't duplicate it in its entirety. The only significant addition to the Pizza Order application is the code that defines the two radio buttons at the bottom-left corner of the scene:

```
ToggleGroup groupTheme = new ToggleGroup();

RadioButton rdoModena =
    new RadioButton("Modena Theme");
rdoModena.setToggleGroup(groupTheme);
rdoModena.setSelected(true);
rdoModena.setOnAction(e ->
    {
        setUserAgentStylesheet(STYLESHEET_MODENA);
    });

RadioButton rdoCaspian =
    new RadioButton("Caspian Theme");
rdoCaspian.setToggleGroup(groupTheme);
rdoCaspian.setOnAction(e ->
    {
        setUserAgentStylesheet(STYLESHEET_CASPIAN);
    });

HBox paneTheme = new HBox(10, rdoModena, rdoCaspian);
```

As you can see, this code creates two radio buttons whose action event handlers set the theme to either Modena or Caspian. These radio buttons are added to a `ToggleGroup` and to an `HBox`. Later in the program, the `HBox` is added to a `GridPane` layout to display in the bottom-left corner of the screen.

Adding a Style Sheet to a Scene

If you want to, you can create a style sheet to replace the Modena or Caspian themes with your own theme, creating an entirely different look and feel for your application. Then, you can apply your style sheet as the application's default style sheet using `Application.setUserAgentStylesheet`, as I describe in the preceding section.

However, creating a completely new theme to apply application-wide can be a difficult task, as your style sheet must provide style information for every possible formattable node element. Instead, you may want to start by creating a smaller style sheet that just provides formatting information for the specific needs of your application. Then, you can apply the style sheet to a specific scene or to an individual node within a scene.

When you apply a style sheet to a scene, any styles contained in that style sheet override any corresponding styles in the application's default style sheet. Similarly, if you apply a style sheet to a specific node, the styles in that style sheet override any corresponding styles in the style sheet applied to the scene.

You can create as many style sheets as you want, applying different style sheets to different parent nodes within the scene. However, you'll find it easier to manage your styles and create consistency if you stick to just one style sheet applied at the scene level.

A style sheet applied to a scene or parent node is actually a separate file with the extension `.css`. The style sheet contains formatting rules that provide the specifics for the formatting you want applied to your application.

You can read about the details of creating a style sheet in the section "Creating a Style Sheet" later in this chapter. For now, I introduce a very simple style sheet named `Simple.css` that specifies the font to use for text and a background color. The `Simple.css` style sheet consists of the following lines:

```
.root
{
    -fx-background-color: lightgray;
    -fx-font-family: "serif";
    -fx-font-size: 12pt;
}
```

The first line specifies that the formatting between the curly braces that follow applies through the entire scene graph. Then, within the curly braces, three formatting rules are used to specify that the background color should be `lightgray`, the font should be `serif`, and the font size should be 12 points.

The easiest way to add a style sheet to a scene is to get the scene's style sheet collection (a scene can have more than one style sheet), use the `add` method to add the style sheet, like this:

```
scene.getStylesheets().add("Simple.css");
```

To keep the code examples in this book simple, the rest of the examples in this chapter use the simple technique shown in the preceding example. However, simply specifying the stylesheet name as the parameter to the `add` method code will work only if the style sheet file resides in the same folder as the application's class file. If the style sheet resides elsewhere, use the following code instead:

```
scene.getStylesheets().add(
    getClass().getResource("Simple.css")
            .toExternalForm());
```

Instead of simply providing the name of the style sheet as a string, this technique calls the getClass method of the Object class, which returns a reference to the application's class. Then, it calls the Class getResource method, which accepts a string parameter that names an external resource (such as a file) that's located on the application's class path. This returns the URL of the Simple.css file. Finally, the toExternalForm method massages the URL into a form acceptable to the getStylesheets.add method.

The window in the top-left part of Figure 12-2 shows a JavaFX application with the Simple.css added to the scene. For comparison, the figure also shows the application without the Simple.css file. As you can see, the style sheet has changed the background color to a darker shade of gray and changed the font to a serif-style font (on Windows computers, Times New Roman is used).

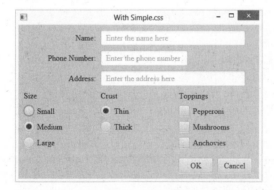

Figure 12-2:
A JavaFX application with and without the Simple.
css file style sheet.

Using Inline Styling

In addition to using separate .css style sheet files, JavaFX lets you apply style rules directly to any node in a scene graph by calling the node's setStyle method, passing the formatting rule as a string argument. For example, the following example sets the font size for a button to 15 points:

```
Button btnOK = new Button("OK");
btnOK.setStyle("-fx-font-size: 15pt");
```

As a general rule, I recommend against using inline styles except for unusual situations. That's because inline styles make it more difficult to change the formatting of your application's user interface. Imagine if you were to apply all style elements using inline styles. If you then decided to make even a simple change, you'd have to search through the entire application code to find the inline styles that need to be changed. Then, you'd have to recompile the program.

In contrast, external style sheets make it easy to change the appearance of your GUI. All you have to do is edit the .css file, and the formatting automatically reflects your changes.

Creating a Style Sheet

Now that you know how to attach styles to an application, scene, or individual node, it's time to turn your attention to the task of actually creating styles. As I mention earlier, a *style sheet* is a simple text file with the extension .css. You can create your style sheets with any standard text editor, including full-featured development studios, such as Eclipse or NetBeans, as well as simple text editors, such as TextPad or Notepad. Save the .css file in the same folder as the application's .java folder.

A style sheet consists of one or more *style rules* that determine the formatting that's applied to various types of elements in a scene. Each style rule consists of a *selector,* which determines which elements the style rule applies to, followed by a *declaration block,* which is a list of *style declarations* contained within a pair of braces. Each declaration consists of a property *name* followed by a colon and a value. Each declaration is terminated by a semi-colon.

For example:

```
.root
{
    -fx-background-color: lightgray;
    -fx-font-family: "serif";
    -fx-font-size: 12pt;
}
```

Here, the first line (.root) indicates that the style applies to all nodes in the scene. The declaration block includes three declarations, which supply values for the three properties named -fx-background-color, -fx-font-family, and -fx-font-size.

The following sections provide additional details about selectors and declarations.

Using type selectors

The most commonly used variety of selectors is a *type selector;* it corresponds to a JavaFX node type, such as Button or TextField. Type selectors begin with a period followed by the *style class name,* which is associated with all JavaFX node types. (**Note:** The terms *style class* and *style type* are used interchangeably.)

For most controls, the name of the style class is similar to the name of the corresponding JavaFX class. To convert a JavaFX class name to a CSS style class name, use all lowercase letters and use a hyphen between words if the JavaFX class name consists of two or more words. The following list includes the CSS style class name for most of the JavaFX classes that have been presented so far in this book.

JavaFX Class	*CSS Style Class*
Button	button
CheckBox	check-box
ChoiceBox	choice-box
ComboBox	combo-box
Label	label
ListCell	list-cell
ListView	list-view
Menu	menu
MenuBar	menu-bar
MenuButton	menu-button
MenuItem	menu-item
RadioButton	radio-button
Separator	separator
TableView	table-view
TextField	text-field
ToggleButton	toggle-button
Tooltip	tooltip
TreeCell	tree-cell
TreeView	tree-view

Creating your own style class names

Every node has a `getStyleClass` method that returns an observable list of style class names. As a result, a given node can have more than one style class name. This can come in handy for scenes that have complicated formatting requirements because it allows you to group controls together for formatting purposes. For example, you can create additional class names to use for buttons if you want one set of buttons to be formatted differently than another set of buttons.

For example, suppose you want to set the font size for some buttons to 16 points. You could do that by creating a style type called `button-large` in the style sheet, like this:

```
.button-large
{
    -fx-font-size: 16pt;
}
```

Then, you could add the `button-large` style class to the list of style classes for the buttons you want formatted with larger type. For example:

```
Button btn1 = new Button("Wow!");
btn1.getStyleClass().add("button-large");
```

When a node has more than one style class name, all the class names will be used when matching selectors in the style sheet. In other words, the buttons that have the additional class named `button-large` will match style rules for both `button` and `button-large`.

Note: For many JavaFX node classes, the default style class collection is empty. For example, layout panes, such as `HBox` and `BorderPane`, do not have a default style class, nor do shape classes such as `Rectangle` or `Circle`. If you want to apply a CSS style to one of these nodes using style types, you must call `getStyleClass().add` to create a style class name for the node.

Using id selectors

If you want to create a style that applies to one and only one node in your scene graph, you can give that node a unique id by calling the node's `setId` method, like this:

```
Button btnOK = new Button("OK");
btnOK.setId("btn-wow");
```

Then, you can create a style rule that applies only to the node whose id is `btnOK`. In the selector, you must prefix the id with a hash mark, like this:

```
#btn-wow
{
    -fx-font-weight: bold;
}
```

The hash mark (#) is not used in the `setId` method to create the id, but it is required in the style sheet.

Node ids must be unique across the entire scene graph. In other words, you cannot create two nodes with the same id. Unfortunately, JavaFX does not enforce this, so it's up to you to make sure that your node ids are unique.

Using multiple selectors

A *style selector* can list more than one style type or id. To do that, you list all the types or ids as part of the selector, separating them with commas. For example, here is a style that's applied to all buttons, radio buttons, and check boxes:

```
.button, .radio-button, .check-box
{
    -fx-font-family: "serif";
}
```

Here's an example that includes several ids:

```
#btn1, #btn2, #btn3, #btn4
{
    -fx-fill: GREEN;
}
```

Specifying Style Properties

Within the declaration block of a style rule, each declaration specifies a style property and a value. For example, to set the font size to 12 points, use `-fx-font-size` as the property name and `12pt` as the value. In all, hundreds of style properties exist. Not all properties apply to all node types, however. Thus, each JavaFX node class has its own set of style properties.

All JavaFX style properties begin with the prefix `-fx-`. The following sections describe some of the more commonly used style properties.

Specifying font properties

For nodes that display text, you can use the properties shown in Table 12-1 to control the text style.

Table 12-1	Font Style Properties
Property	*Value*
`-fx-font-family`	The actual name of the font, or one of the following generic font types: `serif`, `sans-serif`, `cursive`, `fantasy`, or `monospace`.
`-fx-font-size`	A number followed by the unit of measure, which is usually `pt` (points) or `px` (pixels).
`-fx-font-style`	`normal`, `italic`, or `oblique`.
`-fx-font-weight`	`normal`, `bold`, `bolder`, `lighter`, `100`, `200`, `300`, `400`, `500`, `600`, `700`, `800`, or `900`.
`-fx-font`	A shorthand property that combines all other properties mentioned here into a single value that lists the style, weight, size, and family. Separate the values with spaces. If you want, you can omit the style and weight.

The following example sets the font for all button controls:

```
.button
{
    -fx-font-family: sans-serif;
    -fx-font-size: 10pt;
    -fx-font-style: normal;
    -fx-font-weight: normal
}
```

This version does the same thing using the shorthand `font` property:

```
.button
{
    -fx-font: 10pt sans-serif;
}
```

Specifying background colors

The `Region` class has a property named `-fx-background-color` that lets you specify the background color. Because both the `Layout` and `Control` classes inherit `Region`, you can use this property with any layout pane or control.

To apply a background color to a layout pane, you must first give the layout pane a style class name or id so that you can refer to it in a selector.

The following paragraphs describe the possible values you can supply for this property:

- **Named color:** JavaFX defines 148 distinct colors by name, including basic colors such as `black`, `white`, `red`, `orange`, and `blue` as well as exotic colors such as `cornsilk` and `thistle`.

    For example:

    ```
    -fx-background-color: red
    ```

    or

    ```
    -fx-background-color: papayawhip
    ```

    For a complete list of all 148 named colors, consult the CSS reference page online at `http://docs.oracle.com/javase/8/javafx/api/javafx/scene/doc-files/cssref.html#typecolor`.

- **RGB color:** The red-green-blue number of the color. This is usually expressed in hex, with two hex digits for each component of the color. The entire thing is prefixed with a hash like this:

    ```
    -fx-background-color: #f5f5f5
    ```

- **Gradient:** Lets you specify the color as a gradient that creates a smooth transition from one color to another.

    For information about creating gradients, flip to Chapter 13.

- **Lookup color:** A *lookup color* lets you define a set of color names in the `.root` section of the style sheet and then refer to the color name anywhere else within the style sheet.

You can create any name you wish for the color, provided the name doesn't conflict with a JavaFX property. For example:

```
.root
{
    my-color: aliceblue;
}

.button
{
    -fx-background-color: my-color;
}
```

Here, `aliceblue` will be used as the background color for all buttons.

Specifying border properties

The `Region` class also has several style properties that let you create a border around the region. These properties allow you to add borders to layout panes or to add or change the borders in controls. Table 12-2 lists the border style properties.

Table 12-2	Border Style Properties
Property	**Value**
`-fx-border-width`	A number followed by the unit of measure, usually expressed in pixels (px)
`-fx-border-style`	none, solid, dotted, or dashed
`-fx-border-color`	A color

For example, the following style rule applies a dashed border to a style class named `bordered`:

```
.bordered
{
    -fx-border-width: 4px;
    -fx-border-color: black;
    -fx-border-style: dashed;
}
```

Chapter 13

Drawing Shapes

• •

In This Chapter

▶ Creating basic shapes such as lines, rectangles, circles, and ellipses

▶ Creating shapes you can see through

▶ Creating gradient fills

▶ Rotating, translating, and scaling shapes

▶ Drawing some text

▶ Combining shapes with `union`, `intersect`, and `subtract` operations

• •

*W*ere you one of those kids who, way back in school, passed away the boring hours of algebra class by doodling in the margins of the book? If so, you're in luck. Now that you're a grownup and you're mastering JavaFX programming, you don't have to doodle in the book. Instead, you can write programs that doodle onscreen.

This chapter is a brief introduction to the fascinating world of drawing in JavaFX. Specifically, you figure out how to draw two-dimensional objects such as lines, arcs, rectangles, ellipses, and so on. You can set the style used to draw the shape's outline, and you can fill the shape with a solid color, a gradient fill, or text that's created from an image. You can make your shapes solid or transparent, and you can rotate, clip, skew, and do all sorts of other unspeakable things to them.

Introducing the Shape Class

So far in this book, you've read about two types of nodes you can add to a scene graph: controls, which inherit the `Control` class, and layout panes, which inherit the `Pane` class. In this section, you read about how to work with a third type of node: shapes, which (as you might guess) inherit the `Shape` class. Table 13-1 lists some of the most commonly used methods of the `Shape` class.

Table 13-1	The Shape Class
Method	*Description*
`void setFill(Paint value)`	Sets the fill color.
`void setSmooth(boolean value)`	If `true`, anti-aliasing is used to draw the shape more precisely.
`void setStroke(Paint value)`	Sets the color of the stroke used to draw the shape's outline.
`void setStrokeWidth(double value)`	Sets the width of the stroke used to draw the shape's outline.
`void setStrokeType (StrokeType value)`	Sets the position of the stroke relative to the actual outline of the shape. Allowable values are `StrokeType.CENTERED`, `StrokeType.INSIDE`, and `StrokeType.OUTSIDE`.
`void setStrokeLineJoin(Stroke LineJoin value)`	Sets the method used to draw corners. Allowable values are `StrokeLineJoin.MITER`, `StrokeType.BEVEL`, and `StrokeType.ROUND`.
`void setStrokeEndCap(Stroke EndCap value)`	Sets the method used to draw the ends of the stroke line. Allowable values are `StrokeLineCap.BUTT`, `StrokeLineCap.ROUND`, and `StrokeLineCap.SQUARE`.
`static Shape intersect(Shape shape1, Shape shape2)`	Returns a new shape that consists only of those parts of `shape1` and `shape2` that overlap.
`static Shape subtract(Shape shape1, Shape shape2)`	Returns a new shape that is formed by subtracting the `shape2` from `shape1`.
`static Shape union(Shape shape1, Shape shape2)`	Returns a new shape that is formed by adding `shape1` to `shape2`.

There are a total of 12 shapes that inherit the `Shape` class: `Arc`, `Circle`, `CubicCurve`, `Ellipse`, `Line`, `Path`, `Polygon`, `Polyline`, `QuadCurve`, `Rectangle`, `SVGPath`, and `Text`. Table 13-2 shows a basic constructor for each of these classes, and Figure 13-1 shows a scene with a sample of several of them. The code that created this figure is shown in Listing 13-1, later in the chapter.

Table 13-2	Twelve Kinds of Shape Classes
Class Constructor	*Description*
``Arc(double centerX,
double centerY,
double radiusX,
double radiusY,
double startAngle,
double length)```	Creates an *arc,* which is a segment of an ellipse defined by the first four parameters. `startAngle` is the angle in degrees of the starting point of the arc, and `length` is the angular extent of the arc in degrees.
	The `Arc` class also includes a method named `setType` that lets you set the type of the arc. Allowable values are `ArcType.CHORD`, `ArcType.OPEN`, and `ArcType.ROUND`.
``Circle(double centerX,
double centerY,
double radius)```	Creates a circle with the specified center point and radius.
``CubicCurve(double startX,
double startY,
double controlX1,
double controlY1,
double controlX2,
double controlY2,
double endX,
double endY)```	Creates a curve with the specified start and end points and the specified control points.

(continued)

Table 13-2 *(continued)*

Class Constructor	Description

`Ellipse(double centerX,`
`        double centerY,`
`        double radiusX,`
`        double radiusY)`
	Creates an ellipse. `centerX` and `centerY` specify the center point of the ellipse. `radiusX` specifies the horizontal radius of the ellipse, and `radiusY` species the vertical radius.

`Line(double startX,`
`     double startY,`
`     double endX,`
`     double endY)`
	Creates a line with the specified start and end points.

`Path(PathElement...` `elements)`	Creates a path with the specified path elements.
`Polygon (Double... points)`	Creates a polygon with the specified `x,` `y` points as its vertices.
`Polyline (Double... points)`	Creates a polyline with the specified `x,` `y` points as its segments.

`QuadCurve(double startX,`
`          double startY,`
`          double controlX1,`
`          double controlY1,`
`          double controlX2,`
`          double controlY2,`
`          double endX,`
`          double endY)`
	Creates a quadratic curve with the specified start and end points and the specified control points.

`Rectangle(double x,`
`          double y,`
`          double width,`
`          double height)`
	Creates a rectangle. `x` and `y` specify the top-left corner of the rectangle.

`SVGPath()`	Creates a Scalable Vector Graphics (SVG) path.

`Text(double x,`
`     double y,`
`     String text)`
	Creates a text shape with the specified text at the specified `x` and `y` coordinates.

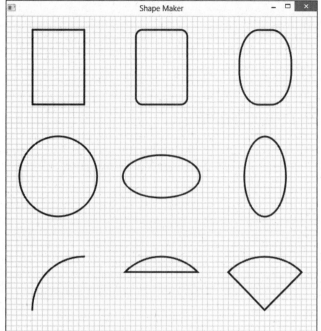

Figure 13-1:
A bunch of
shapes.

Creating lines

The most basic type of shape is a line, created with the Line class. To create a line, you specify the x and y coordinates of the start and end of the line, as in this example:

```
Line line1 = new Line(0, 0, 100, 200);
```

This code creates a line that goes from (0,0) to (100, 200).

The grid lines in Figure 13-1 were drawn by line shapes inside a for loop, like this:

```
for (int i = 0; i <600; i+=10)
{
    Line line1 = new Line(i, 0, i, 600);
    line1.setStroke(Color.LIGHTGRAY);
    Line line2 = new Line(0, i, 600, i);
    line2.setStroke(Color.LIGHTGRAY);
    group1.getChildren().addAll(line1, line2);
}
```

The `for` loop iterates a variable `i` from 0 to 600 in increments of 10. On each iteration of the loop, two lines are created: a vertical line that uses the variable `i` as its x-axis and a horizontal line that uses the variable `i` as its y-axis. The stroke color for each line is set to light gray, and the lines are then added to a `Group` object named `group1`.

Creating rectangles

A rectangle requires an `(x, y)` starting point, a width, and a height. Here's the code that creates the first rectangle shown in Figure 13-1 earlier in this chapter:

```
Rectangle r1 = new Rectangle(50,25,100,140);
r1.setStroke(Color.BLACK);
r1.setFill(null);
r1.setStrokeWidth(3);
```

Here the rectangle starts at `(50, 25)`. Its width is 100, and its height is 140. Notice that the fill color is set to `null` so that the rectangle will be transparent.

You can create a rectangle with rounded corners by calling the `setArcWidth` and `setArcheight` methods. Here's the rounded rectangle in the middle of the first row of shapes shown in Figure 13-1:

```
Rectangle r2 = new Rectangle(250,25,100,140);
r2.setStroke(Color.BLACK);
r2.setFill(null);
r2.setStrokeWidth(3);
r2.setArcWidth(25);
r2.setArcHeight(25);
```

Here, the corners are rounded with an arc whose height and width are both 25.

You can create some interesting shapes by using unequal values for the arc's width and height. For the third shape in the first row of Figure 13-1, arc width is set to 75 and the height to 125:

```
Rectangle r3 = new Rectangle(450,25,100,140);
r3.setStroke(Color.BLACK);
r3.setFill(null);
r3.setStrokeWidth(3);
r3.setArcWidth(75);
r3.setArcHeight(125);
```

Creating circles and ellipses

To create a circle, you use the `Circle` class, specifying the x- and y-coordinates of the center of the circle and the radius. Here's the code that creates the circle in Figure 13-1:

```
Circle c1 = new Circle(100, 300, 75);
c1.setStroke(Color.BLACK);
c1.setFill(null);
c1.setStrokeWidth(3);
```

An *ellipse* is similar to a circle, but has two radii: one in the x-axis, the other in the y-axis. You specify both radii in the constructor. Here's the code that creates the first ellipse in Figure 13-1:

```
Ellipse e1 = new Ellipse(300, 300, 75, 40);
e1.setStroke(Color.BLACK);
e1.setFill(null);
e1.setStrokeWidth(3);
```

The second ellipse is similar, but the x- and y-radii are reversed:

```
Ellipse e2 = new Ellipse(300, 300, 40, 75);
```

Creating arcs

Another useful type of shape is an *arc,* which is a segment of an ellipse. To create an arc, you supply the parameters for the ellipse and then you supply the angle at which the arc begins: 0 is due east (3:00 on a clock face). Finally, you supply the *length,* which represents how much of the ellipse the arc spans and is also expressed in degrees.

The important thing to know is that the arc travels counterclockwise from the starting point. If you specify /90 as the starting point and 90 as the extent, the arc travels from 12:00 high to 9:00, as shown in the first shape in the third row in Figure 13-1.

JavaFX can create three types of arcs, which you can specify via the `setType` method:

✔ **ArcType.OPEN:** Indicates that you want to draw just the arc itself

✔ **ArcType.CHORD:** Means that you want to draw the arc and then connect the ends with a straight line to create a closed shape

✔ **ArcType.ROUND:** Means that you want to use straight lines to connect the ends to the center of the ellipse, thereby creating a shape that looks like a piece of pie

Here's an example that creates the first arc shown in Figure 13-1:

```
Arc a1 = new Arc(150, 550, 100, 100, 90, 90);
a1.setType(ArcType.OPEN);
a1.setStroke(Color.BLACK);
a1.setFill(null);
a1.setStrokeWidth(3);
```

The second arc is created with these statements:

```
Arc a2 = new Arc(300, 550, 100, 100, 45, 90);
a2.setType(ArcType.CHORD);
a2.setStroke(Color.BLACK);
a2.setFill(null);
a2.setStrokeWidth(3);
```

Finally, the third arc (the pie slice) is created by these statements:

```
Arc a3 = new Arc(500, 550, 100, 100, 45, 90);
a3.setType(ArcType.ROUND);
a3.setStroke(Color.BLACK);
a3.setFill(null);
a3.setStrokeWidth(3);
```

Looking at the ShapeMaker program

Now that you've seen how to create a variety of shapes, you're ready to take a glance at Listing 13-1, which draws the shapes shown in Figure 13-1 earlier in this chapter.

Listing 13-1:   The ShapeMaker Program

```
import javafx.application.*;
import javafx.stage.*;
import javafx.scene.*;
import javafx.scene.shape.*;
import javafx.scene.paint.*;

public class ShapeMaker extends Application
{
    public static void main(String[] args)
```

```
{

    launch(args);
}

@Override public void start(Stage primaryStage)
{

    Group group1 = new Group();

    // The background grid
    for (int i = 0; i <600; i+=10)
    {
        Line line1 = new Line(i, 0, i, 600);
        line1.setStroke(Color.LIGHTGRAY);
        Line line2 = new Line(0, i, 600, i);
        line2.setStroke(Color.LIGHTGRAY);
        group1.getChildren().addAll(line1, line2);
    }

    // A rectangle
    Rectangle r1 = new Rectangle(50,25,100,140);
    r1.setStroke(Color.BLACK);
    r1.setFill(null);
    r1.setStrokeWidth(3);
    group1.getChildren().add(r1);

    // A rounded rectangle
    Rectangle r2 = new Rectangle(250,25,100,140);
    r2.setStroke(Color.BLACK);
    r2.setFill(null);
    r2.setStrokeWidth(3);
    r2.setArcWidth(25);
    r2.setArcHeight(25);
    group1.getChildren().add(r2);

    // Another rounded rectangle
    Rectangle r3 = new Rectangle(450,25,100,140);
    r3.setStroke(Color.BLACK);
    r3.setFill(null);
    r3.setStrokeWidth(3);
    r3.setArcWidth(75);
    r3.setArcHeight(125);
    group1.getChildren().add(r3);

    // A circle
    Circle c1 = new Circle(100, 300, 75);
    c1.setStroke(Color.BLACK);
    c1.setFill(null);
    c1.setStrokeWidth(3);
    group1.getChildren().add(c1);
```

(continued)

Listing 13-1 *(continued)*

```java
        // A ellipse
        Ellipse e1 = new Ellipse(300, 300, 75, 40);
        e1.setStroke(Color.BLACK);
        e1.setFill(null);
        e1.setStrokeWidth(3);
        group1.getChildren().add(e1);

        // Another ellipse
        Ellipse e2 = new Ellipse(500, 300, 40, 75);
        e2.setStroke(Color.BLACK);
        e2.setFill(null);
        e2.setStrokeWidth(3);
        group1.getChildren().add(e2);

        // An open arc
        Arc a1 = new Arc(150, 550, 100, 100, 90, 90);
        a1.setType(ArcType.OPEN);
        a1.setStroke(Color.BLACK);
        a1.setFill(null);
        a1.setStrokeWidth(3);
        group1.getChildren().add(a1);

        // A chord arc
        Arc a2 = new Arc(300, 550, 100, 100, 45, 90);
        a2.setType(ArcType.CHORD);
        a2.setStroke(Color.BLACK);
        a2.setFill(null);
        a2.setStrokeWidth(3);
        group1.getChildren().add(a2);

        // A round arc
        Arc a3 = new Arc(500, 550, 100, 100, 45, 90);
        a3.setType(ArcType.ROUND);
        a3.setStroke(Color.BLACK);
        a3.setFill(null);
        a3.setStrokeWidth(3);
        group1.getChildren().add(a3);

        // Create the scene and the stage
        Scene scene = new Scene(group1);
        primaryStage.setScene(scene);
        primaryStage.setTitle("Shape Maker");
        primaryStage.show();
    }
}
```

Fancy Fills

If you've followed along so far, you've already seen that you can fill a shape with a solid color by calling the shape's setFill method and specifying a Color, as in this example:

```
Rectangle r1 = new Rectangle(0,0,100,100);
r1.setFill(Color.RED);
```

Here the rectangle is filled with the color red.

You've also already seen that you can create a fully transparent object by setting the fill color to null. The ShapeMaker program shown in Listing 13-1 used null fills so that the gridlines would show through the shapes.

There's more to filling than solid colors, however. In the following sections, you find out how to create fills that are partially transparent and fills that gradually fade from one color to another.

Drawing transparently

JavaFX lets you create partially transparent colors by setting an opacity value for the color. An opacity value of 1.0 indicates that the color is completely opaque, whereas a value of 0.0 means the color is completely transparent. To create a partially transparent color, you set the opacity value somewhere between 0.0 and 1.0.

There are several ways to do that, but the easiest is to use one of the several static methods of the Color class that create a color from its constituent parts. For your purposes here, I use the rgb method, which accepts four parameters: three integers representing the red, green, and blue components of the color (values can be 0 to 255), and a double that represents the opacity.

For example, to create a 50% transparent black, you'd use the rgb method, like this:

```
Color.rgb(0, 0, 0, 0.5);
```

To create a 20% transparent red, use this:

```
Color.rgb(255, 0, 0, 0.2);
```

Figure 13-2 shows a scene with three rectangles, two of which have transparency applied. The following snippet shows the code used to create these three rectangles:

```
Rectangle r1 = new Rectangle(0,75,350,40);
r1.setStroke(Color.BLACK);
r1.setFill(Color.rgb(200, 200, 200, 1.0));
r1.setStrokeWidth(3);

Rectangle r2 = new Rectangle(50,5,100,200);
r2.setStroke(Color.BLACK);
r2.setFill(Color.rgb(200, 200, 200, 0.5));
r2.setStrokeWidth(3);

Rectangle r3 = new Rectangle(200,5,100,200);
r3.setStroke(Color.BLACK);
r3.setFill(Color.rgb(200, 200, 200, 0.5));
r3.setStrokeWidth(3);
```

As you can see, all three of these rectangles specify a shade of gray by using the values 200, 200, and 200 for the red, green, and blue color components. The first rectangle specifies 1.0 for the opacity; the other two specify 0.5 for the opacity. As a result, you can see the first rectangle behind the other two rectangles.

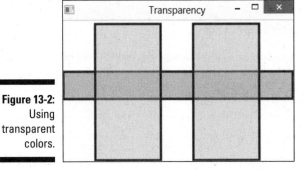

Figure 13-2:
Using
transparent
colors.

Using a gradient fill

Instead of using a solid color, you can specify a *gradient fill,* which blends two colors evenly across the shape. JavaFX provides two classes for working with gradients: `LinearGradient` and `RadialGradient`.

A *linear gradient* is created from two color points. Imagine a line drawn between these two points. The gradient fill varies the color smoothly from the color that's set at the first point to the color set at the second point. Then it extends the colors on this line at 90-degree angles to the line to fill an entire area.

A *radial gradient* is created from a center point of one color and a second color on the radius of a circle. The fill varies the color smoothly from the center color to the outside color.

Table 13-3 shows the constructors for the LinearGradient and Radial Gradient classes, along with the constructor for the Stop class, which is used to specify the colors used for the gradient.

Table 13-3	Constructors for Gradient Classes
Class Constructor	**Description**

`LinearGradient (double startX,`
`                 double startY,`
`                 double endX,`
`                 double endY,`
`                 boolean proportional,`
`                 CycleMethod cycleMethod,`
`                 Stop... stops)`
	Creates a linear gradient. The stops appear along the line defined by the start and end points. Cyclemethod can be `CycleMethod.NO_CYCLE`, `CycleMethod.REPEAT`, or `CycleMethod.REFLECT`.

`RadialGradient (double focusAngle,`
`                 double focusDistance,`
`                 double centerX,`
`                 double centerY,`
`                 double radius,`
`                 boolean proportional,`
`                 CycleMethod cycleMethod,`
`                 Stop... stops)`
	Creates a radial gradient. The stops are circular, starting from the center point of the gradient and extending to the radius. `FocusAngle` is usually set to zero.

(continued)

Table 13-3 *(continued)*

Class Constructor	Description
`Stop(double offset, Color color)`	Defines a color stop on the gradient. The offset is a double that ranges from 0.0 to 1.0. For a linear gradient, 0.0 represents the start point of the gradient and 1.0 represents the end point. For a radial gradient, 0.0 represents the center and 1.0 represents the radius.

Several of the parameters used with these constructors merit a bit of explanation:

- ✔ **Proportional:** This parameter determines the units of measure used for the start and end points for a linear gradient or the center point and radius for a circle. If this parameter is `false`, the coordinates are expressed in pixels. If `true`, the coordinates range from 0.0 to 1.0 and are proportional to the size of the shape being filled. In most cases, it's easier to work with proportional coordinates, so this parameter should usually be set to `true`.

- ✔ **CyclicalMethod:** The default is for a gradient to start with one color, transition to another color, and then end. However, you can create gradients that cycle through their colors repeatedly by using a cycle method other than `NO_CYCLE`. If you specify `REPEAT`, the gradient repeats itself for each cycle. If you specify `REFLECT`, the gradient reverses the order of stops for each cycle.

- ✔ **Stop offset:** The stops represent the colors used for the gradient transition. The offset parameter for a stop determines where along the gradient the stop appears. A value of 0.0 means that the stop appears at the start of a linear gradient or the center of a radial gradient. A value of 1.0 means that the stop appears at the end of the linear gradient or at the radius of a radial gradient.

  All gradients must have at least two stops, one at the start or center and the other at the end or radius. However, you can create more complex gradients by adding additional stops. In that case, the stop offset represents a proportional position along the length of the gradient. For example, a stop offset of 0.5 places the stop at the center of the gradient line or radius.

Also, the start and end stops don't have to be at offset 0.0 or 1.0. For example, if you don't want a bit of solid color on either end of the gradient before the color transition starts, you could specify 0.2 and 0.8 as the start and end stop offsets.

This example creates a gradient fill that varies the color from magenta to yellow:

```
GradientPaint gp =
    new GradientPaint(0, 0, Color.MAGENTA,
                      0, 100, Color.YELLOW);
```

Table 13-4 shows five examples of gradient fills created with the Linear Gradient class and two radial gradients created with the RadialGradient class. Each of the rectangles is 100 × 100 pixels. The table also shows the code used to create each fill.

Table 13-4	Seven Gradient Fills

	`LinearGradient gradient1 =`
	`    new LinearGradient(`
	`        0, 0,`
	`        0, 1,`
	`        true,`
	`        CycleMethod.NO_CYCLE,`
	`        new Stop(0.0, Color.WHITE),`
	`        new Stop(1.0, Color.BLACK));`

	`LinearGradient gradient2 =`
	`    new LinearGradient(`
	`        0, 0,`
	`        1, 0,`
	`        true,`
	`        CycleMethod.NO_CYCLE,`
	`        new Stop(0.0, Color.WHITE),`
	`        new Stop(1.0, Color.BLACK));`

(continued)

Table 13-4 *(continued)*

	`LinearGradient gradient3 =`
	`    new LinearGradient(`
	`        0, 1,`
	`        1, 0,`
	`        true,`
	`        CycleMethod.NO_CYCLE,`
	`        new Stop(0.4, Color.WHITE),`
	`        new Stop(0.6, Color.BLACK));`

	`LinearGradient gradient4 =`
	`    new LinearGradient(`
	`        0, 0,`
	`        0, 0.2,`
	`        true,`
	`        CycleMethod.REPEAT,`
	`        new Stop(0.0, Color.WHITE),`
	`        new Stop(1.0, Color.BLACK));`

	`LinearGradient gradient5 =`
	`    new LinearGradient(`
	`        0, 0,`
	`        0, 0.2,`
	`        true,`
	`        CycleMethod.REFLECT,`
	`        new Stop(0.0, Color.WHITE),`
	`        new Stop(1.0, Color.BLACK));`

	`RadialGradient gradient6 =`
	`    new RadialGradient(`
	`        0, 0,`
	`        0.5, 0.5,`
	`        0.5,`
	`        true,`
	`        CycleMethod.NO_CYCLE,`
	`        new Stop(0.0, Color.WHITE),`
	`        new Stop(1.0, Color.BLACK));`

```
RadialGradient gradient7 =
    new RadialGradient(
        0, 0,
        0.5, 0.5,
        0.1,
        false,
        CycleMethod.REFLECT,
        new Stop(0.2, Color.WHITE),
        new Stop(0.8, Color.BLACK));
```

Translating, Scaling, and Rotating

This section describes several methods of the `Node` class that are especially useful when working with shapes:

- ✔ The `setTranslateX` and `setTranslateY` methods moves the `(0, 0)` point from the top-left corner to any arbitrary point.

- ✔ The `setScaleX` and `setScaleY` methods let you change the scale of a shape so that it appears smaller or larger.

- ✔ The `rotate` method rotates the component's coordinate system so that shapes are drawn at an angle.

Note: These methods can be used for any node in the scene graph, and any transformations you apply to one node are inherited by any children of that node. If you apply a transformation to the root node of a scene, the transformation effectively applies to the entire scene.

For example, Figure 13-3 shows the ShapeMaker program that was presented in Listing 13-1 after its root node has been rotated and translated. The only difference between the program that produces this output and the program in Listing 13-1 is the addition of the following three lines:

```
group1.setRotate(30);
group1.setTranslateX(110);
group1.setTranslateY(110);
```

The first line rotates the root node 30 degrees. Then, the next two lines translate the root node 110 pixels in both the x- and the y-axis.

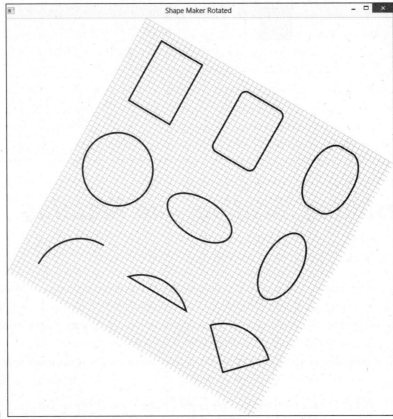

Figure 13-3:
The Shape
Maker
program
rotated and
translated.

Scaling changes the relative size of the x- or the y-axis, which allows you to zoom in or out on a single shape or, if you scale the root node, the entire scene. You'll usually want to scale both the x- and y-axis together, unless you want to intentionally exaggerate just one axis. Here's an example that doubles the size of the entire scene (assuming group1 is the root node):

```
group1.setScaleX(200);
group1.setScaleY(200);
```

Drawing Text

You can use the Text class to draw the text contained in a string. A Text object is similar to a Label object, but with one major difference: A Text object is a Shape, whereas a Label is a Control. Because a text object is a shape, you can format it using any of the methods that apply to shapes. For example, you can apply an outline color to a shape and fill it with a gradient fill or set the fill color to `null`.

The `Text` constructor accepts three parameters: the string to be drawn and the x- and y-coordinates of the bottom-left corner of the first character to be drawn (technically speaking, the start of the *baseline* for the text). Here's an example:

```
Text text1 = new Text("Hello, World!" 100, 50);
```

Here the string `"Hello, World!"` is drawn at point `(100, 50)`.

You can change the font by calling the `setFont` method, which accepts a `Font` object. The constructor for the `Font` class accepts a string value that represents the font name and a size. Here's how to set the font to 60-point Times New Roman:

```
text1.setFont(new Font("Times New Roman", 60));
```

The following example shows how a `Text` shape can be formatted with an outline stroke and a gradient fill:

```
LinearGradient gradient1 =
    new LinearGradient(
        0, 0,
        0, 1,
        true,
        CycleMethod.NO_CYCLE,
        new Stop(0.2, Color.WHITE),
        new Stop(0.8, Color.BLACK));

Text text1 = new Text(100, 300, "Hello, World!");
text1.setFont(new Font("Times New Roman", 200));
text1.setStroke(Color.BLACK);
text1.setStrokeWidth(2);
text1.setFill(gradient1);
```

Figure 13-4 shows how this text object appears when displayed in a scene.

Figure 13-4:
A text shape with an outline and gradient fill.

Combining Shapes

The final topic for this chapter is using three methods of the `Shape` class that let you create complicated shapes by combining shapes in various ways. These methods are

- ✔ `intersect`: Accepts two shapes and returns a new shape that consists only of the parts of the two shapes that overlap
- ✔ `union`: Combines two shapes by adding the shapes to one another
- ✔ `subtract`: Creates a new shape by subtracting one shape from another

These methods are static methods that are defined by the `Shape` class. Each accepts two shape objects and returns a new shape object that's created from the two shapes passed as parameters. For example, the following snippet creates a new shape by combining two existing shapes, named `shape1` and `shape2` using the `union` method:

```
Shape shape3 = Shape.union(shape1, shape2);
```

The best way to understand the difference among `intersect`, `union`, and `subtract` is to see all three in action. Figure 13-5 shows such an example. At the top left, you can see two circles that overlap. The top right shows a `union` of two similar circles. The bottom left shows an `intersect` from two similar circles, and the bottom right shows a `subtract` of two similar circles. The code for this program is shown in Listing 13-2.

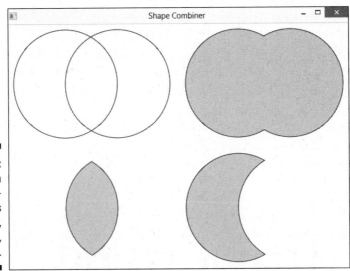

Figure 13-5:
A program that combines circles with union, intersect, and subtract.

Listing 13-2:   The Shape Combiner program

```
import javafx.application.*;
import javafx.stage.*;
import javafx.scene.*;
import javafx.scene.shape.*;
import javafx.scene.paint.*;

public class ShapeCombiner extends Application
{
    public static void main(String[] args)
    {
        launch(args);
    }

    @Override public void start(Stage primaryStage)
    {

        Group group1 = new Group();                            →17

        Circle circle1 = new Circle(110, 110, 100);            →19
        Circle circle2 = new Circle(210, 110, 100);
        Circle circle3 = new Circle(440, 110, 100);
        Circle circle4 = new Circle(540, 110, 100);
        Circle circle5 = new Circle(110, 340, 100);
        Circle circle6 = new Circle(210, 340, 100);
        Circle circle7 = new Circle(440, 340, 100);
        Circle circle8 = new Circle(540, 340, 100);

        Shape union = Shape.union(circle3, circle4);           →28
        Shape intersect = Shape.intersect(circle5, circle6);   →29
        Shape subtract = Shape.subtract(circle7, circle8);     →30

        circle1.setFill(null);                                 →32
        circle1.setStroke(Color.BLACK);

        circle2.setFill(null);
        circle2.setStroke(Color.BLACK);

        union.setStroke(Color.BLACK);                          →38
        union.setFill(Color.LIGHTGRAY);

        intersect.setStroke(Color.BLACK);
        intersect.setFill(Color.LIGHTGRAY);

        subtract.setStroke(Color.BLACK);
        subtract.setFill(Color.LIGHTGRAY);
```

(continued)

Listing 13-2 *(continued)*

```
        group1.getChildren().addAll(circle1, circle2, union,      →47
            intersect, subtract);
        Scene scene = new Scene(group1);
        primaryStage.setScene(scene);
        primaryStage.setTitle("Shape Combiner");
        primaryStage.show();
    }
}
```

The following paragraphs describe the high points of the Shape Combiner program:

→ **17:** A Group is created to hold the circles and composite shapes displayed by this program.

→ **19:** These lines create eight circle objects, positioned on the scene in four groups of two.

→ **28:** The Shape.union method is called to create a Shape object named union by combining circles 3 and 4.

→ **29:** The Shape.intersect method is called to create a Shape object named intersect that is the overlapping portions of circles 5 and 6.

→ **30:** The Shape.subtract method is called to create a Shape object named subtract that is the result of subtracting circle 8 from circle 7.

→ **32:** These lines set the stroke and fill for circles 1 and 2.

→ **38:** These lines set the stroke and fill for the union, intersect, and subtract shapes.

→ **47:** This line adds circles 1 and 2 as well as the union, intersect, and subtract shapes to the group container, which serves as the root container for the scene.

Chapter 14

Adding Special Effects

• •

• •

W*elcome to the Special Effects chapter! Here, you read about how to embellish the appearance of the nodes in your scene graph by adding special effects such as blurs, shadows, color displacements, glows, and so on. You can even add perspective to give your application a three-dimensional look without having to do actual 3D programming.

You probably won't win an Oscar for any of the special effects described in this chapter, but at the least you'll have fun!

Introducing Special Effects

Special effects in JavaFX derive from the `Effect` class, an abstract class that has a wide variety of subclasses you can use to create a special effect. There are a total of 17 subclasses of the `Effect` class, but I don't have room to cover all 17 of them here. Instead, this chapter focuses on those effects that let you make your shapes look more realistic by adding blurriness, shadows, reflections, and glow.

All the effects presented in this chapter work in a similar way. First, you create an instance of the effect's class by calling its default constructor. Then, you optionally set the properties of the effect by calling one or more `set` methods. (In many cases, the default property values are appropriate, so you can often skip this step.) Finally, you apply the effect to a node by calling the node's `setEffect` method.

For example, here's a bit of code that creates a rectangle, fills it, and then adds a drop shadow:

```
Rectangle r1 = new Rectangle(50, 50, 100, 100);
r1.setFill(Color.LIGHTGRAY);
r1.setStroke(Color.BLACK);
r1.setStrokeWidth(2);

DropShadow shadow1 = new DropShadow();
r1.setEffect(shadow1);
```

Figure 14-1 shows the outcome of this effect. As you can see, the rectangle is surrounded by a subtle shadow.

Figure 14-1:
A rectangle with a shadow.

The setEffect method is defined by the Node class, which means that you can apply an effect to any node in your scene graph. The effect is applied not only to the node whose setEffect method you call, but also to any children of that node. In fact, if you call setEffect on a scene's root node, the effect will be applied to the entire scene.

Adding Shadows

You may have noticed that the shadow in the example shown in Figure 14-1 doesn't look very realistic. That's because it's directly behind the rectangle, as if the light source causing the shadow were dead ahead. Usually, we expect shadows to be at a slight angle from the object casting the shadow, most often below the object and offset to one side.

Fortunately, the DropShadow class has several properties that let you control the size and positioning of the shadow. Those methods are listed in Table 14-1, which lists the details not only of the DropShadow class but also of its sister class, InnerShadow. The InnerShadow class creates a shadow inside of a shape instead of outside the shape. I get to the InnerShadow class in a moment. For now, I focus on DropShadow.

Table 14-1   The DropShadow and InnerShadow Classes

Constructor	Explanation
DropShadow()	Creates a new DropShadow effect with default settings.
InnerShadow()	Creates a new InnerShadow effect with default settings.
Common Methods	**Explanation**
void setColor(Color value)	Sets the color to use for the shadow. The default is BLACK.
void setWidth(double value)	Sets the width of the shadow. The default is 21.
void setHeight(double value)	Sets the height of the shadow. The default is 21.
void setOffsetX(double value)	The horizontal offset for the shadow. The default is 0.
void setOffsetY(double value)	The vertical offset for the shadow. The default is 0.
void setRadius(double value)	The radius of the shadow's blur effect. The default is 10.
DropShadow Only	**Explanation**
void setSpread (double value)	The proportion (from 0.0 to 1.0) of the shadow that should be a solid color rather than blurred. The default is 0.
InnerShadow only	**Explanation**
void setChoke (double value)	The proportion (from 0.0 to 1.0) of the shadow that should be a solid color rather than blurred. The default is 0.

The methods of the DropShadow class allow you to specify the exact geometry of the shadow you want applied. The setWidth and setHeight methods let you specify the size of the shadow, and the setOffsetX and setOffsetY methods let you change the location of the shadow relative to the center of the shape. Typically, you'll add a positive x- and y-offset so that the shadow appears below and to the right of the shape, like this:

```
DropShadow shadow1 = new DropShadow();
shadow1.setOffsetX(10);
shadow1.setOffsetY(10);
```

In this example, the shadow is placed 10 pixels to the right and 10 pixels below the shape.

The `setRadius` method lets you specify the size of the blur effect applied to the edges of the shadow. The larger this number, the fuzzier the shadow will appear. You can also control the *spread*, which indicates what portion of the shadow's blur should be solid color before the blur effect kicks in. (I find that the effect of the spread setting is difficult to discern, so I usually don't set it.)

Figure 14-2 shows a JavaFX application that demonstrates nine variations of the basic drop shadow.

Figure 14-2:
Drop
shadows.

To create these shadowed rectangles, I created a utility method named createShadowedBox. Here's the code for this method:

```
Rectangle createShadowedBox(double size,
    double shadowWidth, double shadowHeight,
    double offsetX, double offsetY,
    double radius)
{
    Rectangle r = new Rectangle(size, size);
    r.setFill(Color.LIGHTGRAY);
    r.setStroke(Color.BLACK);
    r.setStrokeWidth(2);

    DropShadow e = new DropShadow();
    e.setWidth(shadowWidth);
    e.setHeight(shadowHeight);
    e.setOffsetX(offsetX);
    e.setOffsetY(offsetY);
    e.setRadius(radius);
    r.setEffect(e);
    return r;
}
```

As you can see, this method accepts six parameters: the size of the rectangle to create (the rectangle is actually a square, so the size is used for both the width and the height), the width and height of the shadow, the x- and y-offsets for the shadow, and the shadow's blur radius. The method starts by creating a rectangle. Then, it creates a drop shadow, applies the width, height, x-offset, y-offset, and radius, and then applies the effect to the rectangle and returns the rectangle.

To create the actual shadowed rectangles, I called the createShadowBox method nine times, using different parameter values:

```
Rectangle r1 = createShadowedBox(100, 10, 10,  5,  5, 10);
Rectangle r2 = createShadowedBox(100, 20, 20, 10, 10, 10);
Rectangle r3 = createShadowedBox(100, 30, 30, 15, 15, 10);

Rectangle r4 = createShadowedBox(100, 20, 20,  0,  0, 10);
Rectangle r5 = createShadowedBox(100, 20, 20,  0, 10, 10);
Rectangle r6 = createShadowedBox(100, 20, 20, 10,  0, 10);

Rectangle r7 = createShadowedBox(100, 20, 20, 10, 10,  0);
Rectangle r8 = createShadowedBox(100, 20, 20, 10, 10, 20);
Rectangle r9 = createShadowedBox(100, 20, 20, 10, 10, 50);
```

For the first set of three, I varied the size and offset of the shadow, in each, using the same values for width and height and for the x-offset and the y-offset. Thus, the first row of rectangles in Figure 14-2 show various placements of the shadow below and to the right of the rectangles.

For the next set of three, I set the x-offset or y-offset to zero to demonstrate variations of the offset. And for the final set of three, I varied the radius. Notice that when the radius is set to 0, the shadow's edges are crisp. With larger radius values, the shadow gets more blurry.

Figure 14-3 shows how inner shadows work. For this figure, I changed just one line of code in the `createShadowBox` method: Instead of creating a `DropShadow`, I created an `InnerShadow`:

```
InnerShadow e = new InnerShadow();
```

As you can see, the `InnerShadow` class places the shadow on the inside of the rectangle rather than on the outside.

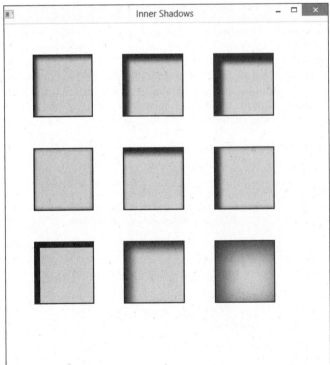

Figure 14-3:
Inner
shadows.

Creating Reflections

A *reflection* projects an inverted copy of the shape in front of and below the shape, creating the impression that the shape is sitting on a reflective surface. You can create a reflection by using the Reflection class, whose members are shown in Table 14-2.

Table 14-2	The Reflection Class
Constructor	*Explanation*
Reflection()	Creates a new Reflection effect with default settings.
Methods	*Explanation*
void setBottomOpacity (double value)	The opacity (0.0 to 1.0) at the bottom edge of the reflection. The default is 0.
void setFraction(double value)	The portion of the shape that will be reflected. The default is 0.75.
void setTopOffset(double value)	The distance between the bottom of the shape and the start of the reflection. The default is 0.
void setTopOpacity(double value)	The opacity (0.0 to 1.0) at the top of the reflection. The default is 0.5.

Figure 14-4 shows a Text shape with a reflection applied. I used the following code to create this shape:

```
Text t = new Text("Reflection");
t.setFont(new Font("Times New Roman", 96));
t.setFill(Color.LIGHTGRAY);
t.setStroke(Color.BLACK);
t.setEffect(new Reflection());
```

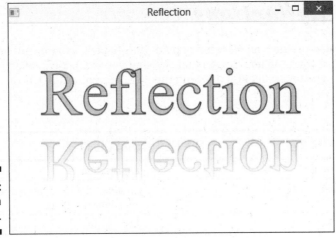

Figure 14-4:
A text with a
reflection.

Making Things Blurry

JavaFX provides three effects classes that can make an object blurry. Each of these classes uses a different method for applying the blur:

- ✔ **BoxBlur:** Applies a simple and efficient blurring technique in which each pixel in the blurred region is calculated by averaging its neighboring pixels in the input image.
- ✔ **GaussianBlur:** Uses a Gaussian blurring algorithm, which is more accurate but less efficient than a box blur.
- ✔ **MotionBlur:** Blurs the shape directionally, creating the effect of motion.

Table 14-3 shows the members of the three blur effect classes.

Table 14-3   The BoxBlur, GaussianBlur, and MotionBlur Classes

Constructors	Explanation
BoxBlur()	Creates a new BoxBlur effect with default settings.
GaussianBlur()	Creates a new GaussianBlur effect with default settings.
MotionBlur()	Creates a new MotionBlur effect with default settings.

BoxBlur Methods	Explanation
`void setHeight(double value)`	Sets the vertical size of the blur effect.
`void setWidth(double value)`	Sets the horizontal size of the blur effect.
`void setIterations(int value)`	Sets the number of times the effect should be repeated. The default is `1`.
GaussianBlur Methods	**Explanation**
`void setRadius(double value)`	The radius of the blur effect. The default is `10.0`.
MotionBlur Methods	**Explanation**
`void setAngle(double value)`	The angle of the motion effect, in degrees. The default is `0.0`.
`void setRadius(double value)`	The radius of the blur effect. The default is `10`.

Figure 14-5 shows the effect of each of these blur types on a text shape. I used the following code to create these three blurs:

```
Text t1 = new Text("BoxBlur");
t1.setFont(new Font("Times New Roman", 60));
t1.setFill(Color.LIGHTGRAY);
t1.setStroke(Color.BLACK);
t1.setEffect(new BoxBlur());

Text t2 = new Text("GaussianBlur");
t2.setFont(new Font("Times New Roman", 60));
t2.setFill(Color.LIGHTGRAY);
t2.setStroke(Color.BLACK);
t2.setEffect(new GaussianBlur());

Text t3 = new Text("MotionBlur");
t3.setFont(new Font("Times New Roman", 60));
t3.setFill(Color.LIGHTGRAY);
t3.setStroke(Color.BLACK);
t3.setEffect(new MotionBlur());
```

As you can see, I used default values for each of the blurs. If you wish, you can use the methods listed in Table 14-3 to tweak the appearance of the blur effects.

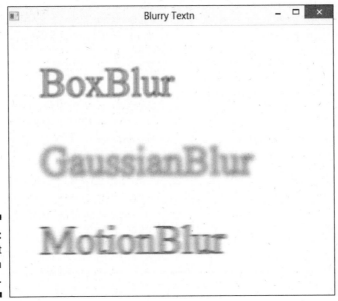

Figure 14-5:
Three text
objects with
blur effects.

Blooming and Glowing

Tonight, on a very special episode of *Blossom* (or should that be, a very special episode of *The Big Bang Theory?*), you find out how to make your ordinary JavaFX shapes bloom and glow, all with the help of two simple classes, unsurprisingly named `Bloom` and `Glow`. Table 14-4 shows the members of these two classes.

Table 14-4	The Bloom and Glow Classes
Constructor	*Explanation*
`Bloom()`	Creates a new `Bloom` effect with default parameters.
`Glow()`	Creates a new `Glow` effect with default parameters.
Bloom Method	*Explanation*
`void setThreshhold (double value)`	Sets the luminosity threshold. The bloom effect will be applied to portions of the shape that are brighter than the threshold. The value can be 0.0 to 1.0. The default value is `0.3`.
Glow Method	*Explanation*
`void setLevel(double value)`	Sets the intensity of the effect's glow level. The value can be 0.0 to 1.0. The default value is `0.3`.

Figure 14-6 shows the effect of the `Bloom` and `Glow` effects. All three of the text shapes shown in the figure are combined with a rectangle in a group. I used the following code to create the first group (shown at the top of the figure):

```
Rectangle r1 = new Rectangle(50, 50, 400, 100);
r1.setFill(Color.BLACK);
r1.setStroke(Color.BLACK);

Text t1 = new Text("Plain Text");
t1.setX(130);
t1.setY(125);
t1.setFont(new Font("Times New Roman", 60));
t1.setFill(Color.LIGHTGRAY);

Group g1 = new Group();
g1.getChildren().addAll(r1, t1);
```

I used the similar code to create the second group (shown in the middle of the figure), but added a `Bloom` effect:

```
Rectangle r2 = new Rectangle(50, 50, 400, 100);
r2.setFill(Color.BLACK);
r2.setStroke(Color.BLACK);

Text t2 = new Text("Blooming Text");
t2.setX(70);
t2.setY(125);
t2.setFont(new Font("Times New Roman", 60));
t2.setFill(Color.LIGHTGRAY);

Group g2 = new Group();
g2.getChildren().addAll(r2, t2);

Bloom e1 = new Bloom();
e1.setThreshold(0.3);
g2.setEffect(e1);
```

For the third group, I added a `Glow` effect instead:

```
Rectangle r3 = new Rectangle(50, 50, 400, 100);
r3.setFill(Color.BLACK);
r3.setStroke(Color.BLACK);

Text t3 = new Text("Glowing Text");
t3.setX(80);
t3.setY(125);
t3.setFont(new Font("Times New Roman", 60));
t3.setFill(Color.LIGHTGRAY);
```

```
Group g3 = new Group();
g3.getChildren().addAll(r3, t3);
Glow e2 = new Glow();

e2.setLevel(1.0);
g3.setEffect(e2);
```

The difference between the bloom and glow effect is subtle. To be honest, it's barely noticeable. If you look very closely, you'll see that the glowing text is just a tad brighter than the blooming text. (The distinction between glow and bloom is more noticeable when colors other than black and white are used.)

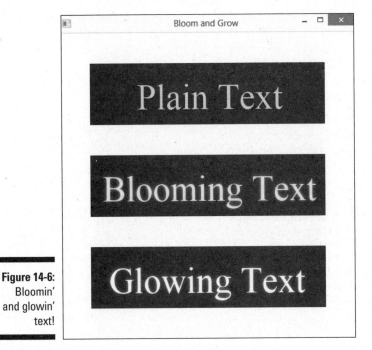

Figure 14-6:
Bloomin'
and glowin'
text!

Gaining Perspective

The `PerspectiveTransform` class lets you distort a shape so that it appears to have a three-dimensional effect. *Note:* This is not the same thing as creating actual three-dimensional shapes in your scene graph; it simply distorts the geometry of a node to create a perspective effect.

The `PerspectiveTransform` class works by mapping the corners of the original shape's bounding rectangle to an arbitrary quadrilateral. (The *bounding rectangle* is a rectangle that fully contains a shape, and a *quadrilateral* is any four-cornered shape.) All you have to supply is the x- and y-coordinates of each corner of the quadrilateral, using the methods listed in Table 14-5.

Table 14-5	The PerspectiveTransform Class
Constructor	**Explanation**
`PerspectiveTransform()`	Creates a new `Perspective Transform` effect with default parameters.
Methods	**Explanation**
`void setUlx(double value)`	Sets the upper-left corner x-coordinate.
`void setUly(double value)`	Sets the upper-left corner y-coordinate.
`void setUrx(double value)`	Sets the upper-right corner x-coordinate.
`void setUry(double value)`	Sets the upper-right corner y-coordinate.
`void setLlx(double value)`	Sets the lower-left corner x-coordinate.
`void setLly(double value)`	Sets the lower-left corner y-coordinate.
`void setLrx(double value)`	Sets the lower-right corner x-coordinate.
`void setLry(double value)`	Sets the lower-right corner y-coordinate.

To illustrate how the perspective transform works, I apply it to a chessboard created with the following bit of code:

```
Group board = new Group();
boolean isLight = true;
int size = 50;

for (int rank = 0; rank < 8; rank++)
{
    for (int file = 0; file < 8; file++)
```

```
        {
            Rectangle r = new Rectangle(size, size);
            r.setX(file * size);
            r.setY(rank * size);
            if (isLight)
                r.setFill(Color.LIGHTGRAY);
            else
                r.setFill(Color.DARKGRAY);
            isLight = !isLight;
            board.getChildren().add(r);
        }
        isLight = !isLight;
}
```

This code uses a set of nested `for` loops to draw the ranks (rows) and files (columns) of the chessboard using 50x50 rectangles of alternating color. The `isLight` Boolean variable is used to keep track of the color of each square; this value is inverted after each rectangle is drawn. The `isLight` value is inverted after each file is drawn so that the subsequent file starts with the opposite color. Figure 14-7 shows how the chessboard appears when displayed in a scene.

Figure 14-7:
A chess-board with no perspective.

The entire chessboard occupies a 400x400 square. To add perspective, I create a `PerspectiveTransform` effect that maps the 400x400 square chessboard to a quadrilateral with the following corner coordinates:

Corner	Original x, y	New x, y
Upper Left	0, 0	100, 100
Upper Right	400, 0	450, 100
Lower Left	0, 400	0, 300
Lower Right	400, 400	400, 300

The code to accomplish this transformation looks like this:

```
PerspectiveTransform e = new PerspectiveTransform();

e.setUlx(100);      // Upper left
e.setUly(100);

e.setUrx(450);      // Upper right
e.setUry(100);

e.setLlx(0);        // Lower left
e.setLly(300);

e.setLrx(400);      // Lower right
e.setLry(300);

board.setEffect(e);
```

Figure 14-8 shows how the chessboard looks when this perspective transform is applied.

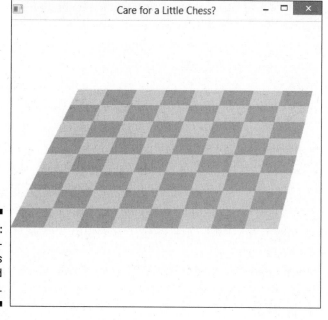

Figure 14-8: The chessboard has gained perspective.

Combining Effects

By now, I hope you'll agree that JavaFX special effects can have a major impact on the appearance of your scenes. But wait, there's more! JavaFX lets you improve the appearance of your scenes even more by allowing you to combine special effects, essentially laying one effect atop another.

To combine effects, you use the setInput method, which is available for all the effects classes I cover in this chapter. Simply put, you create an instance of an effect class, create an instance of a second effects class, and chain the first to the second by calling the first effect's setInput method and specifying the second effect as the input.

For example, suppose you want to combine a reflection with a shadow and then apply the combined effect to a rectangle. You can do so like this:

```
Rectangle rect = new Rectangle(100,100);
DropShadow shadow = new DropShadow();
Reflection reflect = new Reflection();
reflect.setInput(shadow);
rect.setEffect(reflect);
```

In this example, the shadow effect will first be rendered on the rectangle. Then, the reflection effect will be rendered on the rectangle, creating a reflection of both the rectangle and its shadow.

Figure 14-9 shows how the chessboard that was created in the preceding section appears with a drop shadow chained to the perspective transform. The code that creates the perspective and shadow effects is as follows:

```
PerspectiveTransform e = new PerspectiveTransform();

e.setUlx(100);     // Upper left
e.setUly(100);

e.setUrx(450);     // Upper right
e.setUry(100);

e.setLlx(0);       // Lower left
e.setLly(300);

e.setLrx(400);     // Lower right
e.setLry(300);

DropShadow shadow = new DropShadow();
shadow.setWidth(20);
shadow.setHeight(20);
```

```
shadow.setOffsetX(20);
shadow.setOffsetY(20);
shadow.setRadius(30);
e.setInput(shadow);board.setEffect(e);

board.setEffect(e);
```

As you can see, the perspective transform is applied to the chessboard and its shadow, creating a realistic effect of the chessboard floating above a surface.

Figure 14-9:
The chess-
board with a
shadow.

Part IV
Making Your Programs Come Alive

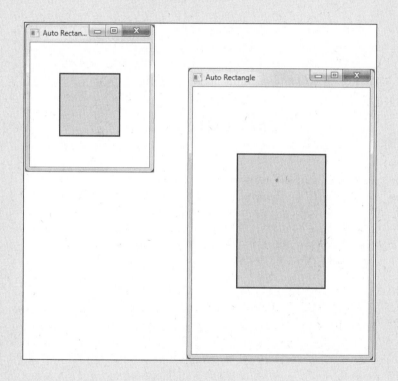

In this part . . .

- ✔ Working with properties
- ✔ Adding visuals and sound
- ✔ Incorporating animation effects
- ✔ Gesturing with touch devices
- ✔ Visit `www.dummies.com/extras/javafx` for great Dummies content online.

Chapter 15

Using Properties to Create Dynamic Scenes

*I*n this chapter, you discover how to use a powerful feature of JavaFX — properties. Simply put, a JavaFX *property* is an observable value that's exposed by a class. Properties are observable in the sense that you can attach listeners to them. These listeners can be invoked whenever the value of the property changes or becomes unknown.

One of the best features of properties is that you can *bind* to them, or connect properties together so that when one property changes, the other property is adjusted automatically. In other words, binding allows two properties to be synchronized. When one property changes, the other property changes as well.

In this chapter, I discuss the basics of working with properties. First, you read about how to create your own properties. Then, you figure out how to attach listeners to properties so your code can respond when the property value changes or becomes invalid. And finally, I tell you how to bind.

Introducing JavaFX Properties

In object-oriented programming parlance, a *property* is a value that represents the state of an instantiated object which can be retrieved and in some cases set by users of the object. In some object-oriented programming languages, such as C#, the concept of properties is built in to the language. Alas, such is not the case with Java. Java has no built-in features for implementing properties . . . at least, not until now.

Prior to Java 8, Java developers usually followed the pattern of using property getters and setters to retrieve and set property values. A property *getter* is a public method that retrieves the value of a property, and a *setter* is a public method that sets the value of a property.

For example, suppose you're creating a class that represents a customer, and each customer is identified by a unique customer number. You might store the customer number internally as a private field named `customerNumber`. Then, you'd provide a public method named `getCustomerNumber` to return the customer's number and another public method named `setCustomerNumber` to set the customer number. The resulting code would look like this:

```
class Customer
{
    private int customerNumber;

    public int getCustomerNumber()
    {
        return customerNumber;
    }

    public void setCustomerNumber(int value)
    {
        customerNumber = value;
    }
}
```

This pattern of using getter and setter methods has a name: the *accessor pattern*. (No, this has nothing to do with property taxes. Property taxes are determined by an *assessor,* not an *accessor.*)

JavaFX 8 introduces a new scheme for implementing properties, which dutifully follows the accessor pattern. As a result, JavaFX classes that implement properties must provide a getter and a setter that returns and sets the value of the properties (unless the property is read-only, in which case only a `get` method is required).

However, instead of using a simple field to represent the value of the property, JavaFX uses special property classes to represent properties. These classes encapsulate the value of a property in an object that provides the new whiz-bang features that enable you to listen for changes in the property value or bind properties together.

When JavaFX properties are used, the getter and setter methods return the value that's encapsulated by the property object. In addition to the getter and setter methods, JavaFX properties introduce a third method which returns the actual property itself. This allows users of the property to directly access the property object, which in turn lets them access those new whiz-bang features.

Naming conventions are an essential aspect of using JavaFX properties correctly. Every property has a name, which by convention begins with a lowercase letter. For example, a property that represents a person's first name might be called firstName. The getter and setter methods are created by capitalizing the property name and prefixing it with the word get or set. The method that returns the property object is the name of the property (uncapitalized) followed by the word Property.

Thus, a class that implements a read/write property named firstName must expose three methods:

```
getFirstName

setFirstName

firstNameProperty
```

If the property is read-only, the setFirstName method would be omitted.

Java API Properties

All the JavaFX API classes that are presented in this book make extensive use of properties. In fact, just about every API get or set method is actually a property getter or setter, and has a corresponding method that returns the property itself.

For example, consider the TextField class, which has methods named getText and setText that get and set the text contained in the text field. These methods are actually getters and setters for a property named text, and the TextField class has a method named textProperty that provides direct access to the text property.

Likewise with the HBox class: It has properties named alignment, hgrow, padding, and spacing which correspond to the getAlignment, setAlignment, getHgrow, setHgrow, getPadding, setPadding, getSpacing, and setSpacing methods.

So far in this book, you've had no need to access the properties directly, so you've relied on the getter and setter methods to manipulate the property values. Later in this chapter, when you discover how to bind property values, you see that accessing these properties can be very useful.

In the next few sections, I discuss how to create your own JavaFX properties. Even if you never create JavaFX properties for your own classes, knowing how to do so will help you understand the benefits of working with the properties that are defined as part of the standard JavaFX API classes.

JavaFX Property Classes

At the heart of JavaFX properties is a collection of classes that create property objects. There are a lot of them, as JavaFX provides four important classes for each of its basic data types, and property classes are provided for ten different data types. Do the math: That means there are 40 property classes. The following paragraphs describe the four classes for String properties:

- **ReadOnlyStringProperty:** An abstract class that represents a read-only property whose value can be read but not modified.

- **StringProperty:** Another abstract class that represents a read-write property. This class extends ReadOnlyStringProperty.

- **SimpleStringProperty:** This is the class that you instantiate to create a read/write string property.

- **ReadOnlyStringWrapper:** This is the class you instantiate to create a read-only string property. The use of this class is a bit confusing, so I won't explain it quite yet. You see how it works in the section "Creating a Read-Only Property" later in this chapter.

For your reference, Table 15-1 lists all 40 of the classes used to create properties of the various types.

Table 15-1	JavaFX Property Classes
Boolean Classes	***Long Classes***
ReadOnlyBooleanProperty	ReadOnlyLongProperty
BooleanProperty	LongProperty
SimpleBooleanProperty	SimpleLongProperty
ReadOnlyBooleanWrapper	ReadOnlyLongWrapper
Double Classes	***Map***
ReadOnlyDoubleProperty	ReadOnlyMapProperty<K,V>
DoubleProperty	MapProperty<K,V>
SimpleDoubleProperty	SimpleMapProperty<K,V>
ReadOnlyDoubleWrapper	ReadOnlyMapWrapper<K,V>
Float Classes	***Object Classes***
ReadOnlyFloatProperty	ReadOnlyObjectProperty<T>
FloatProperty	ObjectProperty<T>
SimpleFloatProperty	SimpleObjectProperty<T>
ReadOnlyFloatWrapper	ReadOnlyObjectWrapper<T>
Integer Classes	***Set Classes***
ReadOnlyIntegerProperty	ReadOnlySetProperty<E>
IntegerProperty	SetProperty<E>
SimpleIntegerProperty	SimpleSetProperty<E>
ReadOnlyIntegerWrapper	ReadOnlySetWrapper<E>
List Classes	***String Classes***
ReadOnlyListProperty<E>	ReadOnlyStringProperty
ListProperty<E>	StringProperty
SimpleListProperty<E>	SimpleStringProperty
ReadOnlyListWrapper<E>	ReadOnlyStringWrapper

Note that four of the types shown in Table 15-1 — List, Map, Object, and Set — are generic. For the List and Set classes, you must specify the element type for the underlying list and set collections; for the Map type, you need to specify types for the keys and values. The Object property classes let you create properties of any type you wish, but you must specify the type so that JavaFX can enforce type safety.

Creating a Read/Write Property

To create a basic property whose value can be read and written, you need to use two of the classes for the property type: the property class of the correct type and the corresponding simple property. For example, to create a property of type `Double`, you need to use both the `DoubleProperty` class and the `SimpleDoubleProperty` class.

Here are the steps to create a read/write property:

1. **Create a local field for the property using the property class for the correct type.**

   The field should be defined with `private` visibility, and it should be `final`. For example:

   ```
   private String Property firstName;
   ```

2. **Create an instance of the property using the simple property class of the correct type.**

   The constructor for the simple property type accepts three parameters, representing the object that contains the property (usually specified as `this`, a string that represents the name of the property, and the property's default value). For example:

   ```
   firstName = new SimpleStringProperty(this,
       "firstName", "");
   ```

   Here, `this` is specified as the containing object, `firstName` is the name of the property, and the default value is an empty string.

   It is often convenient to declare the private property field and instantiate the property in the same statement, like this:

   ```
   StringProperty firstName =
       new SimpleStringProperty(this,
           "firstName", "");
   ```

3. **Create a getter for the property.**

   The getter method name should be `public` or `protected`, it should be `final`, it should follow the property naming convention (`get` followed by the name of the property with an initial cap), and it should return a value of the underlying property type. It should then call the private property's `get` method to retrieve the value of the property, like this:

   ```
   public final String getFirstName
   {
       return firstName.get();
   }
   ```

4. Create a setter for the property.

The setter method name should by `public` or `protected`, it should be `final`, it should follow the property naming convention (`set` followed by the name of the property with an initial cap), and it should accept a parameter value of the underlying property type. It should then call the private property's `set` method to set the property to the passed value. For example:

```
public final void setFirstName(String value)
{
    firstName.set(value);
}
```

5. Create the property accessor.

This method should return the property object itself:

```
public final StringProperty firstNameProperty()
{
    return firstName;
}
```

Notice that the type is `StringProperty`, not `SimpleStringProperty`.

6. Repeat the entire procedure for every property in your class.

Here's a complete example that implements a read/write property named `firstName` in a class named `Customer`:

```
public class Customer
{
    StringProperty firstName =
        new SimpleStringProperty(this,
            "firstName", "");

    public final String getFirstName
    {
        return firstName.get();
    }

    public final void setFirstName(String value)
    {
        firstName.set(value);
    }

    public final StringProperty firstNameProperty()
    {
        return firstName;
    }
}
```

Creating a Read-Only Property

Although a read-only property has less functionality than a read/write property, it's actually more complicated to implement. Why? Because internally — within the class that contains the read-only property — you need to be able to read or write the value of the property. But externally — that is, outside of the class that defines the read-only property — you must ensure that users can read but not write the property value.

You might think that omitting the setter method would be enough to create a read-only property. But the problem is that in addition to getter and setter methods, JavaFX properties also expose a property accessor method that provides direct access to the property object itself.

The following is an example of how *not* to create a read-only property:

```
StringProperty firstName =
    new SimpleStringProperty(this,
        "firstName", "");

public final String getFirstName()
{
    return firstName.get();
}

public final StringProperty firstNameProperty()
{
    return firstName;
}
```

This code is the same as the code used to create a read/write property in the preceding section, except that I omitted the setFirstName method. Unfortunately, this property definition does not prevent users of the class that defines the property from modifying the property. To do so, all the user would need to do is access the property and then call the property's set method directly.

For example, suppose this property is part of a class named Customer, an instance of which is referenced by the variable cust. The following code would set the value of the read-only property:

```
cust.getFirstName().set("Bogus Value");
```

To safely create a read-only property, you must actually create two copies of the property: a read-only version and a read/write version. The read-only version will be exposed to the outside world. The read/write version will be used internally, within the class that defines the property. Then, you must synchronize these two properties so that whenever the value of the internal read/write property changes, the value of the external read-only property is updated automatically.

To accomplish this, JavaFX provides two additional classes for each property data type: a read-only property class and a read-only wrapper class. The read-only property class is the one you share with the outside world via the property accessor method. The read-only wrapper class is the one you use to create the private field used to reference the property within the program.

Here's a complete example that implements a read-only integer property named `customerNumber` in a class named `Customer`:

```
public class Customer
{
    ReadOnlyIntegerWrapper customerNumber =
        new ReadOnlyIntegerWrapper(this,
            "customerNumber", 0);

    public final Integer getCustomerNumber()
    {
        return customerNumber.get();
    }

    public final ReadOnlyIntegerProperty()
        customerNumberProperty()
    {
        return customerNumber.getReadOnlyProperty();
    }

    // more class details go here

}
```

The key to understanding how this works is realizing that the read-only wrapper class is an extension of the simple property class which adds just one new method: `getReadOnlyProperty`, which returns a read-only copy of the simple property. This read-only copy is automatically synchronized with the simple property, so that whenever a change is made to the underlying simple property, the value of the read-only property will be changed as well.

Creating Properties More Efficiently

The advanced capabilities of JavaFX properties, which you'll come to appreciate in the final sections of this chapter, do not come without a cost. Specifically, instantiating a property object takes more memory and processing time than creating a simple field-based property. And in many classes, the advanced capabilities of a JavaFX property object are only occasionally needed. This, instantiating property objects for every property in a class whether the object is needed or not, is wasteful.

In this section, I show you a technique for creating properties in which the property objects themselves are not instantiated until the property accessor itself is called. That way, the property object is not created unless it is actually needed. Here are the details of this technique:

1. **Declare a private field to hold the data represented by the property.**

   For example, for a string property, you create a `String` variable. For the variable name, use the name of the property prefixed by an underscore, like this:

   ```
   private final String _firstName = "";
   ```

2. **Create, but do not instantiate, a private variable to represent the property object.**

   In other words, declare the variable but do not call the class constructor:

   ```
   private final SimpleStringProperty firstName;
   ```

3. **Create the getter.**

   In the getter, use an `if` statement to determine whether the property object exists. If it does, return the value from the property. If it doesn't, return the value of the private field. For example:

   ```
   public final String getFirstName()
   {
       if (firstName == null)
           return _firstName;
       else
           return firstName.get();
   }
   ```

4. **Create the setter.**

   Use the same technique in the setter:

```
public final void setFirstName(String value)
{
    if (firstName == null)
        _firstName = value;
    else
        firstName.set(value);
}
```

5. Create the property accessor.

In this method, first check whether the property object exists and create
the object if it does not exist. Use the value of the private field as the initial value of the property. Then, return the object:

```
public final StringProperty firstNameProperty()
{if (firstName == null)
        firstName = new SimpleStringProperty(
            this, "firstName", _firstName);
    return firstName;
}
```

Here's what it looks like put together in a class named Customer:

```
Public class Customer
{
    private final String _firstName = "";
    private final SimpleStringProperty firstName;

    public final String getFirstName()
    {
        if (firstName == null)
            return _firstName;
        else
            return firstName.get();
    }

    public final void setFirstName(String value)
    {
        if (firstName == null)
            _firstName = value;
        else
            firstName.set(value);
    }

    public final StringProperty firstNameProperty()

    {           if (firstName == null)
            firstName = new SimpleStringProperty(
                this, "firstName", _firstName);
        return firstName;
    }
}
```

Using Property Events

JavaFX properties provide an `addListener` method that lets you add event handlers that are called whenever the value of a property changes. You can create two types of property event handlers:

- ✔ A **change listener,** which is called whenever the value of the property has been recalculated. The change listener is passed three arguments: the property whose value has changed, the previous value of the property, and the new value.

- ✔ An **invalidation listener,** which is called whenever the value of the property becomes unknown. This event is raised when the value of the property needs to be recalculated, but has not yet been recalculated. An invalidation event listener is passed just one argument: the property object itself.

Change and invalidation listeners are defined by functional interfaces named `ChangeListener` and `InvalidationListener`. Because these interfaces are functional interfaces, you can use Lambda expressions to implement them. Here's how you use a Lambda expression to register a change listener on the `text` property of a text field named `text1`:

```
text1.textProperty().addListener(
    (observable, oldvalue, newvalue) ->
        // code goes here
    );
```

Here's an example that registers an invalidation listener:

```
text1.textProperty().addListener(
    (observable) ->
        // code goes here
    );
```

The only way the `addListener` knows whether you are registering a change listener or an invalidation listener is by looking at the arguments you specify for the Lambda expression. If you provide three arguments, `addListener` registers a change listener. If you provide just one argument, an invalidation listener is installed.

Listing 15-1 shows a simple JavaFX application that uses change listeners to vary the size of a rectangle automatically with the size of the stack pane that contains it. A change listener is registered with the stack pane's width property so that whenever the width of the stack pane changes, the width of the rectangle is automatically set to half the new width of the stack pane. Likewise, a change listener is registered on the height property to change the rectangle's height.

Figure 15-1 shows this application in action. This figure shows the initial window displayed by the application as well as how the window appears after the user has made the window taller and wider. As you can see, the rectangle has increased in size proportionately.

Listing 15-1: The Auto Rectangle Program

```
import javafx.application.*;
import javafx.stage.*;
import javafx.scene.*;
import javafx.scene.layout.*;
import javafx.scene.shape.*;
import javafx.scene.paint.*;

public class AutoRectangle extends Application
{
    public static void main(String[] args)
    {
        launch(args);
    }

    @Override public void start(Stage primaryStage)
    {

        Rectangle r = new Rectangle(100,100);              →18
        r.setFill(Color.LIGHTGRAY);
        r.setStroke(Color.BLACK);
        r.setStrokeWidth(2);

        StackPane p = new StackPane();                     →23
        p.setMinWidth(200);
        p.setPrefWidth(200);
        p.setMaxWidth(200);
        p.setMinHeight(200);
```

(continued)

Listing 15-1 *(continued)*

```
        p.setPrefHeight(200);
        p.setMaxHeight(200);

        p.getChildren().add(r);

        p.widthProperty().addListener(                        →33
            (observable, oldvalue, newvalue) ->
                r.setWidth((Double)newvalue/2)
            );

        p.heightProperty().addListener(                       →38
            (observable, oldvalue, newvalue) ->
                r.setHeight((Double)newvalue/2)
            );

        Scene scene = new Scene(p);
        primaryStage.setScene(scene);
        primaryStage.setTitle("Auto Rectangle");
        primaryStage.show();
    }

}
```

The following paragraphs describe the highlights:

→ **18:** These lines create a 100x100 rectangle and set the rectangle's fill color, stroke color, and stroke width.

→ **23:** These lines create a stack pane and set its width and height properties.

→ **33:** These lines use a Lambda expression to register a change handler with the stack pane's width parameter. When the stack pane's width changes, the width of the rectangle is set to one half of the stack pane's width.

→ **38:** These lines use a Lambda expression to register a change handler with the stack pane's height parameter. When the stack pane's height changes, the height of the rectangle is set to one half of the stack pane's height.

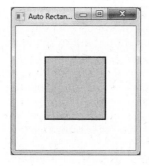

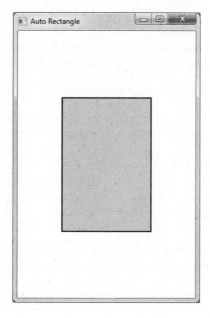

Figure 15-1:
The Auto
Rectangle
program in
action.

Binding Properties

JavaFX *property binding* allows you to synchronize the value of two properties so that whenever one of the properties changes, the value of the other property is updated automatically. Two types of binding are supported:

- ✔ **Unidirectional binding:** With unidirectional binding, the binding works in just one direction. For example, if you bind property A to property B, the value of property A changes when property B changes, but not the other way around.

- ✔ **Bidirectional binding:** With bidirectional binding, the two property values are synchronized so that if either property changes, the other property is automatically changed as well.

Setting up either type of binding is surprisingly easy. Every property has a bind and a bindBiDirectional method. To set up a binding, simply call this method, specifying the property you want to bind to as the argument.

Here's an example that creates a unidirectional binding on the text property of a label to the text property of a text field, so that the contents of the label always displays the contents of the text field:

```
lable1.textProperty().bind(text1.textProperty());
```

With this binding in place, the text displayed by label1 is automatically updated, character by character, when the user types data into the text field.

The following example shows how to create a bidirectional binding between two text fields, named text1 and text2:

```
text1.textProperty()
    .bindBidirectional(text2.textProperty());
```

With this binding in place, any text you type into either text field will be replicated automatically in the other.

To show how binding can be used in a complete program, Listing 15-2 shows a program with two text fields with a pair of labels bound to each. The first text field accepts the name of a character in a play, and the second text field accepts the name of an actor. The labels display the actor who will play the role, as shown in Figure 15-2.

Listing 15-2:   The Role Player Program

```java
import javafx.application.*;
import javafx.stage.*;
import javafx.scene.*;
import javafx.scene.layout.*;
import javafx.geometry.*;
import javafx.scene.control.*;

public class RolePlayer extends Application
{
    public static void main(String[] args)
    {
        launch(args);
    }
```

```
TextField txtCharacter;
TextField txtActor;

@Override public void start(Stage primaryStage)
{

    // Create the Character label
    Label lblCharacter = new Label("Character's Name:");
    lblCharacter.setMinWidth(100);
    lblCharacter.setAlignment(Pos.BOTTOM_RIGHT);

    // Create the Character text field
    txtCharacter = new TextField();
    txtCharacter.setMinWidth(200);
    txtCharacter.setMaxWidth(200);
    txtCharacter.setPromptText("Enter the name of the character here.");

    // Create the Actor label
    Label lblActor = new Label("Actor's Name:");
    lblActor.setMinWidth(100);
    lblActor.setAlignment(Pos.BOTTOM_RIGHT);

    // Create the Actor text field
    txtActor = new TextField();
    txtActor.setMinWidth(200);
    txtActor.setMaxWidth(200);
    txtActor.setPromptText("Enter the name of the actor here.");

    // Create the Role labels
    Label lblRole1 = new Label("The role of ");
    Label lblRole2 = new Label();
    Label lblRole3 = new Label(" will be played by ");
    Label lblRole4 = new Label();

    // Create the Character pane
    HBox paneCharacter = new HBox(20, lblCharacter, txtCharacter);
    paneCharacter.setPadding(new Insets(10));

    // Create the Actor pane
    HBox paneActor = new HBox(20, lblActor, txtActor);
    paneActor.setPadding(new Insets(10));

    // Create the Role pane
    HBox paneRole = new HBox(lblRole1, lblRole2, lblRole3, lblRole4);
    paneRole.setPadding(new Insets(10));
```

(continued)

Listing 15-2 *(continued)*

```
        // Add the Character and Actor panes to a VBox
        VBox pane = new VBox(10, paneCharacter, paneActor, paneRole);

        // Create the bindings
        lblRole2.textProperty().bind(txtCharacter.textProperty());
        lblRole4.textProperty().bind(txtActor.textProperty());


        // Set the stage
        Scene scene = new Scene(pane);
        primaryStage.setScene(scene);
        primaryStage.setTitle("Role Player");
        primaryStage.show();      }
}
```

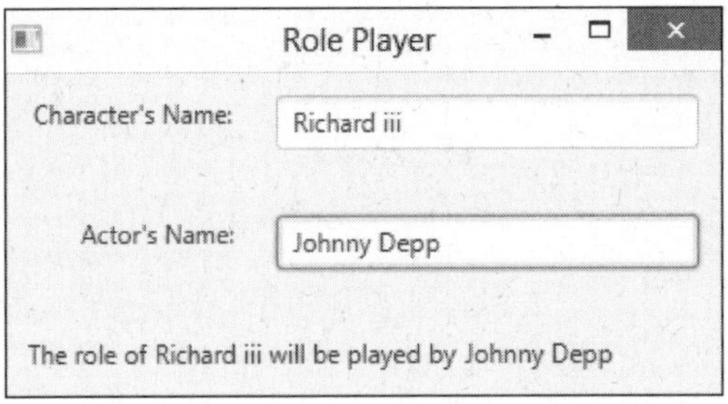

Figure 15-2:
The Role
Player appli-
cation in
action.

Chapter 16

Using Images and Media

So far in this book, all the JavaFX applications have been pretty boring. They've had plenty of labels, text fields, combo boxes, and the like, but no pictures, sounds, or movies!

This chapter remedies that situation. You find out how to incorporate graphic images (that is, pictures — not necessarily images of a graphic nature) into your JavaFX applications. Just to make things interesting, I show you how to throw in sound effects and music, as well as video, too.

Using Images

An *image* is a file that contains a picture. Java supports pictures in several formats, including .jpg, .png, .gif, and .bmp. To incorporate images into your applications, you need to use two classes: Image and ImageView. The Image class represents an image in memory, whereas the ImageView class is a Node that you can add to a scene graph to display an Image on the screen.

Both of these classes are in the package javafx.scene.image, so you need to add the following statement to your programs:

```
import javafx.scene.image.*;
```

Using the Image class

To load an image from an external source, such as a disk file or a web location, you use the Image class. This class has six constructors, detailed in Table 16-1.

Table 16-1	The Image Class
Constructor	**Description**
Image(InputStream in)	Creates an image by reading from the specified input stream.
Image(InputStream in, double width, double height, boolean preserveRatio, boolean smooth)	Creates an image by reading from the specified input stream and resizes it according to the width and height you specify. preserveRatio indicates whether the aspect ratio of the original image should be preserved, and smooth indicates whether image smoothing should be applied.
Image(String url)	Creates an image by reading from the specified URL.
Image(String url, boolean backgroundLoading)	Creates an image by reading from the specified URL. If backgroundLoading is true, the image is loaded in the background (that is, on a separate thread).
Image(String url, double width, double height, boolean preserveRatio, boolean smooth)	Creates an image by reading from the specified URL. This constructor specifies the width and height of the resulting image and indicates whether the aspect ratio of the original image should be preserved and whether image smoothing should be applied.
Image(String url, double width, double height, boolean preserveRatio, boolean smooth, boolean backgroundLoading)	Creates an image by reading from the specified web path and resizes it according to the width and height you specify. preserveRatio indicates whether the aspect ratio of the original image should be preserved, and smooth indicates whether image smoothing should be applied. If backgroundLoading is true, the image is loaded in the background (that is, on a separate thread).

The easiest way to load an image is to do so directly from a file on your local computer by specifying a file path in the `Image` constructor. The file path string should be prefaced by the protocol string `file:`. For example, the following constructor creates an `Image` object from a file named `pic001.jpg` in the folder `C:\Pictures`:

```
Image img = new Image("file:C:\\Pictures\\pic001.jpg");
```

You can also specify a web location using the `http:` protocol, as in this example:

```
Image img = new Image("http://www.domain.com/pic001.jpg");
```

Notice in the web example that you don't have to double the slashes because HTTP addresses use forward slashes, not backward slashes.

In many cases, you want to load an image from a `File` object. To do that, use the `File` object's `toURI` method to get the correct path from the file. ***Note:*** `toURI` returns an object of type `URI`; you must then call `getString` to convert the `URI` to a string:

```
File f = new File("C:\\Pictures\\pic001.jpg");
Image img = new Image(f.toURI().toString());
```

Here, a file is created from the path `C:\Pictures\pic001.jpg`. Then, an image is created from the file.

When you create an `Image` object, you can specify that the image should be resized by providing the width and height parameters. You'll also need to provide two `boolean` arguments. The first specifies whether you want JavaFX to preserve the image's aspect ratio (that is, the ratio of width to height). If you specify `true`, the image may contain blank areas above and below or left and right as needed to preserve the image's aspect ratio. If you specify `false`, the image may be distorted.

The second `boolean` argument specifies whether you want JavaFX to apply a smoothing algorithm to improve the clarity of the image. The smoothing process makes the image look better, but takes time.

Finally, you can specify an optional third `boolean` argument that indicates that you want the image to load in the background. This causes the image loading process to be spun off to a separate thread so that your main application thread can continue without waiting for the image to load.

Using the ImageView class

While the `Image` class holds an image in memory, the `ImageView` class displays an image on the screen. `ImageView` is a subclass of `Node`, which allows you to add an image view to the scene graph. The basic constructor accepts an `Image` object, like this:

```
Image img = new Image("file:C:\\Pictures\\pic001.jpg");
ImageView iview1 = new ImageView(img);
```

Then, you can add the image view to a layout pane and display it in your scene, just like any other node.

By default, the image view will display the image at full size. More often than not, you want to constrain the size by calling the `setFitWidth` and `setFitHeight` methods, and you want to call the `setPreserveRatio` method to ensure that the aspect ratio of the original image is preserved when it is resized. For example:

```
iview1.setFitWidth(200);
iview1.setFitWidth(200);
iview1.setPreserveRatio(true);
```

Here, the size of the displayed image is 200x200. Figure 16-1 shows how this image appears when displayed in a scene.

Figure 16-1:
Displaying
an image.

Displaying a single image in two or more image views is perfectly acceptable. For example:

```
Image img = new Image("file:C:\\Pictures\\pic001.jpg");
ImageView iview1 = new ImageView(img);
ImageView iview2 = new ImageView(imt);
```

Because an image view is a node, you can apply special effects to it, as I describe in Chapter 14. For example, here's a snippet of code that loads an image, places it into two image views, and then applies a motion blur to the second image view:

```
Image img = new Image("file:C:\\Pictures\\pic001.jpg");

ImageView iview1 = new ImageView(img);
iview1.setFitWidth(300);
iview1.setFitHeight(300);
iview1.setPreserveRatio(true);

ImageView iview2 = new ImageView(img);
iview2.setFitWidth(300);
iview2.setFitHeight(300);
iview2.setPreserveRatio(true);

MotionBlur blur = new MotionBlur();
blur.setRadius(25);
blur.setAngle(180);
iview2.setEffect(blur);
```

Figure 16-2 shows how this image appears in the two image views, the second of which has a motion blur effect.

Figure 16-2:
Applying an effect to an image.

Normal   Motion Blur

Viewing an Image example

To show how the elements presented in the preceding two sections work together, Listing 16-1 shows a complete program that uses the Image and ImageView class to display all the images contained in a folder named C:\Pictures on the local file system.

This program uses the Java File class to access the files in the folder. If you want more information about this class, please see my book, *Java All-in-One For Dummies,* 4th Edition (Wiley Publishing, Inc., of course).

Figure 16-3 shows the screen displayed by this program. As you can see, the name of the folder being accessed is displayed in the window title bar, and the name of each image is displayed by a Text field beneath each image. The images are placed in a TilePane so that they are automatically laid out in rows and columns and scroll bars are displayed as necessary.

Figure 16-3:
The Photo
Viewer
application
in action.

Listing 16-1:   The Photo Viewer Application

```
import javafx.application.*;
import javafx.stage.*;
import javafx.scene.*;
import javafx.scene.layout.*;
import javafx.scene.control.*;
import javafx.scene.image.*;
import javafx.scene.shape.*;
import javafx.scene.text.*;
import javafx.geometry.*;
import java.io.*;
import java.util.*;
```

```
public class PhotoViewer extends Application
{
    public static void main(String[] args)
    {
        launch(args);
    }

    private final String PATH = "C:\\Pictures";                    →19

    @Override public void start(Stage primaryStage)
    {
        TilePane tile = new TilePane();                            →23
        tile.setHgap(20);
        tile.setVgap(20);
        tile.setPadding(new Insets(20));
        tile.setPrefColumns(4);

        File dir = new File(PATH);                                 →29
        File[] files = dir.listFiles();                            →30
        for (File f : files)                                       →31
        {
            Image img = new Image(f.toURI().toString(),            →33
                200, 200, true, true);

            ImageView iview = new ImageView(img);                  →36
            iview.setFitWidth(200);
            iview.setFitHeight(200);
            iview.setPreserveRatio(true);

            Text txt = new Text(f.getName());                      →41
            txt.setFont(new Font("Times New Roman", 16));

            Region spacer = new Region();                          →44

            VBox box = new VBox(10, iview, spacer, txt);           →46
            box.setVgrow(spacer, Priority.ALWAYS);
            box.setAlignment(Pos.CENTER);

            tile.getChildren().add(box);                           →50
        }

        ScrollPane scroll = new ScrollPane(tile);                  →53
        scroll.setMinWidth(920);
        scroll.setMinHeight(450);

        Scene scene = new Scene(scroll);                           →57
        primaryStage.setScene(scene);
        primaryStage.setTitle("Photo Viewer - " + PATH);
        primaryStage.show();
    }
}
```

The following paragraphs hit the highlights of this program:

→ **19:** The PATH variable is declared here so that the class can access it.

→ **23:** A TilePane is created, and its properties initialized. The tile pane will have a horizontal and vertical gap of 20 pixels and padding of 20 pixels on all four sides. Each row will show four images.

→ **29:** Next, a File object is created to access the folder specified in the PATH variable. For simplicity, no error handling is provided for the file processing. In an actual program, of course, this section of code should be enclosed in a try block.

→ **30:** A list of the files in the directory is retrieved by the listFiles method. The list is returned as an array of File objects.

→ **31:** A for loop iterates over the list of files in the folder.

→ **33:** For each file, an Image object is created. The toURI method is called to get the path to the file, and the image is resized to 200x200 pixels. Because this loop may process a lot of images, resizing the images is necessary to conserve memory.

→ **36:** An ImageView is then created for the image. Its width and height are set to 200.

→ **41:** A Text object is created to show the filename for the image. The font is set to 16-point Times New Roman.

→ **44:** A Region is created to use as a spacer so that the Text objects will be aligned properly even if the images in the row are of different heights.

→ **46:** A VBox is created to hold the image view, spacer, and text nodes. Note that the vgrow property of the spacer is set to always expand. This forces the text objects to align across the row.

→ **50:** The VBox is added to the TilePane.

→ **53:** The TilePane is added to a scroll pane.

→ **57:** The ScrollPane is added to the scene, and the scene is displayed on the stage.

Playing Audio Files

JavaFX provides built-in support for playing audio files in common formats such as .mp3, .wav, and .aiff. Video files can be .mp4 or .flv. You only need to concern yourself with two classes: Media and MediaPlayer, designed to be analogous to the Image and ImageViewer classes you can read about earlier in this chapter.

Both the `Media` and `MediaPlayer` classes are in the package `javafx.scene.media`, so you need to add the following `import` statement to your program:

```
import javafx.scene.media.*;
```

To create a `Media` object, call the `Media` class constructor and specify the URI (Uniform Resource Identifier) to the media file. If you're accessing a file from the local file system, the best way to get a valid URI is to first create a `File` object using a standard file path for the file. Then, call `toURI().toString()` on the `File` object to get the correct URI. Here's an example that assumes the local file path is in the variable named `PATH`:

```
File f = new File(PATH);
Media media = new Media(f.toURI().toString());
```

After you obtain a `Media` object, you can easily play it by using the `MediaPlayer` class:

```
MediaPlayer mplayer = new MediaPlayer(media);
mplayer.setAutoPlay(true);
```

Here, the `MediaPlayer` constructor accepts the `Media` object as its only parameter. The `setAutoPlay` method directs the media player to play the audio clip as soon as it finishes loading.

The `MediaPlayer` class is *not* a subclass of `Node`. That means that you can't add a media player to the scene graph. If you want to display standard media controls such as play, stop, and pause buttons, you must manually create those buttons and use them to manipulate the media player object. The `MediaPlayer` has methods named `play`, `pause`, and `stop` to accomplish this.

Listing 16-2 shows a complete example that loads and plays a media clip when the user clicks a button. The example assumes that the media clip is named `574928main_houston_problem.mp3`. This is a recording of astronaut Jim Lovell saying his famous line, "Houston, we've had a problem," from the Apollo 13 mission. I chose this audio clip because you can freely download it from NASA's website. Just browse to `www.nasa.gov/connect/sounds`, scroll down to the Apollo and Mercury section, right-click Apollo 13: Houston, We've Had a Problem, and choose Save Target As. I saved it to the folder `C:\Media`. If you save it to a different location or use a different `.mp3` file, you have to adjust the `PATH` variable accordingly.

Listing 16-2:   Playing an Audio File

```
import javafx.application.*;
import javafx.stage.*;
import javafx.scene.*;
import javafx.scene.layout.*;
import javafx.scene.control.*;
import javafx.scene.media.*;
import javafx.geometry.*;
import java.io.*;

public class AudioApp extends Application
{
    public static void main(String[] args)
    {
        launch(args);
    }

    private final String PATH =                                    →17
        "C:\\Media\\574928main_houston_problem.mp3";

    @Override public void start(Stage primaryStage)
    {
        Button btn = new Button("Play Audio");                     →22
        btn.setOnAction(e -> playMedia());

        HBox box = new HBox(20, btn);                              →25
        box.setPadding(new Insets(20));

        Scene scene = new Scene(box);                              →28
        primaryStage.setScene(scene);
        primaryStage.setTitle("Media Player");
        primaryStage.show();
    }

    private void playMedia()                                       →34
    {
        File f = new File(PATH);
        Media media = new Media(f.toURI().toString());
        MediaPlayer mplayer = new MediaPlayer(media);
        mplayer.setAutoPlay(true);
    }
}
```

The following paragraphs describe the high points of this program:

→ **17:** A final variable named PATH specifies the path to the audio file to be loaded.

→ **22:** A button is used to initiate the playing of the media file. The button's action event handler calls the playMedia method.

→ **25:** The button is added to an HBox.

→ **28:** The HBox is added to the scene, and the scene is displayed.

→ **34:** The playMedia method loads the audio file into a Media object and then creates a MediaPlayer to play the sound.

If your application needs to frequently play short sounds, use the AudioClip class instead of the Media and MediaPlayer classes for those sounds. The AudioClip class is designed to quickly load small sound files and then let you play them at will by calling the play method. Here's an example that loads a file whose path is specified by the PATH variable:

```
AudioClip clip1 = new AudioClip(PATH);
```

After the clip loads, you can play it at will by calling the play method:

```
clip1.play();
```

Playing Video Files

Playing video files is similar to playing audio files, with one crucial difference: To play a video file, you must first add a MediaView control to the scene graph. Unlike MediaPlayer, MediaView *is* a subclass of Node, so you can manipulate it in the same manner you can manipulate any other node. In other words, you can control its size and position, and you can even translate or rotate it or apply special effects.

The MediaView class accepts a MediaPlayer in its constructor. To play a video file, you first create a Media object that loads the video file. Then, you create a MediaPlayer object that plays the video. And finally, you use a MediaView object to visualize the video file.

Listing 16-3 shows a simple example that loads and plays a video file that I downloaded from NASA's website. I obtained this video file, named `Solar_System_Birth_ipod_sm.mp4`, from NASA's website at `www.jwst.nasa.gov/videos_science.html`; just scroll to the bottom of the page and right-click the `mp4` link next to the last video on the page.

Figure 16-4 shows this media clip being played in the media viewer shown by the program in Listing 16-3.

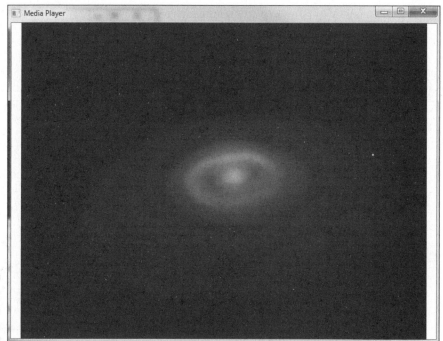

Figure 16-4:
Playing a
video file.

Listing 16-3: The VideoApp Program

```
import javafx.application.*;
import javafx.stage.*;
import javafx.scene.*;
import javafx.scene.layout.*;
import javafx.scene.control.*;
import javafx.scene.media.*;
import java.io.*;
```

```java
public class VideoApp extends Application
{
    public static void main(String[] args)
    {
        launch(args);
    }

    private final String PATH =
        "C:\\Media\\Solar_System_Birth_ipod_sm.mp4";

    @Override public void start(Stage primaryStage)
    {
        File f = new File(PATH);
        Media media = new Media(f.toURI().toString());

        MediaPlayer mplayer = new MediaPlayer(media);
        mplayer.setAutoPlay(true);

        MediaView mview = new MediaView(mplayer);
        mview.setFitWidth(700);
        mview.setFitHeight(500);

        StackPane pane = new StackPane(mview);

        Scene scene = new Scene(pane);
        primaryStage.setScene(scene);
        primaryStage.setTitle("Media Player");
        primaryStage.show();
    }

}
```

Chapter 17

Animating Your Scenes

. . . .

In This Chapter

▶ Looking at the various ways to create JavaFX animations

▶ Using JavaFX transitions

▶ Using the KeyFrame and Timeline classes

▶ Creating bouncing balls

. . . .

*Y*ou can go a long way toward improving the look and feel of your applications by applying special effects as described in Chapter 14, incorporating property bindings to make your controls more responsive, and using sound and media to provide audio and visual interest. In this chapter, I discuss how to take your applications one step further by incorporating simple animation effects. The effects you read about in this chapter make your applications come alive by enabling objects on the screen to move.

Please don't get your hopes set on winning an Oscar for Best Animation next year. No one will be fooled into thinking that you collaborated with Pixar on your application. Still, you can add some interesting whiz-bang to your applications using these techniques.

Introducing JavaFX Animation

The basic idea of JavaFX animations is to manipulate the value of one or more node properties at regular intervals. For example, suppose you have a circle that represents a ball and you want to move it from the left side of the screen to the right. Assuming the width of the screen is 600 pixels, you'd animate the circle by varying its posX property from 0 to 600.

Two factors will affect how fast the ball moves across the screen: the amount of time that elapses between each change to the posX property, and the increment you add to the posX property at each time interval. For example, if you add 3 to the posX property at each time interval, it will take 200 intervals to get to 600 (3 x 200 = 600). If the intervals occur every 10 milliseconds (100 times per second), it will take 2,000 milliseconds — 2 full seconds — for the ball to traverse the screen from left to right.

Without JavaFX animations, you could implement the moving ball by using the Java Timer object to move the ball at regular intervals. The Timer class can be difficult to set up and use correctly. The JavaFX animation classes make animating your nodes a much simpler proposition.

JavaFX provides two basic ways to create animations, which I refer to in this chapter using extremely technical terms — the *hard way* and the *easy way:*

- The **hard way** requires that you set up timer events manually, and then write event listeners that are called when the timer events occur. In the event listeners, you manipulate the properties of the nodes you want to animate. For example, to move a ball across the screen, you'd set up a timer interval that ticks every 10 milliseconds. At each tick, you'd increase the x position of the ball by 3. You'd then set the timer to run a total of 200 times to move the ball. Setting up this animation requires that you use two classes: Timeline and KeyFrame, and that you write an ActionEvent listener to move the ball.

- The **easy way** takes advantage of shortcut classes provided by JavaFX to easily implement common types of animations. For example, you can use the TranslateTransition class to easily move a circle from one side of the screen to the other over a specified period of time. You just set up a TranslateTransition specifying that you want to vary the ball's x position from 0 to 600 over the course of 2 seconds. The TranslateTransition class will take care of the details.

In the remainder of this chapter, you discover both the easy way and the hard way. I start with the easy way.

Using Transition Classes

JavaFX comes with eight predefined animation effects — dubbed *transition classes* — that you can use to easily create an animation on most any node in your scene graph. (Most of the transitions will work with any node, but some will work only on shapes.) The eight transition types are

✔ **FadeTransition:** Varies the opacity value of any node. You can use this transition to fade an object in or out. Or, you can use it to make an object "wink" by quickly fading it out and then back in. You can also use it to create a flashing light that repeatedly fades in and then out.

✔ **FillTransition:** Varies the color of a shape's fill from a starting color to an ending color. For example, you can make a circle change from red to green.

✔ **PathTranslation:** Causes a shape to move along a predefined path. You can use any shape for the path.

✔ **PauseTransition:** This handy transition simply pauses for a moment; it's often used between two transitions to cause a break in the action.

✔ **RotateTransition:** Causes a node to rotate.

✔ **ScaleTransition:** Causes an object to increase or decrease in size.

✔ **StrokeTransition:** Varies the color used for a shape's outline stroke.

✔ **TranslateTransition:** Moves a node by translating it from one location to another.

These eight transition classes are all subclasses of the Transition class, which is in turn a subclass of the Animation class. Table 17-1 lists the methods that are defined by the Transition and Animation classes, and are therefore available to all transition classes.

Table 17-1   Methods of the Transition and Animation Classes

Method	Explanation
void play()	Plays the animation from its current position.
void playFromStart()	Plays the animation from the start.
void pause()	Temporarily suspends the animation. You can start it again by calling play.
void stop()	Stops the animation.
void setCycleCount(int value)	Sets the number of times the animation should repeat. To repeat the animation an indefinite number of times, specify Animation. INDEFINITE.

(continued)

Table 17-1 *(continued)*

Method	Explanation
setAutoReverse(boolean value)	If true, the animation reverses direction each time the cycle is repeated.
setInterpolator(Interpolator value)	Determines the method used to calculate the intermediate values of the property controlled by the transition. The possible values are Interpolator.DISCRETE Interpolator.LINEAR Interpolator.EASE_IN Interpolator.EASE_OUT Interpolator.EASE_BOTH The default setting is EASE_BOTH.

Most of the methods in Table 17-1 are straightforward, but the setInterpolator method merits a bit of explanation. The *interpolator* is the method used to calculate the intermediate values of the property being controlled by the transition. For example, in a FadeTransition, the interpolator determines how the value of the node's opacity is varied during the time that the animation is running; for a TranslateTransition, the interpolator determines how the x- and y-coordinates change during the animation.

The default interpolator setting is Interpolator.EASE_BOTH, which means that the change begins slowly, then speeds up though the middle of the animation, then slows down again just before the animation ends. For a TranslateTransition, this causes the movement of the node to start slowly, speed up, and then slow down toward the end.

The EASE_IN interpolator speeds up at the beginning but ends abruptly, while the EASE_OUT interpolator starts abruptly but slows down at the end. The LINEAR interpolator varies the property controlled by the transition at a constant rate throughout the animation. And the DISCRETE interpolator doesn't change the property value at all until the end of the animation has been reached; then, it immediately changes to the ending value.

Table 17-2 lists the most commonly used constructors and methods for each of the transition types.

Table 17-2	Transition Classes
FadeTransition	**Explanation**
`FadeTransition(Duration duration, Node node)`	Creates a fade transition of the given duration for the specified node.
`void setFromValue(Double value)`	Sets the starting opacity for the fade transition.
`void setToValue(Double value)`	Sets the ending opacity for the fade transition.
`void setByValue(Double value)`	If the ending opacity is not specified, this value is added to the starting value to determine the ending value.
FillTransition	**Explanation**
`FillTransition(Duration duration, Shape shape)`	Creates a fill transition of the given duration for the specified shape.
`void setFromValue(Color value)`	Sets the starting color for the fade transition.
`void setToValue(Color value)`	Sets the ending color for the fade transition.
PathTransition	**Explanation**
`PathTransition(Duration duration, Shape path, Shape shape)`	Creates a path transition of the given duration. The path translation causes the specified shape to travel along the specified path.
`void setFromValue(Color value)`	Sets the starting color for the fade transition.
`void setToValue(Color value)`	Sets the ending color for the fade transition.
PauseTransition	**Explanation**
`PauseTransition(Duration duration)`	Causes a delay of the specified duration.
RotateTransition	**Explanation**
`RotateTransition(Duration duration, Node node)`	Creates a rotate transition of the given duration on the specified node.
`void setFromAngle(Double value)`	Sets the starting angle for the rotation.

(continued)

Table 17-2 *(continued)*

RotateTransition	*Explanation*
`void setToAngle(Double value)`	Sets the ending angle for the rotation.
`void setByAngle(Double value)`	If the ending angle is not specified, this value is added to the starting angle to determine the ending angle.

ScaleTransition	*Explanation*
`ScaleTransition(Duration duration, Node node)`	Creates a scale transition of the given duration on the specified node.
`void setFromX(Double value)`	Sets the starting scale for the x-axis.
`void setFromY(Double value)`	Sets the starting scale for the y-axis.
`void setFromZ(Double value)`	Sets the starting scale for the z-axis.
`void setToX(Double value)`	Sets the ending scale for the x-axis.
`void setToY(Double value)`	Sets the ending scale for the y-axis.
`void setToZ(Double value)`	Sets the ending scale for the z-axis.
`void setByX(Double value)`	Sets the increment scale for the x-axis.
`void setByY(Double value)`	Sets the increment scale for the y-axis.
`void setByZ(Double value)`	Sets the increment scale for the z-axis.

StrokeTransition	*Explanation*
`StrokeTransition(Duration duration, Shape shape)`	Creates a stroke transition of the given duration for the specified shape.
`void setFromValue(Color value)`	Sets the starting color for the stroke transition.
`void setToValue(Color value)`	Sets the ending color for the stroke transition.

TranslateTransition	*Explanation*
`TranslateTransition(Duration duration, Node node)`	Creates a translate transition of the given duration on the specified node.
`void setFromX(Double value)`	Sets the starting point for the x-axis.
`void setFromY(Double value)`	Sets the starting point for the y-axis.
`void setFromZ(Double value)`	Sets the starting point for the z-axis.
`void setToX(Double value)`	Sets the ending point for the x-axis.
`void setToY(Double value)`	Sets the ending point for the y-axis.
`void setToZ(Double value)`	Sets the ending point for the z-axis.
`void setByX(Double value)`	Sets the increment point for the x-axis.
`void setByY(Double value)`	Sets the increment point for the y-axis.
`void setByZ(Double value)`	Sets the increment point for the z-axis.

Setting properties by, from, or to?

The `setFrom`, `setTo`, and `setBy` methods that appear in several of the transition classes listed in Table 17-2 deserve a little explanation.

By default, both the start and end values of a transition are the node's current values for the property being animated. Thus, the default starting and ending locations for a `TranslateTransition` are the node's current x and y positions.

Here are several ways to specify a different starting value, ending value, or both:

- Let the node's current values stand as the starting values and specify a new ending value by using the `setTo` methods.

- Let the node's current values stand as the starting values and specify a displacement to the ending value by using a `setBy` method. The value you specify in the `setBy` method will be added to the starting value to determine the ending value.

- Use the `setFrom` location to change the starting location from the node's current value. Then, omit both the `setTo` and `setBy` values to let the node's current value be the ending value.

- Use the `setFrom` location to change the starting location from the node's current value and use `setTo` to set the ending value.

- Use the `setFrom` location to change the starting location from the node's current value and use `setBy` to set a displacement value that will be added to the starting location to determine the ending location.

Looking at a Transition Example

The nine transitions listed in Table 17-2 all work essentially the same. To use any of them, you simply create the transition by calling its constructor and specifying the duration of the transition and the node you want animated. Then, if necessary, you call additional methods to set the transition parameters. Finally, you call the `play` method to start the animation.

The following example shows a transition that moves a circle named c from the top-left corner of the scene to location 300, 300:

```
TranslateTransition t = new TranslateTransition(
    Duration.millis(2000), c);
t.setFromX(0);
t.setFromY(0);
t.setToX(300);
t.setToY(300);
t.play();
```

Here, the duration of the animation is set to 2 seconds (2,000 milliseconds).

Listing 17-1 shows how this transition can be incorporated into a complete program. As you can see, the program is short. It simply displays a red ball at the left edge of the scene and then moves the ball to the right edge of the scene. The transition's cycle count is set to indefinite, and the autoreverse setting is set to true. As a result, the animation repeats itself indefinitely, giving the appearance that the ball is bouncing back and forth between the right and left edges of the screen.

Listing 17-1:   The BouncingBall Program

```
import javafx.application.*;
import javafx.stage.*;
import javafx.scene.*;
import javafx.scene.layout.*;
import javafx.scene.shape.*;
import javafx.scene.paint.*;
import javafx.animation.*;
import javafx.util.*;

public class BouncingBall extends Application
{
    public static void main(String[] args)
    {
        launch(args);
    }
```

```
@Override public void start(Stage primaryStage)
{

    RadialGradient g = new RadialGradient(                    →20
        0, 0,
        0.35, 0.35,
        0.5,
        true,
        CycleMethod.NO_CYCLE,
        new Stop(0.0, Color.WHITE),
        new Stop(1.0, Color.RED));

    Circle ball = new Circle(0,0,20);                         →29
    ball.setFill(g);

    Group root = new Group();                                 →32
    root.getChildren().add(ball);
    Scene scene = new Scene(root, 600, 600);
    primaryStage.setScene(scene);
    primaryStage.setTitle("Bouncing Ball");
    primaryStage.show();

    TranslateTransition t = new TranslateTransition(          →39
        Duration.millis(2000), ball);
    t.setFromX(ball.getRadius());                             →41
    t.setToX(scene.getWidth() - ball.getRadius());            →42
    t.setFromY(scene.getHeight() / 2);                        →43
    t.setToY(scene.getHeight() / 2);
    t.setCycleCount(Transition.INDEFINITE);                   →45
    t.setAutoReverse(true);                                   →46
    t.setInterpolator(Interpolator.LINEAR);                   →47
    t.play();                                                 →48
    }

}
```

The following paragraphs highlight the key points in this program:

→ **20:** A radial gradient is created to give the ball a three-dimensional appearance.

→ **29:** The circle is created. Its radius is 20 pixels, and its fill is the gradient created in line 20.

→ **32:** A group object is created to serve as the root node for the scene. Then, the ball is added to the group and the group is used to create and display a scene.

→ **39:** A `TranslateTransition` is created to translate the ball. The duration is set to 2 seconds.

→ **41:** The `fromX` property is set to the radius of the ball. That positions the ball with its left edge on the left edge of the scene.

→ **42:** The `toX` property is set to the width of the screen less the radius of the ball. This positions the ball at the right edge of the screen at the end of the animation cycle.

→ **43:** The `fromY` and `toY` properties are set to half the height of the scene. That way, the ball will travel along a horizontal path centered vertically in the scene.

→ **45:** The cycle count is set to `INDEFINITE` so the ball will bounce forever.

→ **46:** `AutoReverse` is set to `true` so that each cycle will reverse the direction of the ball's travel.

→ **47:** The interpolator is set to linear so that the ball does not slow down at as it approaches the edges of the scene.

→ **48:** Play!

Figure 17-1 shows the Bouncing Ball program in action.

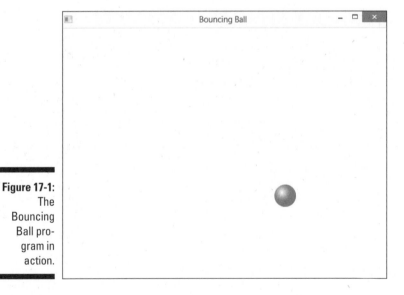

Figure 17-1:
The
Bouncing
Ball pro-
gram in
action.

Combining Transitions

JavaFX provides two transition classes that are designed to let you combine transitions so that two or more transitions run one after the other or at the same time. The SequentialTransition class lets you run several transitions one after the other, whereas the ParallelTransition class lets you run several transitions at once.

Both classes have simple constructors that accept a list of transitions as arguments and a play method that lets you start the animations. For example, if you have three transitions named t1, t2, and t3 already created, you can run them in sequence like this:

```
SequentialTransition s =
            new SequentialTransition(t1, t2, t3)
s.play();
```

When the play method is called, transition t1 will run until completion and then transition t2 will run. When t2 finishes, transition t3 will be run.

To run all three transitions simultaneously, use the ParallelTransition class instead:

```
ParallelTransition p =
    new ParallelTransition(t1, t2, t3)
p.play();
```

If you prefer, you can add animations after the constructor has been called by using the getChildren method. For example:

```
ParallelTransition p = new ParallelTransition()
p.getChildren().add(t1);
p.getChildren().add(t2);
p.getChildren().add(t3);
p.play();
```

Or:

```
ParallelTransition p = new ParallelTransition()
p.getChildren().addAll(t1, t2, t3);
p.play();
```

Note: An animation added to a SequentialTransition or Parallel Transition can itself be a SequentialTransition or a Parallel Transition. For example, suppose you have three transitions that animate one node (t1, t2, and t3) and a fourth transition that animates a second node (t4) and you want to run t1, t2, and t3 in sequence while t4 runs at the same time as the sequence. Here's how you can achieve that:

```
SequentialTransition s =
    new SequentialTransition(t1, t2, t3)
ParallelTransition p = new ParallelTransition(s, t4);
p.play();
```

To illustrate how transitions can be combined into a complete program, Listing 17-2 shows a variation of the BouncingBall program that was presented in Listing 17-1.

Listing 17-2:   The TwoBouncingBalls Program

```java
import javafx.application.*;
import javafx.stage.*;
import javafx.scene.*;
import javafx.scene.layout.*;
import javafx.scene.shape.*;
import javafx.scene.paint.*;
import javafx.animation.*;
import javafx.util.*;

public class TwoBouncingBalls extends Application
{
    public static void main(String[] args)
    {
        launch(args);
    }

    @Override public void start(Stage primaryStage)
    {

        RadialGradient g = new RadialGradient(
            0, 0,
            0.35, 0.35,
            0.5,
            true,
            CycleMethod.NO_CYCLE,
            new Stop(0.0, Color.WHITE),
            new Stop(1.0, Color.RED));

        Circle ball1 = new Circle(0,0,20);
        ball1.setFill(g);

        Circle ball2 = new Circle(0,0,20);
        ball2.setFill(g);
```

```
        Group root = new Group();
        root.getChildren().addAll(ball1, ball2);

        Scene scene = new Scene(root, 600, 600);
        primaryStage.setScene(scene);
        primaryStage.setTitle("Two Bouncing Balls");
        primaryStage.show();

        // Bounce ball 1
        TranslateTransition t1 = new TranslateTransition(
            Duration.millis(2000), ball1);
        t1.setFromX(ball1.getRadius());
        t1.setToX(scene.getWidth() - ball1.getRadius());
        t1.setFromY(scene.getHeight() / 3);
        t1.setToY(scene.getHeight() / 3);
        t1.setCycleCount(Transition.INDEFINITE);
        t1.setAutoReverse(true);
        t1.setInterpolator(Interpolator.LINEAR);

        // Bounce ball 2
        TranslateTransition t2 = new TranslateTransition(
            Duration.millis(2000), ball2);
        t2.setFromX(scene.getWidth() - ball2.getRadius());
        t2.setToX(ball2.getRadius());
        t2.setFromY(scene.getHeight() / 3 * 2);
        t2.setToY(scene.getHeight() / 3 * 2);
        t2.setCycleCount(Transition.INDEFINITE);
        t2.setAutoReverse(true);
        t2.setInterpolator(Interpolator.LINEAR);

        // Bounce both balls at the same time
        ParallelTransition pt = new ParallelTransition(t1, t2);
        pt.play();
    }
}
```

This version of the program animates two balls traveling in opposite directions. A transition is created on the first ball to bounce it from left to right one third of the way down the scene. A transition is created for the second ball to animate it in the opposite direction two thirds of the way down the scene. Then, a `ParallelTransition` is used to animate both balls at the same time. Figure 17-2 shows the program in action.

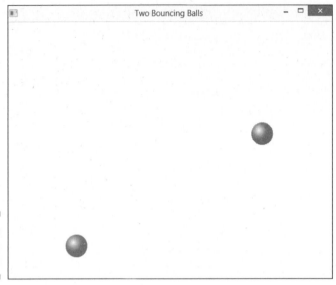

Figure 17-2:
Bouncing
two balls.

Animating the Hard Way

Now that you've seen the easy way to create animations (using transition classes), it's time to have a look at the more difficult way. Of course, as you might envision, the more difficult way is also the more flexible way.

For example, the bouncing balls shown in Listings 17-1 and 17-2 are interesting but not very practical, as they bounce back in forth in a strictly horizontal direction. If you wanted to use these balls to create a game, you'd want them to bounce around at angles, bouncing off all four edges of the scene. And you'd want them to bounce off each other as well. To achieve that, you need to work with two advanced animation classes: KeyFrame and TimeLine:

✓ **KeyFrame:** A KeyFrame is a timing interval that raises an ActionEvent when the time interval has expired.

When you create a KeyFrame, you specify the duration of the time interval and provide an ActionEvent listener. Then, in the action listener, you provide the code that implements your animation. In the case of this bouncing ball program, the action event will examine each ball that's in motion and calculate the next position for each ball, taking into account the effect of balls bouncing off the edges of the scene or bouncing off each other.

✔ **Timeline:** A `Timeline` is a sequence of `KeyFrames`.

When you call the `TimeLine`'s play method, each `KeyFrame` is executed in sequence. A `Timeline` also has a `cycleCount` property, which indicates how many times the timeline should be repeated, and `play`, `pause`, and `stop` methods that control the execution of the timeline. You can set the cycle count to `INDEFINATE` to continue the animation indefinitely.

To create a `KeyFrame`, call the `KeyFrame` constructor with two arguments: the duration of the keyframe (usually in milliseconds) and the `ActionEvent` listener that will be called when the timer expires. Here's an example that uses a Lambda expression to define a simple listener:

```
KeyFrame k = new KeyFrame(Duration.millis(10),
    e ->
    {
        // Action event listener code goes here
    } );
```

To add this `KeyFrame` to a `Timeline` and run the animation, use this code:

```
Timeline t = new Timeline(k);
t.setCycleCount(Timeline.INDEFINITE);
t.play();
```

Listing 17-3 shows a program that uses the `KeyFrame` and `Timeline` classes to send a ball bouncing off all four of the edges of a scene.

Listing 17-3:   The Hard BouncingBall Program

```
import javafx.application.*;
import javafx.stage.*;
import javafx.scene.*;
import javafx.event.*;
import javafx.scene.layout.*;
import javafx.scene.shape.*;
import javafx.scene.paint.*;
import javafx.animation.*;
import javafx.util.*;

public class HardBouncingBall extends Application {

    public static void main(String[] args)
    {
        launch(args);
    }
```

(continued)

Listing 17-3 *(continued)*

```
private Circle ball;                                              →18
private double x_speed = 2;
private double y_speed = 3;
final private int WIDTH = 600;
final private int HEIGHT = 500;
final private int BALL_SIZE = 20;

@Override public void start(final Stage primaryStage)
{
    Group root = new Group();

    RadialGradient g = new RadialGradient(                       →29
        0, 0,
        0.35, 0.35,
        0.5,
        true,
        CycleMethod.NO_CYCLE,
        new Stop(0.0, Color.WHITE),
        new Stop(1.0, Color.RED));

    ball = new Circle(BALL_SIZE, g);                             →38
    ball.setCenterX(BALL_SIZE);
    ball.setCenterY(BALL_SIZE);

    root.getChildren().addAll(ball);                             →42
    Scene scene = new Scene(root, WIDTH, HEIGHT);
    primaryStage.setTitle("Bouncing Ball");
    primaryStage.setScene(scene);
    primaryStage.show();

    KeyFrame k = new KeyFrame(Duration.millis(10),              →48
        e ->
        {
            ball.setCenterX(ball.getCenterX() + x_speed);       →51
            ball.setCenterY(ball.getCenterY() + y_speed);

            if (ball.getCenterX() <= BALL_SIZE ||               →54
                ball.getCenterX() >= WIDTH - BALL_SIZE)
                x_speed = -x_speed;

            if (ball.getCenterY() <= BALL_SIZE ||               →58
                ball.getCenterY() >= HEIGHT - BALL_SIZE)
                y_speed = -y_speed;
        } );

    Timeline t = new Timeline(k);                               →63
    t.setCycleCount(Timeline.INDEFINITE);
    t.play();
}

}
```

The following paragraphs draw attention to the key points in this program:

→ **18:** These class variables are used within the `ActionEvent` handler.

→ **29:** The gradient that will be used to fill the ball is created here.

→ **38:** The ball is created. The initial x- and y-coordinates place the ball at the top-left corner of the scene.

→ **42:** The scene is set and the stage is displayed.

→ **48:** A `KeyFrame` is created with a timing duration of 10 milliseconds. A Lambda expression is used to create the event listener.

→ **51:** Within the event listener, the ball is moved by adding the current `x_speed` and `y_speed` values to the center x and y positions of the ball.

→ **54:** Next, the ball's x position is checked against the left and right edges of the scene. If the ball is at the edge, the `x_speed` value is inverted so that the ball will travel in the opposite x direction.

→ **58:** Similarly, the ball's y position is checked against the top and bottom edges of the scene. If the ball is at the edge, the `y_speed` value is inverted.

→ **63:** A `Timeline` is created using the `KeyFrame`. The cycle count is set to `INDEFINITE`, and the `play` method is called to start the ball moving.

Figure 17-3 shows the bouncing ball in action.

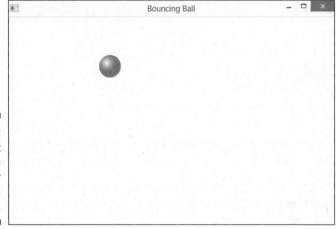

Figure 17-3:
A ball that bounces off all four edges of the scene.

Improving the Ball Bouncer

The program shown in Listing 17-3 is finally beginning to resemble something that might be useful in a game program. With a little more programming effort, you can convert this program into something resembling the classic Pong game.

But to be more useful, the ball bouncing program needs to support more than one ball at a time within the scene. And after you add a second ball, the program should provide for the balls bouncing not only off the walls, but also off each other. Figure 17-4 shows a program that does just that. Here, a total of ten balls are flying around within the crowded scene. The balls bounce off the walls and each other.

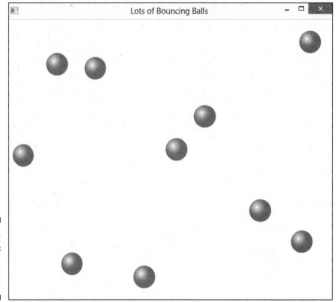

Figure 17-4:
Lots of
bouncing
balls!

To implement this program, I created a separate class named `Ball` that extends the `Circle` class. The `Ball` class provides the following features:

- ✔ You specify the radius of the ball via the constructor. The ball is filled automatically with a red gradient to give it a three-dimensional appearance.

- ✔ You also specify the width and height of the bouncing area in the constructor. The ball is given an initial random position within this area, and automatically travels at a random speed within this specified area, bouncing off the edges when they're encountered.

✔ In addition, you pass an `ArrayList` of other balls to the constructor. As the ball moves, it automatically bounces off any other balls in this list that the ball happens to collide with. When balls collide, they trade their x and y speeds.

✔ The `Ball` class provides a `move` method that should be called from the animation `KeyFrame` action listener.

Listing 17-4 shows the complete code for the program, which includes the `Ball` class.

Listing 17-4:   The ManyBalls Program

```
import javafx.application.*;
import javafx.stage.*;
import javafx.scene.*;
import javafx.event.*;
import javafx.scene.layout.*;
import javafx.scene.shape.*;
import javafx.scene.paint.*;
import javafx.animation.*;
import javafx.util.*;
import java.util.*;

public class ManyBalls extends Application {

    public static void main(String[] args)
    {
        launch(args);
    }

    final private int WIDTH = 600;
    final private int HEIGHT = 500;
    final private int BALL_SIZE = 20;

    private ArrayList<Ball> balls = new ArrayList<Ball>();          →23

    @Override public void start(final Stage primaryStage)
    {
        Group root = new Group();

        for (int i = 0; i < 10; i++)                               →29
            balls.add(new Ball(BALL_SIZE, WIDTH, HEIGHT, balls));

        root.getChildren().addAll(balls);                          →34

        Scene scene = new Scene(root, WIDTH, HEIGHT);              →36
        primaryStage.setTitle("Lots of Bouncing Balls");
        primaryStage.setScene(scene);
        primaryStage.show();
```

(continued)

Listing 17-4 *(continued)*

```
    KeyFrame k = new KeyFrame(Duration.millis(10),           →41
        e ->
        {
            for (Ball ball : balls)
                ball.move();
        });

    Timeline t = new Timeline(k);                            →48
    t.setCycleCount(Timeline.INDEFINITE);
    t.play();
}

public class Ball extends Circle                             →53
{
    public double x_speed;                                   →55
    public double y_speed;
    public double radius;
    private double fieldWidth;
    private double fieldHeight;

    public Ball(double radius,                               →61
                double fieldWidth,
                double fieldHeight,
                ArrayList<Ball> balls)
    {
        super();                                             →66

        this.radius = radius;                                →68
        this.fieldWidth = fieldWidth;
        this.fieldHeight = fieldHeight;

        super.setRadius(radius);                             →72

        super.setCenterX(                                    →74
            Math.random() * (fieldWidth - this.radius) + 1);
        super.setCenterY(
            Math.random() * (fieldHeight - this.radius) + 1);
        this.x_speed = Math.random() * 5 + 1;
        this.y_speed = Math.random() * 5 + 1;

        RadialGradient g = new RadialGradient(               →81
            0, 0,
            0.35, 0.35,
            0.5,
            true,
            CycleMethod.NO_CYCLE,
            new Stop(0.0, Color.WHITE),
            new Stop(1.0, Color.RED));
        super.setFill(g);
    }
```

```
public void move()                                                    →92
{
    super.setCenterX(super.getCenterX() + this.x_speed);
    super.setCenterY(super.getCenterY() + this.y_speed);

    // Detect collision with left edge                                →97
    if (super.getCenterX() <= this.radius)
    {
        super.setCenterX(this.radius);
        this.x_speed = -this.x_speed;
    }

    // Detect collision with right edge                              →104
    if (super.getCenterX() >= this.fieldWidth - this.radius)
    {
        super.setCenterX(this.fieldWidth - this.radius);
        this.x_speed = -this.x_speed;
    }

    // Detect collision with top edge                                →111
    if (super.getCenterY() <= this.radius)
    {
        super.setCenterY(this.radius);
        this.y_speed = -this.y_speed;
    }

    // Detect collision with bottom edge                             →118
    if (super.getCenterY() >= this.fieldHeight - this.radius)
    {
        super.setCenterY(this.fieldHeight - this.radius);
        this.y_speed = -this.y_speed;
    }

    // Detect collision with other balls                             →125
    for (Ball b : balls)
    {
        if (b != this &&
            b.intersects(super.getLayoutBounds()))
        {
            double tempx = this.x_speed;                             →131
            double tempy = this.y_speed;
            this.x_speed = b.x_speed;
            this.y_speed = b.y_speed;
            b.x_speed = tempx;
            b.y_speed = tempy;
            break;                                                   →137
        }
    }
}
}
}
```

The following paragraphs explain the key points of this program:

→ **23:** An `ArrayList` named `balls` is used to hold the balls that will be animated by this program.

→ **29:** A `for` loop creates ten `Ball` objects and adds them to the array list. The constructor for the `Ball` objects passes the ball size, the width and height of the scene, and the `balls` array list.

→ **34:** The `balls` array list is added to the scene root.

→ **36:** The root is added to the scene, and the scene is displayed.

→ **41:** A `KeyFrame` is created with an interval of 10 milliseconds. The action listener is very simple: It simply calls the `move` method for every `Ball` in the `balls` collection.

→ **48:** A `Timeline` is created using the `KeyFrame` created in line 41. Then, the timeline is played to set the balls in motion.

→ **53:** The `Ball` class extends the `Circle` class.

→ **55:** Class fields are used to hold the internal values for the x and y speeds, the circle radius, and the playing field's width and height.

→ **61:** The constructor accepts four parameters: the radius, the playing field width and height, and an array list containing other `Ball` objects that should be checked for collisions.

→ **66:** The `Ball` constructor starts by calling the `super` constructor to create the `Circle` object from which this ball will be extended.

→ **68:** The radius, width, and height class variables are initialized from the values passed into the constructor.

→ **72:** The radius of the circle is set to match the radius passed to the constructor.

→ **74:** The center x and y positions as well as the x and y speed fields are set to random values.

→ **81:** The gradient fill is created.

→ **92:** The `move` method begins by adding the x and y speed fields to the circle's center x and y positions.

→ **97:** An `if` statement is used to detect a collision with the left edge. If the left edge collision occurs, the position of the ball is adjusted to bring it back within the playing field and the x speed is inverted so that the ball will change directions. The reason for repositioning the ball is that, depending on the previous position and the speed of the ball, the ball may have actually crossed outside the playing field.

→ **104:** Another `if` statement checks for a collision with the right edge.

→ **111:** And the top edge.

→ **118:** And the bottom edge.

→ **125:** Now it gets interesting. These lines check for collisions with other balls in the `balls` array. A `for` loop iterates over all the balls in the array list. The `if` statement first eliminates the current ball by checking if `b != this`. After all, a ball can't really collide with itself.

Next, the `if` statement checks to see whether the current ball has collided with any other ball. It does this by calling the `intersects` method, which is defined by the `Shape` class. This method accepts a `Bounds` object that represents the bounding rectangle within which a shape fits. You can get the bounding rectangle by calling the shape's `getLayoutBounds` method. Thus, this test works by checking whether a ball in the `balls` collection intersects with the bounding rectangle of the current ball. ***Note:*** This collision test isn't perfect; it sometimes treats near misses as collisions. But it's close enough.

→ **131:** If a collision is detected, the x and y speed values of the two balls are swapped. Not only do the balls bounce away from each other, but also the slower ball picks up speed and the faster ball slows down.

→ **137:** A `break` statement is executed if a collision is detected to prevent detecting collisions with more than one ball. Without this `break` statement, collisions that involve more than two balls usually result in pretty strange behavior. Try removing the `break` statement to see what happens. (Even with this `break` statement, the balls sometimes behave in unexpected ways. I think it's kind of fun to watch, but then again, I'm pretty easily entertained.)

Chapter 18

Targeting Touch Devices

. . . .

In This Chapter

▶ Discovering gestures on touch devices

▶ Adding listeners that respond to gesture events

▶ Creating a program that lets the user manipulate a shape with gestures

. . . .

*T*ouch devices are everywhere nowadays. Tablets and smartphones are the most common types of touch devices, but even some desktop users have installed touch-capable monitors. At one time, touch devices ran primarily non-Microsoft operating systems, such as Apple's iOS or Google's Android. But now, with Windows 8, many touch devices even run Windows.

Fortunately, JavaFX can run on all those platforms. In this chapter, you discover how to develop JavaFX applications that take advantage of the unique user interactions that are possible with touch devices, including basic touch and swiping and scrolling as well as multi-touch gestures such as zooming and rotating.

Introducing Gestures and Touch Events

Before I get into the details of working with gestures and touch events, I want to point out that the support for basic touch devices for JavaFX controls is already built-in and requires no programming to enable. For example, Button controls respond to taps on a touch device just as they respond to mouse clicks. So no special programming is needed to enable the basic operation of JavaFX controls on a touch device.

The good news is that the programming required to handle more advanced touch gestures, such as zooming or rotating, is pretty straightforward. JavaFX handles the difficult tasks of figuring out what gestures the user is making when he touches the screen. For example, when JavaFX sees that the user has touched the screen with two fingers and then rotated the fingers in opposite directions, the user is attempting to rotate an object on the screen. JavaFX figures out which object is the target of the rotation, figures out how much the user has rotated the object, and then sends a ROTATE event to the target. All you have to do is provide an event listener for the ROTATE event.

Actually, when the user does a rotate gesture, JavaFX will likely send dozens of separate ROTATE events to the target of the rotation. Each of those events represents an incremental step along the way to the complete rotation. Your program will respond to those events by rotating the target object by the amount indicated by the ROTATE event; the result will be that the object smoothly follows the user's fingers as the user continues the rotation gesture.

JavaFX provides event handling for four distinct types of touch gestures:

- ✔ **Rotate:** A *rotate* gesture is recognized when the user places two fingers on the screen and rotates them in opposite directions. Three distinct events are generated when a rotate gesture is recognized:

  - ROTATE_STARTED: This event occurs once, as soon as the rotation gesture is recognized.

  - ROTATE: This event can occur multiple times throughout the rotation gesture. It is usually the event you'll want to handle.

  - ROTATE_FINISHED: This event occurs once, after the end of the rotation gesture is recognized.

  All rotation events are represented by a RotateEvent object, which defines two key methods:

  - getAngle: Returns the angle of rotation for this particular event.

  - getTotalAngle: Returns the cumulative angle for the entire rotation gesture.

- ✔ **Zoom:** A *zoom* gesture is recognized when the user places two fingers on the screen and then spreads them apart or brings them together. As with rotate gestures, zoom gestures create three types of events:

  - ZOOM_STARTED: This event occurs when the zoom gesture begins.

  - ZOOM: This event occurs multiple times throughout the zoom gesture.

  - ZOOM_FINISHED: This event occurs when the zoom gesture ends.

  Zoom events are defined by the ZoomEvent class, which has two important methods:

  - getZoomFactor: Returns the amount of the zoom for this particular event.

  - getTotalZoomFactor: Returns the accumulated zoom factor for the entire zoom gesture.

The zoom factor is a multiplier you can use to determine the new size of the zoomed object. For example, if the user doubles the size of the target object, the zoom factor will be 2.0.

✔ **Scroll:** A *scroll* gesture is recognized when the user places one finger on the screen and drags it to another location. Once again, three types of events are generated for scroll gestures:

• SCROLL_STARTED: Occurs at the start of the scroll gesture.

• SCROLL: Occurs multiple times throughout the scroll gesture.

• SCROLL_FINISHED: Occurs when the scroll gesture ends.

Scroll events are represented by the ScrollEvent class, which provides several methods to retrieve the scroll amount:

• getDeltaX: Returns the horizontal change for this scroll event.

• getDeltaY: Returns the vertical change for this scroll event.

• getTotalDeltaX: Returns the total horizontal change for this scroll gesture.

• getTotalDeltaY: Returns the total vertical change for this scroll gesture.

✔ **Swipe:** A *swipe* gesture is recognized when the user places one finger on the screen and quickly swipes it either horizontally or vertically. Unlike the other gestures, swipe gestures do not generate events to indicate the start and end of the gesture. Instead, one of the following events is generated to indicate the direction of the swipe:

• SWIPE_LEFT

• SWIPE_RIGHT

• SWIPE_UP

• SWIPE_DOWN

Swipe events are represented by the SwipeEvent class.

Swipe events and scroll events are difficult to distinguish because a swipe is simply a fast scroll in either a horizontal or vertical direction. Thus, when the user performs a swipe gesture, scroll events are generated in addition to the swipe event.

Listening for Gestures

You can install a listener for any gesture on any node object by calling one of the methods listed in Table 18-1. As with all JavaFX events, these events use functional interfaces, so you can easily implement the event listeners with Lambda expressions.

Table 18-1   Node Methods for Installing Gesture Event Listeners

Method	Explanation
void setOnRotate(Rotate Event listener)	Creates a listener for the ROTATE event.
void setOnRotateStarted (RotateEvent listener)	Creates a listener for the ROTATE_ STARTED event.
void setOnRotateFinished (RotateEvent listener)	Creates a listener for the ROTATE_ FINISHED event.
void setOnZoom(ZoomEvent listener)	Creates a listener for the ZOOM event.
void setOnZoomStarted (ZoomEvent listener)	Creates a listener for the ZOOM_ STARTED event.
void setOnZoomFinished (ZoomEvent listener)	Creates a listener for the ZOOM_ FINISHED event.
void setOnScroll (ScrollEvent listener)	Creates a listener for the SCROLL event.
void setOnScrollStarted (ScrollEvent listener)	Creates a listener for the SCROLL_ STARTED event.
void setOnScrollFinished (ScrollEvent listener)	Creates a listener for the SCROLL_ FINISHED event.
void setOnSwipeLeft (SwipeEvent listener)	Creates a listener for the SWIPE_ LEFT event.
void setOnSwipeRight (SwipeEvent listener)	Creates a listener for the SWIPE_ RIGHT event.
void setOnSwipeUp (SwipeEvent listener)	Creates a listener for the SWIPE_UP event.
void setOnSwipeDown (SwipeEvent listener)	Creates a listener for the SWIPE_ DOWN event.

Here's an example that creates a rectangle, and then installs a listener for the rotate event and adjusts the rectangles rotation when the rotate event is fired:

```
Rectangle r = new Rectangle(150, 150, 200, 200);
r.setFill(Color.DARKGRAY);
r.setOnRotate(e ->
    {
        r.setRotate(r.getRotate() + e.getAngle());
        e.consume();
    });
```

Here, the rotation of the rectangle is modified by first retrieving the current rotation and then adding the angle retrieved from the rotate event.

This event handler calls the `consume` method to discard the event. This is important when dealing with gesture events. If you don't consume the event, the event will be passed up the chain and may be processed again by other objects.

One other detail you should know about is that gesture events have a characteristic know as *inertia,* which causes events to continue to be raised after the user completes the gesture. For example, when the user completes a scroll gesture, the SCROLL_FINISHED event occurs, but several SCROLL events are generated after the SCROLL_FINISHED event. This creates a more realistic experience for the user, but can complicate your programming.

You can call the gesture event's `isInertia` method to determine whether an event was created as a result of inertia. Then, if you want to suppress the effect of inertia, you can ignore the event if `isInertia` returns `true`. For example:

```
Rectangle r = new Rectangle(150, 150, 200, 200);
r.setFill(Color.DARKGRAY);
r.setOnRotate(e ->
    {
        if (!isInertia())
        {
            r.setRotate(r.getRotate() + e.getAngle());
            e.consume();
        }
    });
```

Here, the rectangle is rotated only if the event is not generated as a result of inertia.

Looking at an Example Program

In this section, you look at a sample program — the Gesturator. The Gesturator program displays a simple rectangle on the screen and allows the user to manipulate the rectangle using gestures. Figure 18-1 shows the scene displayed by the Gesturator program.

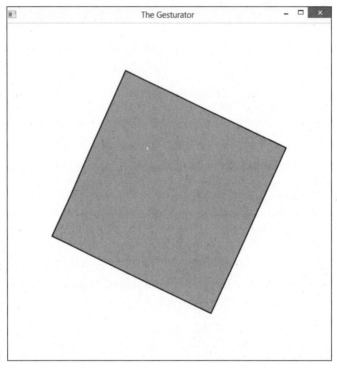

Figure 18-1:
The
Gesturator
program in
action.

Here are the key features of the Gesturator program:

- ✔ Initially, the rectangle is centered in the screen.
- ✔ The user can rotate the rectangle using a rotate gesture.
- ✔ The user can change the size of the rectangle by using a zoom gesture.
- ✔ The user can move the rectangle by dragging it with a single finger. The movement is constrained so that the entire rectangle stays within the bounds of the scene.

✔ The user can shove the rectangle to one edge of the screen by swiping the rectangle in the correct direction. The program responds to the swipe gesture by moving the rectangle all the way to edge of the screen.

Listing 18-1 provides the complete source code for the Gesturator program.

Listing 18-1:   The Gesturator Program

```
import javafx.application.*;
import javafx.scene.*;
import javafx.stage.*;
import javafx.scene.control.*;
import javafx.scene.paint.*;
import javafx.scene.shape.*;
import javafx.scene.input.*;
import javafx.event.*;

public class Gesturator extends Application
{

    public static void main(String[] args)
    {
        launch(args);
    }

    private final double RECT_X = 200;                              →18
    private final double RECT_Y = 200;
    private final double SCENE_X = 600;
    private final double SCENE_Y = 600;

    @Override public void start(Stage primaryStage)
    {
        Group root = new Group();

        Rectangle r =                                               →27
            new Rectangle((SCENE_X - RECT_X)/2,
                          (SCENE_Y - RECT_Y)/2,
                          RECT_X,
                          RECT_Y);
        r.setFill(Color.DARKGRAY);
        r.setStroke(Color.BLACK);
        r.setStrokeWidth(2);

        r.setOnZoom(e ->                                            →36
            {
                r.setScaleX(r.getScaleX() * e.getZoomFactor());
                r.setScaleY(r.getScaleY() * e.getZoomFactor());
                e.consume();
            });
```

(continued)

Listing 18-1 *(continued)*

```
    r.setOnRotate(e ->                                              →43
        {
            r.setRotate(r.getRotate() + e.getAngle());
            e.consume();
        });

    r.setOnScroll(e ->                                              →49
        {
            if (!e.isInertia())                                     →51
            {
                double newX = r.getX() + e.getDeltaX();             →53
                if ( (newX >= 0) &&
                     (newX <= SCENE_X - r.getWidth()) )
                {
                    r.setX(newX);
                }
                double newY = r.getY() + e.getDeltaY();             →59
                if ( (newY >= 0) &&
                     (newY <= SCENE_Y - r.getHeight()) )
                {
                    r.setY(newY);
                }
            }
            e.consume();
        });

    r.setOnSwipeLeft(e ->                                           →69
        {
            r.setX(0);
            e.consume();
        });

    r.setOnSwipeRight(e ->                                          →75
        {
            r.setX(SCENE_X - r.getWidth());
            e.consume();
        });

    r.setOnSwipeUp(e ->                                             →81
        {
            r.setY(0);
            e.consume();
        });

    r.setOnSwipeDown(e ->                                           →87
        {
            r.setY(SCENE_Y - r.getHeight());
            e.consume();
        });
```

```
        root.getChildren().add(r);                                →93
        Scene scene = new Scene(root, SCENE_X, SCENE_Y);
        primaryStage.setTitle("The Gesturator");
        primaryStage.setScene(scene);
        primaryStage.show();
    }
}
```

The following paragraphs explain the key points of the Gesturator program:

→ **18:** Private fields are used to set the size of the rectangle and the size of the scene. These constants are referred to several times throughout the program.

→ **27:** The rectangle is created using the size specified by RECT_X and RECT_Y. The initial center position is calculated using the size of the scene and the size of the rectangle.

→ **36:** The zoom event listener adjusts the size of the rectangle by multiplying its current size by the zoom factors provided by the ZoomEvent object.

→ **43:** The rotate event listener rotates the rectangle by adding the rotation angle provided by the RotateEvent object to the current rotation value of the rectangle.

→ **49:** The scroll event handler is a little more complicated than the other event handlers because it imposes several constraints on the position of the rectangle.

→ **51:** The scroll event is ignored if it is the result of inertia. That way, the rectangle stops its movement immediately when the user stops the scroll gesture.

→ **53:** To determine the new x position, the scroll event listener first calculates the proposed new x position by adding the amount of horizontal movement (getDeltaX) to the current x position. Then, it sets the rectangles x position to the proposed position only if the proposed position is greater than zero and less than the width of the screen minus the current width of the rectangle. The if statement prevents the user from moving the rectangle past the left or right edge of the scene.

→ **59:** Similar logic is used to change the y position. First, the proposed y position is calculated; then, the proposed y position is applied only if it does not move the rectangle past the top or bottom edges of the scene.

→ 69: The swipe left listener moves the rectangle to the left edge of the screen.

→ 75: The swipe right listener moves the rectangle to the right edge of the screen.

→ 81: The swipe up listener moves the rectangle to the top edge of the screen.

→ 87: The swipe down listener moves the rectangle to the bottom edge of the screen.

→ 93: The rectangle is added to the root node. Then, the scene is created and displayed on the stage.

Part V
The Part of Tens

In this part . . .

- ✓ Applying more powerful controls
- ✓ Building a 3D world
- ✓ Visit `www.dummies.com` for great Dummies content online.

Chapter 19

Ten More JavaFX Controls

*I*n all, JavaFX has about 75 different controls you can choose from to build your user interfaces. So far in this book, you've read about how to work with about 30 of them. In this chapter, you find out about ten more.

So, without further ado, direct from my home office in sunny California, here are ten more JavaFX controls to put in your toolbox.

TitledPane

A *titled pane* is a pane that contains a single content node and draws a title bar and a border around the content to distinguish the content from other content in the scene. In addition, title panes are *collapsible,* which means that the user can collapse the titled pane so that just the title bar is visible. However, you can make the titled pane non-collapsible if you wish.

In spite of its name, `TitledPane` is a control, not a layout pane. In other words, it is a subclass of `Control`, not of `Pane`.

The `TitledPane` class has a simple constructor that accepts a string that will be displayed in the title bar and a node that will be displayed as the content. The node can, of course, be a layout pane that contains child nodes. Thus, a titled pane can contain multiple nodes. Here's an example that creates three radio buttons, adds them to a toggle group and a `VBox`, and then creates a titled pane class to display the group of buttons:

```
RadioButton rbSmall = new RadioButton("Small");
RadioButton rbMedium = new RadioButton("Medium");
RadioButton rbLarge = new RadioButton("Large");

ToggleGroup sizeGroup = new ToggleGroup();
sizeGroup.getToggles().addAll(rbSmall, rbMedium, rbLarge);
rbMedium.setSelected(true);

VBox box = new VBox(10);
box.setPadding(new Insets(10));
box.getChildren().addAll(rbSmall, rbMedium, rbLarge);

TitledPane tpane = new TitledPane("Size", box);
```

If you want to make the titled pane non-collapsible, add the following line:

```
tpane.setCollapsible(false);
```

Then, the user can't collapse the pane. In this case, the main purpose of the titled pane becomes visual: The border creates a visual grouping of the radio buttons, and the title bar lets the user know why these radio buttons are grouped (they let the user choose a size option). Figure 19-1 shows two titled panes: one collapsible, the other non-collapsible.

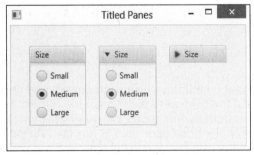

Figure 19-1:
Titled panes.

Accordion

An *accordion* is a stack of titled panes. Only one of the titled panes in the accordion can be opened at any given moment. So if one of the titled panes in the accordion is open and you open a different one, the one that was open automatically closes. Figure 19-2 shows an accordion pane that contains three title panes; the same accordion pane is shown three times in the figure, each time with a different one of the titled panes opened.

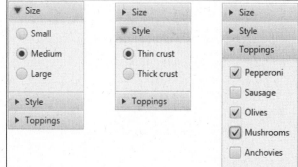

Figure 19-2:
An
accordion.

To create an accordion control, you first create the separate titled panes that will make up the accordion. Then, you create the accordion using the default constructor and add the titled panes using the `getPanes().addAll` method. The following code sample shows how I created the accordion shown in Figure 19-2:

```
// Create the size toggle pane
RadioButton rbSmall = new RadioButton("Small");
RadioButton rbMedium = new RadioButton("Medium");
RadioButton rbLarge = new RadioButton("Large");

ToggleGroup sizeGroup = new ToggleGroup();
sizeGroup.getToggles().addAll(rbSmall, rbMedium, rbLarge);
rbMedium.setSelected(true);

VBox sizeBox = new VBox(10);
sizeBox.setPadding(new Insets(10));
sizeBox.getChildren().addAll(rbSmall, rbMedium, rbLarge);
```

```
TitledPane sizeTpane = new TitledPane("Size", sizeBox);

// Create the style toggle pane
RadioButton rbThin = new RadioButton("Thin crust");
RadioButton rbThick = new RadioButton("Thick crust");

ToggleGroup styleGroup = new ToggleGroup();
styleGroup.getToggles().addAll(rbThin, rbThick);
rbThin.setSelected(true);

VBox styleBox = new VBox(10);
styleBox.setPadding(new Insets(10));
styleBox.getChildren().addAll(rbThin, rbThick);

TitledPane styleTpane = new TitledPane("Style", styleBox);

// Create the toppings toggle pane
CheckBox cbPepperoni = new CheckBox("Pepperoni");
CheckBox cbSausage   = new CheckBox("Sausage");
CheckBox cbOlives    = new CheckBox("Olives");
CheckBox cbMushrooms = new CheckBox("Mushrooms");
CheckBox cbAnchovies = new CheckBox("Anchovies");

VBox toppingsBox = new VBox(10);
toppingsBox.setPadding(new Insets(10));
toppingsBox.getChildren().addAll(cbPepperoni, cbSausage,
    cbOlives, cbMushrooms, cbAnchovies);

TitledPane toppingsTpane = new TitledPane("Toppings", toppingsBox);

// Create the accordion control
Accordion acc = new Accordion();
acc.getPanes().addAll(sizeTpane, styleTpane, toppingsTpane);
```

ColorPicker

A *color picker* is a special type of combo box that lets the user choose a color. When the color picker is initially displayed, it looks like a button. When the user clicks it, a palette of colors appears from which the user may choose, as shown in Figure 19-3.

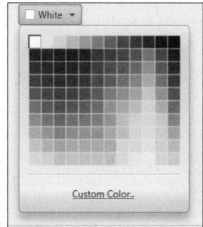

Figure 19-3:
A color
picker.

If the user doesn't like the choices that are displayed in the color picker palette, the user can click the `Custom Colors` link at the bottom of the picker.
This brings up a dialog box that lets the user craft a custom color, as shown
in Figure 19-4.

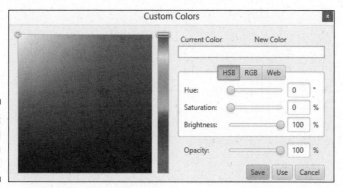

Figure 19-4:
Creating
a custom
color.

To create a color picker, just use the default constructor:

```
ColorPicker cp = new ColorPicker();
```

You can read the color selected by the user via the `getValue` method:

```
Color c = cp.getValue();
```

The following example shows how you can add a listener for a color picker's OnAction event to set the fill color of a rectangle named rect to the selected color:

```
cp.setOnAction(e ->
        r1.setFill(cp.getValue()) );
```

DatePicker

Like a color picker, a *date picker* is a special type of combo box that lets the user choose a date from a calendar-like display. Initially, the date picker looks like a text field. But when the user clicks it, a calendar display appears, as shown in Figure 19-5. The user can then choose a date, which the program can retrieve via the getValue method, which returns the date as a LocalDate.

7/16/2014						▦
<	July	>		<	2014	>
Sun	Mon	Tue	Wed	Thu	Fri	Sat
29	30	1	2	3	4	5
6	7	8	9	10	11	12
13	14	15	16	17	18	19
20	21	22	23	24	25	26
27	28	29	30	31	1	2
3	4	5	6	7	8	9

Figure 19-5: A date picker.

The following example creates a date picker control and an OnAction event handler that sets the text value of a Label control named lbl to the date selected by the user:

```
DatePicker dp = new DatePicker();
dp.setOnAction(e ->
    {
        LocalDate date = dp.getValue();
        lbl.setText(date.toString());
    });
```

Hyperlink

A *hyperlink control* is a button that resembles an HTML hyperlink. It is rendered as simple text that changes format when the mouse rolls over it and when it has been clicked. When clicked, the hyperlink control acts just like a button; you can handle the click by creating a listener for the OnAction event.

Here's a bit of code that creates a hyperlink and responds when the hyperlink is clicked:

```
Hyperlink h1 = new Hyperlink("Show details");
h1.setOnAction(e ->
    {
        // Code goes here
    });
```

ProgressIndicator and ProgressBar

Both the ProgressIndicator and ProgressBar controls are designed to let your users know that some process which takes a long time (such as updating a database or downloading a file) hasn't stalled, but is indeed chugging along toward completion. The difference between the two is the way progress is visualized: The ProgressIndicator is a circular control in which more of the circle fills in as progress is made, whereas the ProgressBar is a horizontal bar that fills in from left to right as progress is made.

To create a progress indicator or progress bar, just call the default constructor:

```
ProgressIndicator pi = new ProgressIndicator();
ProgressBar pb = new ProgressBar();
```

To set the amount of progress indicated by the progress indicator, you call the setProgress method, passing it a double value between 0.0 and 1.0. For example, to set the progress to 45 percent:

```
pb.setProgress(0.45);
```

Until you call the `setProgress` method, the progress indicator is considered to be *indeterminate,* which means that the user can't tell how much progress has been made. An indeterminate `ProgressIndicator` is indicated by a circular pattern of spinning dots; an indeterminate `ProgressBar` is a bar that sweeps back and forth. After you call the `setProgress` method, the indicator will change to show the amount of progress that has been made.

Figure 19-6 shows both indeterminate and determinate examples of a progress indicator and a progress bar.

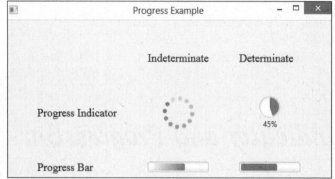

Figure 19-6:
Progress indicators and progress bars.

Slider

A *slider* is a control that's used to indicate a continuous range of values between a given minimum and maximum. A slider is rendered as a vertical or horizontal bar with a knob that the user can slide to indicate the desired value. A slider can also have tick marks and labels to indicate the intervals along the bar. Figure 19-7 shows a scene that resembles an audio equalizer with eight slider controls, each showing tick marks allowing values from 0 to 100. The labels beneath the sliders are not a part of the slider control; they are separate labels whose values are set by the `OnAction` event generated whenever the user moves one of the sliders.

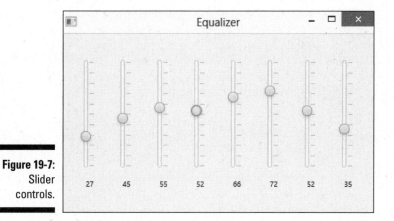

Figure 19-7:
Slider
controls.

To create the slider controls shown in Figure 19-7, I created a helper method named `makeSlider`, which returns a `VBox` object that contains the slider control along with the text that displays its value. The method accepts an `int` value that indicates the starting value for the slider. The slider itself uses the default minimum and maximum values of 0 and 100, although you can easily change those values by calling the `setMin` and `setMax` methods.

Here's the code for the `makeSlider` method:

```
private VBox makeSlider(int value)
{
    Text text = new Text();
    text.setFont(new Font("sans-serif", 10));

    Slider s = new Slider();
    s.setOrientation(Orientation.VERTICAL);
    s.setPrefHeight(150);
    s.setShowTickMarks(true);
    s.setMajorTickUnit(10);
    s.setMinorTickCount(0);
    s.setShowTickLabels(false);

    s.valueProperty().addListener(
        (observable, oldvalue, newvalue) ->
        {
            int i = newvalue.intValue();
            text.setText(Integer.toString(i));
        } );
```

```
        s.setValue(value);

        VBox box = new VBox(10, s, text);
        box.setPadding(new Insets(10));
        box.setAlignment(Pos.CENTER);
        box.setMinWidth(30);
        box.setPrefWidth(30);
        box.setMaxWidth(30);

        return box;
}
```

ScrollBar

The `ScrollBar` control is not usually used by itself; instead, it is used by other controls such as `ScrollPane` or `ListView` to display the scroll bar that lets the user scroll the contents of a panel or other region.

However, there are occasions when you might want to use a scroll bar for some purpose other than scrolling a region. In fact, you can actually use a scroll bar in much the same way as you use a slider, as the two are very similar. One difference is that unlike a slider, a scroll bar does not allow tick marks. But on the other hand, a scroll bar has increment and decrement buttons on either end of the bar, which allows the user to set the scroll bar's value up or down in fixed increments.

Figure 19-8 shows a version of the audio mixer that was shown in Figure 19-7, only implemented with scroll bars. As in the slider version, each scroll bar is paired with a `Text` object that displays the scroll bar's value whenever the user manipulates the control.

I used the following `helper` method to create each combined scroll bar and `Text` object:

```
private Node makeScrollBar(int value)
{
    Text text = new Text();
    text.setFont(new Font("sans-serif", 10));

    ScrollBar sb = new ScrollBar();
    sb.setOrientation(Orientation.VERTICAL);
    sb.setPrefHeight(150);
    sb.valueProperty().addListener(
        (observable, oldvalue, newvalue) ->
```

```
        {
            int i = newvalue.intValue();
            text.setText(Integer.toString(100-i));
        }
        );
    sb.setValue(value);

    VBox box = new VBox(10, sb, text);
    box.setPadding(new Insets(10));
    box.setAlignment(Pos.CENTER);
    box.setMinWidth(30);
    box.setPrefWidth(30);
    box.setMaxWidth(30);

    return box;
}
```

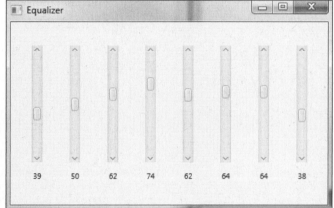

Figure 19-8:
Using scroll
bars to
create a
mixer board.

PasswordField

A *password field* is a special type of text field that hides the characters entered by the user; it's useful whenever the information being entered is sensitive. Figure 19-9 shows a password field in action.

The PasswordField class is a direct subclass of TextField, and it adds no additional methods or constructors. Thus, you can use it exactly the way you use a text field. Here's how you can create a password field:

```
PasswordField pw = new PasswordField();
```

To retrieve the value entered by the user, use the getText method:

```
String pwtext = pw.getText();
```

TIP

In addition to hiding the input entered by the user, a password field has one additional difference from a text field: Its contents cannot be copied or pasted.

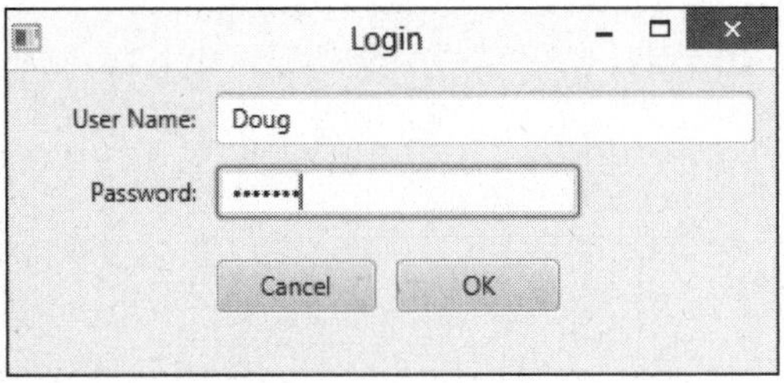

Figure 19-9:
Using a
password
field.

Login	– ☐ ✕
User Name:	Doug
Password:	••••••
	Cancel OK

Chapter 20

Ten Steps to Building a 3D World

*J*avaFX has built-in support for realistic 3D modeling. In fact, the JavaFX scene graph is three-dimensional in nature. Most JavaFX programs work in just two dimensions, specifying just x- and y-coordinates. But all you have to do to step into the third dimension is specify z-coordinates to place the nodes of your scene graph in three-dimensional space.

JavaFX includes a rich set of classes that are dedicated to creating and visualizing 3D objects in 3D worlds. You can create three-dimensional shapes, such as cubes and cylinders. You can move the virtual camera around within the 3D space to look at your 3D objects from different angles and different perspectives. And you can even add lighting sources to carefully control the final appearance of your virtual worlds. In short, JavaFX is capable of producing astonishing 3D scenes.

In this chapter, I discuss in ten short steps how to create a relatively simple 3D program that displays the three-dimensional world shown in Figure 20-1. As you can see, this 3D space includes four shapes: a sphere, a cube, a cylinder, and a pyramid. This program also demonstrates several other key aspects of 3D programming: a perspective camera, a Phong material, a light source, and 3D animation.

Put on your Thinking Cap, as this chapter will get pretty technical at times, and many of the concepts presented in this chapter can be confusing, especially if this is your first experience with 3D programming.

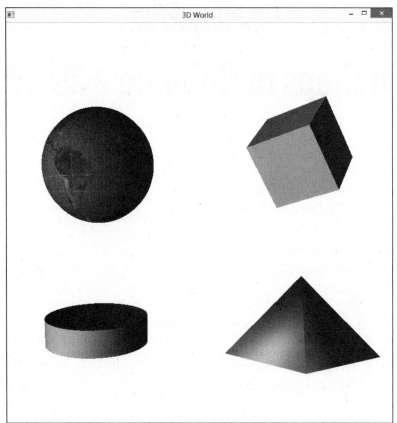

Figure 20-1:
A sample 3D
program.

Step One: Add a Perspective Camera

The first step in creating a three-dimensional JavaFX application is adding a camera to the scene graph. You do that by creating a `PerspectiveCamera` object, fiddling with its settings, and then calling the scene's `setCamera` method. Here's an example:

```
Group root = new Group();
Scene scene = new Scene(root, 800, 800);

PerspectiveCamera camera = new PerspectiveCamera(true);
camera.setTranslateZ(-1000);
camera.setNearClip(0.1);
camera.setFarClip(2000.0);
camera.setFieldOfView(35);
scene.setCamera(camera);
```

Getting used to JavaFX 3D coordinates

In two-dimensional scenes, coordinates are measured in the x-axis (horizontal) and the y-axis (vertical). Two-dimensional points are referenced by a pair of x- and y-coordinates. For example, the point (100, 200) represents the point 100 units to the right of zero on the right axis and 200 units below zero on the y-axis.

When you work in three dimensions, a third axis — called the z-axis — is added. The z-axis is perpendicular to both the x- and y-axis. Imagine a line extending from your eyes into the computer monitor and through the monitor to the wall behind it. That's the z-axis.

Three-dimensional points are represented by three coordinates: x, y, and z. Thus, (100, 200, 300) represents a point 100 units to the right of zero on the x-axis, 200 units below 0 on the y-axis, and 300 units toward you from zero on the z-axis.

A crucial difference between 2D and 3D coordinates is that in a 2D scene, the origin (point 0,0) is located at the top-left corner of the screen. In a 3D scene, the origin (point 0,0,0) is located right at the middle of the space visualized by the 3D scene.

Also, keep in mind that in the JavaFX 3D world, z-coordinates decrease as they move toward you and increase as they move away from you. X- and y-coordinates behave exactly as they do in 2D: X-coordinates increase as they move to the right, and y-coordinates increase as they move down.

This example begins by creating a scene in the same manner as you'd create a scene for a 2D JavaFX application. Then, the example creates an instance of the PerspectiveCamera class and adjusts three properties of this class.

A *perspective camera* is an essential element in any 3D scene. A perspective camera represents the virtual camera that is used to render the three-dimensional world onto a flat surface. The camera is actually a part of the scene graph and has a position indicated by a set of x-, y-, z-coordinates, just like any other object in the 3D scene. The default position for the camera (and any other object you add to the scene) is the origin point (0,0,0). So, the first thing you want to do after you add a camera is move it to a location from which it can get a good view of the objects you'll be adding to the scene. In this example, I call the setTranslateZ method to back the camera away from the scene 1,000 units.

Next, I set the near and far clipping distances. These values mark the range within which the camera will render objects. The near clipping distance is typically set to a very small value (in this case, 0.1) and the far clipping distance to a value large enough to contain the objects you want to appear in the scene.

After setting the clipping distances, I adjusted the field of view of the camera. The field of view is given as an angle and is analogous to using a wide-angle or a telephoto lens in a real camera. The default value is 30, but for this application, I found that 35 gives a better look at the scene.

Finally, I designated the camera as the scene's active camera by calling the scene's setCamera method.

At this stage, you have created a three-dimensional world. However, that world is a pretty lonely place, as it has no inhabitants. In the next step, you add a basic 3D shape to the world.

Step Two: Add a Cylinder

In this step, you add a basic 3D object to your world. JavaFX provides three basic shapes you can add: cylinders, boxes, and spheres. Start by adding a cylinder:

```
Cylinder cylinder = new Cylinder(100,50);
root.getChildren().add(cylinder);
```

The Cylinder class constructor accepts two arguments: the radius of the cylinder and its height. This example creates a cylinder roughly the shape of a hockey puck, four times as wide as it is tall; then, it adds the cylinder to the scene's root node.

At this point, the cylinder exists in the world, but is not visible. Based on what you know of 2D shapes, you may be tempted to make it visible by adding a fill color (setFill) or a stroke color (setStroke). But that's not how 3D objects work. In the next step, you discover how to apply a material to the surface of the cylinder so that it will be visible in the scene.

Step Three: Create a Material

Rendering the faces of a 3D object is much more complicated than rendering flat, two-dimensional objects. For a 2D object, you just apply a Paint object via the setFill method. The paint can be a simple color, a gradient color, or an image.

For 3D objects, you don't apply paint. Instead, you apply a special object called a *Phong material*, represented by the `PhongMaterial` class. A Phong material (named after Bui Tuong Phong, a pioneering computer graphics expert in the 1970's) provides the means by which the faces of a 3D object are realistically rendered.

The following code creates a simple Phong material based on two shades of blue and then applies the material to the cylinder:

```
PhongMaterial blueStuff = new PhongMaterial();
blueStuff.setDiffuseColor(Color.LIGHTBLUE);
blueStuff.setSpecularColor(Color.BLUE);
cylinder.setMaterial(blueStuff);
```

After the Phong material has been applied to the cylinder, the cylinder will be visible within the scene, as shown in Figure 20-2.

Figure 20-2:
The cylin-
der with
a Phong
material.

Step Four: Translate the Cylinder

You undoubtedly noticed that the cylinder in Figure 20-2 doesn't look very three dimensional. That's because you're looking at it edge-on: The camera is pointing straight at the intersection of the x- and y-axes, and the cylinder is centered on that very spot.

To gain some perspective on the cylinder, you can move it to a different location in 3D space by translating the x-, y-, and z-coordinates. For example:

```
cylinder.setTranslateX(-200);
cylinder.setTranslateY(200);
cylinder.setTranslateZ(200);
```

Here, the cylinder is moved 200 units to the left, 200 units down, and 200 units away from the camera. The resulting view looks more like a cylinder, as you can see in Figure 20-3.

Figure 20-3:
The trans-
lated
cylinder.

In Figure 20-3, it looks as if the cylinder has been rotated forward so that you can see a bit of the top surface. This isn't the case, however. What has actually happened is that you're no longer looking at the cylinder edge-on. Instead, because the cylinder is below the camera, you're looking down on it. Thus, you can see a bit of the top face. You're also looking at it from the side, which explains why it appears just a tad tilted.

Step Five: Add a Box

In this step, I add a second object to the 3D world: In this case, a box, represented by the Box class. Here's the code:

```
Box box = new Box(100, 100, 100);
box.setMaterial(blueStuff);
box.setTranslateX(150);
box.setTranslateY(-100);
box.setTranslateZ(-100);
root.getChildren().add(box);
```

The Box constructor accepts three arguments representing the width, height, and depth of the box. In this example, all three are set to 100. Thus, the box will be drawn as a cube with each side measuring 100 units.

The box is given the same material as the cylinder; then, it is translated on all three axes so that you can have a perspective view of the box. Figure 20-4 shows how the box appears when rendered. As you can see, the left and bottom faces of the box are visible because you translated the position of the box up and to the right so that the camera can gain some perspective.

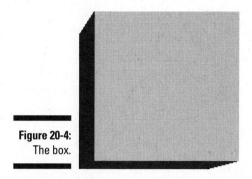

Figure 20-4:
The box.

Step Six: Rotate the Box

In this step, I rotate the box to create an even more interesting perspective view. There are two ways to rotate a 3D object. The simplest is to call the object's `setRotate` method and supply a rotation angle:

```
box.setRotate(25);
```

By default, this will rotate the object on its z-axis. If this is difficult to visualize, imagine skewering the object with a long stick that is parallel to the z-axis. Then, spin the object on the skewer.

If you want to rotate the object along a different axis, first call the `setRotationAxis`. For example, to spin the object on its x-axis, use this sequence:

```
box.setRotationAxis(Rotate.X_AXIS);
box.setRotate(25);
```

Imagine running the skewer through the box with the skewer parallel to the x-axis and then spinning the box 25 degrees.

The only problem with using the `setRotate` method to rotate a 3D object is that it works only on one axis at a time. For example, suppose you want to rotate the box 25 degrees on both the z- and the x-axis. The following code will *not* accomplish this:

```
box.setRotationAxis(Rotate.X_AXIS);
box.setRotate(25);
box.setRotationAxis(Rotate.Z_AXIS);
box.setRotate(25);
```

When the `setRotate` method is called the second time to rotate the box on the z-axis, the x-axis rotation is reset.

To rotate on more than one axis, you must use the `Rotate` class instead. You create a separate `Rotate` instance for each axis you want to rotate the object on and then add all the `Rotate` instances to the object's `Transforms` collection via the `getTransforms().addAll` method, like this:

```
Rotate rxBox = new Rotate(0, 0, 0, 0, Rotate.X_AXIS);
Rotate ryBox = new Rotate(0, 0, 0, 0, Rotate.Y_AXIS);
Rotate rzBox = new Rotate(0, 0, 0, 0, Rotate.Z_AXIS);
rxBox.setAngle(30);
ryBox.setAngle(50);
rzBox.setAngle(30);
box.getTransforms().addAll(rxBox, ryBox, rzBox);
```

The `Rotate` constructor accepts four parameters. The first three are the x-, y-, and z-coordinates of the point within the object through which the rotation axis will pass. Typically, you specify zeros for these parameters to rotate the object around its center point. The fourth parameter specifies the rotation axis.

Figure 20-5 shows how the box appears after it's been rotated.

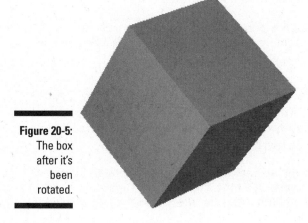

Figure 20-5:
The box after it's been rotated.

Step Seven: Add a Sphere

In this step, I add a sphere, represented by the `Sphere` class. The `Sphere` constructor accepts just a single parameter, which specifies the radius of the sphere. For example, these lines create a sphere whose radius is 100, and then translates it to move it off the center point of your virtual world:

```
Sphere sphere = new Sphere(100);
sphere.setTranslateX(-180);
sphere.setTranslateY(-100);
sphere.setTranslateZ(100);
root.getChildren().add(sphere);
```

Rather than apply the same blue Phong material to the sphere, I decided to do something more interesting: I apply a Phong material constructed from an image of a cylindrical projection of the earth using this code:

```
Image earthImage = new Image("file:earth.jpg");
PhongMaterial earthPhong = new PhongMaterial();
earthPhong.setDiffuseMap(earthImage);
sphere.setMaterial(earthPhong);
```

Figure 20-6 shows the resulting sphere.

Figure 20-6:
A sphere with a cylindrical projection of the earth applied as the Phong material.

You can wrap any image around a sphere (or any other 3D object, for that matter) using this technique. I obtained the image I used for this program from Wikipedia. Just search for *Behrmann Projection* and then download the file. (I used Windows Paint to crop the edges of the image a bit because the image available on Wikipedia has a small border around the edges.)

Step Eight: Add a Mesh Object

The three objects you've added to your virtual world so far have been created using the three built-in 3D shape classes that come with JavaFX: `Cylinder`, `Box`, and `Sphere`. For more complex objects, you must use the `TriangleMesh` class to create the object based on a connected series of triangles.

In this step, I create one of the simplest of all mesh objects: the four-sided pyramid pictured in Figure 20-7. Visually, a four-sided pyramid has a total of five *faces:* the four triangular side faces and the square base. But in a JavaFX triangle mesh, squares are not allowed, only triangles. So the pyramid actually consists of six faces: the four triangular side faces and two adjacent triangles that make up the face.

This section presents probably the most conceptually difficult information in this entire book. If you haven't studied meshes in a Computer Graphics class, be prepared to read through the following paragraphs several times before it starts to make sense. If it still doesn't make sense, grab a latte, pull out a sheet of graph paper, and start doodling. Drawing the pyramid with your own hand will help your understanding. I recommend you use a pencil.

Figure 20-7:
A square
pyramid.

To get the pyramid started, call the `TriangleMesh` constructor like this:

```
TriangleMesh pyramidMesh = new TriangleMesh();
```

To complete the pyramid, you need to populate three collections that define the geometry of the mesh. These collections hold the points, the faces, and the texture coordinates that define the shape.

I start with the texture coordinate collection, because you can pretty much ignore it for this simple pyramid. Texture coordinates are useful when you're using a material that contains an image that should be stretched in a specific way over the framework of the mesh. They allow you to associate a specific x-, y-coordinate in the image with each corner of each face.

Unfortunately, you can't simply leave out the texture coordinates even if you don't need them, so you must load at least one coordinate. Do that with this line of code:

```
pyramidMesh.getTexCoords().addAll(0,0);
```

Now I move on to the other two collections. The next is a collection of the *vertices* (that is, corners) that defines the shape. Your square pyramid has five vertices, which you can envision as the top, the front corner (the point nearest you), the left corner, the back corner, and the right corner. These vertices are numbered 0, 1, 2, 3, and 4.

Given the height h and the length s of each side of the pyramid, you can calculate the x-, y-, and z-coordinates for each vertex using the following formulas:

Vertex	Corner	X	Y	Z
0	Top	0	0	0
1	Front	0	h	$-s/2$
2	Left	$-s/2$	h	0
3	Back	$s/2$	h	0
4	Right	0	h	$s/2$

With all that as background, here's the code to create the Points collection:

```
float h = 150;                      // Height
float s = 300;                      // Side
pyramidMesh.getPoints().addAll(
        0,    0,    0,              // Point 0 - Top
        0,    h,    -s/2,           // Point 1 - Front
        -s/2, h,    0,              // Point 2 - Left
        s/2,  h,    0,              // Point 3 - Back
        0,    h,    s/2             // Point 4 - Right
    );
```

The final collection defines the faces. The faces are defined by specifying the index of each vertex that makes up each face. For example, the front left face is a triangle whose three vertices are the top, the front, and the left. The indexes for these three vertices are 0, 2, and 1.

There are a total of six triangles in the pyramid, and their faces are defined by the following points:

Face	Point 1	Point 2	Point 3
Front left	0	2	1
Front right	0	1	3
Back right	0	3	4
Back left	0	4	2
Bottom rear	4	1	2
Bottom front	4	3	2

Although it may not be evident from this table, the order in which the faces appear is critical to the success of the mesh. In general, the faces are listed in a counter-clockwise and downward order. Thus, the four side faces wrap around the pyramid in counter-clockwise order. They're followed by the two bottom faces.

Each face in the Faces collection is represented by three pairs of numbers, each of which represents the index of one of the vertices of the triangle and the index of the corresponding texture coordinate. Because you have only one item in the Texture Coordinate collection, the second number in each pair will always be zero. Thus, the sequence 0, 0, 2, 0, 1, 0 defines the front left face: The vertex indexes are 0, 2, and 1, and the texture coordinate indexes are all 0.

Here's the code to load the Faces collection:

```
pyramidMesh.getFaces().addAll(
        0,0,  2,0,  1,0,          // Front left face
        0,0,  1,0,  3,0,          // Front right face
        0,0,  3,0,  4,0,          // Back right face
        0,0,  4,0,  2,0,          // Back left face
        4,0,  1,0,  2,0,          // Bottom rear face
        4,0,  3,0,  1,0           // Bottom front face
    );
```

After the three collections of the mesh are ready, the rest of the code fleshes out the pyramid by adding a Phong material, translates the pyramid to get it off the center of the scene, and adds the pyramid to the root:

```
MeshView pyramid = new MeshView(pyramidMesh);
pyramid.setDrawMode(DrawMode.FILL);
pyramid.setMaterial(blueStuff);
pyramid.setTranslateX(200);
pyramid.setTranslateY(100);
pyramid.setTranslateZ(200);
root.getChildren().add(pyramid);
```

Step Nine: Animate the Objects

Whew! Your 3D virtual world now has four objects: a sphere that looks like the earth, a cubic box, a cylinder that looks like a hockey puck, and a pyramid.

In this step, I add an animation to all four objects to get them spinning. Each object gets a simple `RotationTransition` animation. First, the box:

```
RotateTransition rt1 = new RotateTransition();
rt1.setNode(box);
rt1.setDuration(Duration.millis(3000));
rt1.setAxis(Rotate.Z_AXIS);
rt1.setByAngle(360);
rt1.setCycleCount(Animation.INDEFINITE);
rt1.setInterpolator(Interpolator.LINEAR);
rt1.play();
```

After the `play` method is called, the box starts spinning, making one complete turn around its z-axis every three seconds.

The other three animations are similar; the only differences are the node to be rotated, the axis of rotation, and the speed. For the cylinder, the rotation is on the x-axis. The sphere rotates around the y-axis, creating the impression that the world is revolving. For the sphere, the speed is set to one revolution every 10 seconds. And finally, the pyramid rotates on the y-axis.

Step Ten: Add a Light Source

The last step into this foray into the world of 3D programming is to add a light source. The light source will change the whole look of the scene, as shown in Figure 20-8.

To add the light source, I use the following code:

```
PointLight light = new PointLight(Color.WHITE);
light.setTranslateX(-1000);
light.setTranslateY(100);
light.setTranslateZ(-1000);
root.getChildren().add(light);
```

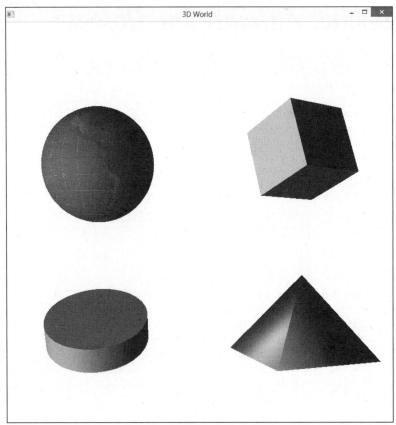

Figure 20-8:
Your 3D
world with a
light source.

The PointLight class defines a light source that originates from a specific point in the scene and projects light of the given color (in this case, good ol' white). To create the lighting effect I want, I relocate the light by translating its coordinates 1,000 to the left, 100 down, and 1,000 units toward the user. The result casts nice shadows on the backsides of the spinning objects.

Putting It All Together: The Complete 3D World Program

Now that you've seen all the pieces, Listing 20-1 shows the entire program. Comments within the program make it clear which sections of the program correspond to the steps outlined in this chapter.

With this as a starting point, you're well on your way to creating virtual 3D worlds of your own. Have fun!

Listing 20-1:   The 3D World Program

```java
import javafx.application.*;
import javafx.stage.*;
import javafx.scene.*;
import javafx.scene.shape.*;
import javafx.scene.paint.*;
import javafx.animation.*;
import javafx.util.*;
import javafx.scene.transform.*;
import javafx.scene.image.*;

public class ThreeDWorld extends Application
{
    public static void main(String[] args)
    {
        launch(args);
    }

    @Override public void start(Stage primaryStage)
    {
        Group root = new Group();
        Scene scene = new Scene(root, 800, 800);


        // STEP ONE:  ADD A CAMERA

        PerspectiveCamera camera = new PerspectiveCamera(true);
        camera.setTranslateZ(-1000);
        camera.setNearClip(0.1);
        camera.setFarClip(2000.0);
        camera.setFieldOfView(35);
        scene.setCamera(camera);


        // STEP TWO: ADD A CYLINDER

        Cylinder cylinder = new Cylinder(100,50);
        root.getChildren().add(cylinder);


        // STEP THREE: CREATE A MATERIAL

        PhongMaterial blueStuff = new PhongMaterial();
        blueStuff.setDiffuseColor(Color.LIGHTBLUE);
        blueStuff.setSpecularColor(Color.BLUE);
        cylinder.setMaterial(blueStuff);
```

(continued)

Listing 20-1 *(continued)*

```
// STEP FOUR: TRANSLATE THE CYLINDER

cylinder.setTranslateX(-200);
cylinder.setTranslateY(200);
cylinder.setTranslateZ(200);


// STEP FIVE: ADD A BOX

Box box = new Box(100, 100, 100);
box.setMaterial(blueStuff);
box.setTranslateX(150);
box.setTranslateY(-100);
box.setTranslateZ(-100);
root.getChildren().add(box);


// STEP SIX: ROTATE THE BOX

Rotate rxBox = new Rotate(0, 0, 0, 0, Rotate.X_AXIS);
Rotate ryBox = new Rotate(0, 0, 0, 0, Rotate.Y_AXIS);
Rotate rzBox = new Rotate(0, 0, 0, 0, Rotate.Z_AXIS);
rxBox.setAngle(30);
ryBox.setAngle(50);
rzBox.setAngle(30);
box.getTransforms().addAll(rxBox, ryBox, rzBox);


// STEP SEVEN: ADD A SPHERE

Sphere sphere = new Sphere(100);
sphere.setTranslateX(-180);
sphere.setTranslateY(-100);
sphere.setTranslateZ(100);
root.getChildren().add(sphere);

Image earthImage = new Image("file:earth.jpg");
PhongMaterial earthPhong = new PhongMaterial();
earthPhong.setDiffuseMap(earthImage);
sphere.setMaterial(earthPhong);


//STEP EIGHT: ADD A MESH OBJECT

TriangleMesh pyramidMesh = new TriangleMesh();

pyramidMesh.getTexCoords().addAll(0,0);

float h = 150;                    // Height
```

```
float s = 300;                    // Side
pyramidMesh.getPoints().addAll(
        0,    0,    0,            // Point 0 - Top
        0,    h,    -s/2,         // Point 1 - Front
        -s/2, h,    0,            // Point 2 - Left
        s/2,  h,    0,            // Point 3 - Back
        0,    h,    s/2           // Point 4 - Right
    );

pyramidMesh.getFaces().addAll(
        0,0,  2,0,  1,0,          // Front left face
        0,0,  1,0,  3,0,          // Front right face
        0,0,  3,0,  4,0,          // Back right face
        0,0,  4,0,  2,0,          // Back left face
        4,0,  1,0,  2,0,          // Bottom rear face
        4,0,  3,0,  1,0           // Bottom front face
    );

MeshView pyramid = new MeshView(pyramidMesh);
pyramid.setDrawMode(DrawMode.FILL);
pyramid.setMaterial(blueStuff);
pyramid.setTranslateX(200);
pyramid.setTranslateY(100);
pyramid.setTranslateZ(200);
root.getChildren().add(pyramid);


// STEP NINE: ANIMATE THE OBJECTS

RotateTransition rt1 = new RotateTransition();
rt1.setNode(box);
rt1.setDuration(Duration.millis(3000));
rt1.setAxis(Rotate.Z_AXIS);
rt1.setByAngle(360);
rt1.setCycleCount(Animation.INDEFINITE);
rt1.setInterpolator(Interpolator.LINEAR);
rt1.play();

RotateTransition rt2 = new RotateTransition();
rt2.setNode(cylinder);
rt2.setDuration(Duration.millis(3000));
rt2.setAxis(Rotate.X_AXIS);
rt2.setByAngle(360);
rt2.setCycleCount(Animation.INDEFINITE);
rt2.setInterpolator(Interpolator.LINEAR);
rt2.play();

RotateTransition rt3 = new RotateTransition();
rt3.setNode(pyramid);
rt3.setDuration(Duration.millis(3000));
```

(continued)

Listing 20-1 *(continued)*

```
    rt3.setAxis(Rotate.Y_AXIS);
    rt3.setByAngle(360);
    rt3.setCycleCount(Animation.INDEFINITE);
    rt3.setInterpolator(Interpolator.LINEAR);
    rt3.play();

    RotateTransition rt4 = new RotateTransition();
    rt4.setNode(sphere);
    rt4.setDuration(Duration.millis(9000));
    rt4.setAxis(Rotate.Y_AXIS);
    rt4.setByAngle(360);
    rt4.setCycleCount(Animation.INDEFINITE);
    rt4.setInterpolator(Interpolator.LINEAR);
    rt4.play();


    // STEP TEN: ADD A LIGHT SOURCE

    PointLight light = new PointLight(Color.WHITE);
    light.setTranslateX(-1000);
    light.setTranslateY(100);
    light.setTranslateZ(-1000);
    root.getChildren().add(light);


    // Finalize and show the stage

    primaryStage.setScene(scene);
    primaryStage.setTitle("3D World");
    primaryStage.show();
  }
}
```

Index

About the Author

Doug Lowe has been writing computer programming books since the guys who invented Java were in grade school. He's written books on COBOL, FORTRAN, Visual Basic, IBM mainframe computers, mid-range systems, PC's, web programming, and probably a few he's completely forgotten about. He's the author of more than 30 *For Dummies* books, including *Java All-In-One For Dummies,* 4th Edition; *Java For Dummies Quick Reference; Networking For Dummies,* 10th Edition; *Networking All-In-One For Dummies,* 4th Edition; *PowerPoint 2013 For Dummies;* and *Electronics All-In-One For Dummies.* He lives in that sunny Formerly-All-American city Fresno, California, where his motto is, "Buster Posey Got Out, Why Can't I?"

Dedication

To my amazing father-in-law Gordon Gearhart, who passed away while I was trying to write this book. Thank you for making this world a better place.

Author's Acknowledgments

I want to thank everyone at Wiley who was involved in the creation of this book, starting with project manager Pat O'Brien, who as usual did a great job managing all the editorial work required to put this book together and was very patient when deadlines came and went. I also want to thank acquisitions editor Connie Santisteban for making the whole project possible (happy trails!), as well as Russ Mullen for his excellent and thorough technical review and copy editor Jen Riggs for crossing all my i's and dotting all my t's — wait, reverse that!

Publisher's Acknowledgments

Project Editor: Pat O'Brien

Copy Editor: Jen Riggs

Technical Editor: Russ Mullen

Editorial Assistant: Claire Johnson

Sr. Editorial Assistant: Cherie Case

Project Coordinator: Sheree Montgomery

Cover Image: ©iStock.com/Henvry